THE
MIDDLE EAST
UNVEILED

Visit our How To website at **www.howto.co.uk**

At **www.howto.co.uk** you can engage in conversation with some of our authors – all of whom have 'been there and done that' in their specialist fields. You can get access to special offers and additional content but, most importantly, you will be able to engage with, and become a part of, a wide and growing community of people just like yourself.

At **www.howto.co.uk** you'll be able to talk to, and share tips with, people who have similar interests and are facing similar challenges in their lives. People who, just like you, have the desire to change their lives for the better – be it through moving to a new country, starting a new business, growing their own vegetables, or writing a novel.

At **www.howto.co.uk** you'll find the support and encouragement you need to help make your aspirations a reality.

How To Books strives to present authentic, inspiring, practical information in their books. Now, when you buy a title from **How To Books**, you get even more than words on a page.

THE
MIDDLE EAST
UNVEILED

A CULTURAL AND PRACTICAL GUIDE
FOR ALL WESTERN BUSINESS PROFESSIONALS

DONNA MARSH

howtobooks

Dedication

To my parents, who encouraged me to learn

How To Books Ltd
Spring Hill House, Spring Hill Road
Begbroke, Oxford OX5 1RX, United Kingdom
Tel: 01865 375794 Fax: 01865 379162
info@howtobooks.co.uk
www.howtobooks.co.uk

British Library Cataloguing in Publication Data
A catalogue record for this book is available from
the British Library.

First published 2010

ISBN: 978 1 84528 416 9

Typeset by *specialist* publishing services ltd, Montgomery
Produced for How To Books by Deer Park Productions, Tavistock

Photos & images:
Shutterstock.com: p4: © Olinchuk; p80: © Mahesh Patil; p124: © ronfromyork;
p200: © Izabela Zaremba
iStock.com: p178: © Catherine Yeulet; p260: © Alex Jeffries; p298: © Catherine Yeulet;
p324: © Holger Mette; p336: © Nafe Al Yasi; p340: © Alex Jeffries.

Printed and bound in Great Britain by Bell & Bain Ltd, Glasgow

CONTENTS

Introduction

Until recently, working in the Middle East was perceived by many Westerners to be a difficult challenge. Few businesses other than those in the oil, military or diplomatic fields even had the region on their corporate radar. General knowledge about the region was very low. The few Westerners who were sent to live as expatriates in parts of the Middle East were often considered to be on a hardship posting.

From a Western point of view, the economic climate started to change perceptibly in the late 1990s. Many Western companies were globalising, usually prioritising the large markets of China and India first. Some companies then turned to the Middle East as the next step in their strategy to expand their business; others stumbled into the region, often through business connections from elsewhere in the world.

With the arrival of Western businesses new to the Middle East, some organisations have become very successful. Others struggle; some have failed. Often, the difference between a successful organisation and one that fails is the organisation's level of cultural intelligence. Cultural intelligence has never been more important as businesses globalise, especially to parts of the world that are very different from markets in the West. Cultural and social mistakes can cost business. Learning how to do business in the Middle East without causing offence is crucial.

It is the intention of this book to provide cultural intelligence for the Westerner who will be travelling to the Middle East on business. It focuses on Arab and Islamic topics. Geographical focus is given firstly to the countries of the Gulf, then the Levant and Egypt. Iraq has been excluded, as mainstream business professionals have not been travelling to this destination for quite some time and are not expected to travel there for mainstream business reasons in the near future.

Issues relating to Israel will be raised where relevant. It is not the intention of this book to be a comprehensive guide for Western business professionals working in Israel. This decision has been taken for practical reasons, and should not be interpreted politically.

Similarly, issues relating to Iran will be raised only where relevant. This decision has also been taken for practical reasons, recognising that there are sanctions currently in place that restrict many Western organisations from doing business in that country.

This book focuses on practical business issues, cultural values and social etiquette of the Middle East; is it not a substitute for Lonely Planet or any other tourist guide. Many other books are available for readers who wish to learn more about daily living issues in the region for ex-pats as well as dealing with bureaucracy.

Donna Marsh

Notes

There is some repetition in this book. As the author recognises that many readers may read this book out of sequence, the repetitions are intentional so that readers do not miss important points.

All Arabic words have been transliterated into English. It is important to note that transliteration between the two alphabets is an inexact exercise. It is common to find multiple spellings and pronunciations of the same words in both languages. The author has tried to use words and spellings most familiar to Westerners that are also considered correct by Arabic speakers.

1

Culture, stereotypes and generalisations

CULTURE

Defining culture is not an easy task. We think we know what it is, but often find it difficult to articulate: it's 'how we do things around here'. For the purpose of this book, we will define culture as a set of typical beliefs, values and behaviour that distinguishes one group of people from another. Culture includes traditions and eccentricities. People belong to many cultures throughout their life, including family, religion, nationality, and outside cultural influences such as the workplace.

It is important to recognise that any study of culture will almost certainly include judgments and opinions of the cultures being discussed. Cultural theorists point out that most people see another culture through a 'cultural lens', i.e. their own set of values and beliefs, often applying what they believe to be right and wrong to the new culture. Whilst it may be useful to try to understand another culture by comparing it to what a person already knows, it can also lead to misunderstandings.

By exploring the differences between stereotypes and generalisations, we set the stage for minimising these misunderstandings.

STEREOTYPES

Stereotypes are a fixed set of assumptions about a group of people. The person may believe that specific characteristics apply to all people within this group.

Stereotypes are often verbalised by using phrases such as 'All xxxx are yyyy' or 'you know what xxxx are like'. It is a simplified and inaccurate view that is applied to an entire group of people without regard to individual variation.

GENERALISATIONS

Generalisations are a set of characteristics that often apply to many members of a group. However, it is not assumed that all members of the group will share the characteristics of the group. Generalisations are often verbalised by using phrases such as 'xxxx are often yyyy' or 'many xxxx are typically yyyy'. It recognises the frequency of a characteristic without making the assumption that all individuals within that group share that characteristic.

THE BELL CURVE OF HUMAN CHARACTERISTICS

Most human behaviour falls into a neat Bell Curve, where the majority of a group of people exhibit similar characteristics. However, there is a minority of individuals who fall outside of the range on either side of the curve.

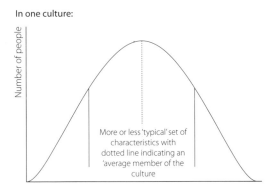

In one culture:

Number of people

More or less 'typical' set of characteristics with dotted line indicating an 'average member of the culture

As a Western business professional working with people from the Middle East, it is important to keep these concepts in mind. You may find that your preconceived notion about someone or something in the Middle East is far off the mark. You may also find that, at least once in a while, you encounter someone who is an exception to the particular characteristics shared by most of a group.

For example, many people in the West think that women in the Middle East are uneducated, oppressed and forbidden to work outside the home. If you hold this stereotype, then you will be in for a big surprise the first time you meet a Lebanese bank executive in her French designer suit, an Iranian exporter shuttling between her offices in the Gulf and Tehran, or an Emirati business owner in traditional veil managing a staff of dozens of employees, both making multimillion *dirham* (or *riyal*, *dinar*, dollar, pound, euro) decisions.

It is also suggested that the concepts of stereotypes and generalisations are considered throughout this book. Whilst every attempt has been made to portray an accurate and objective description of all topics raised, it is impossible to avoid presenting some points of view that may be disputed by some readers.

2

Defining the Middle East

In most of the world, defining regional and national geographies is reasonably straightforward. Most of us understand each other when we refer to North America, Continental Europe or Sub-Saharan Africa, for example. However, like most things regarding the Middle East, even this simple question is complicated. Defining the Middle East entails interpreting history, geography, anthropology, religion, economics and politics.

A GEOGRAPHICAL OVERVIEW OF THE MIDDLE EAST

The modern day Middle East includes the countries of the Arabian Peninsula, along with adjacent countries to the north of the peninsula that border or nearly border the Eastern Mediterranean referred to as the Levant. Most people would be in agreement that these are the core countries of the Middle East.

Countries of the Arabian Peninsula

Common Name	Official Name
Bahrain	Kingdom of Bahrain
Kuwait	State of Kuwait
Oman	Sultanate of Oman
Qatar	State of Qatar
Saudi Arabia (KSA)	Kingdom of Saudi Arabia
United Arab Emirates (UAE)	United Arab Emirates
Yemen	Republic of Yemen

With the exception of Yemen, the countries of the Arabian Peninsula are also known as the Gulf Countries, due to their border with the body of water known both as the Persian Gulf and the Arabian Gulf, found between the Arabian Peninsula and Iran. Although most Westerners have been taught to refer to these waters as the Persian Gulf, the politically neutral way to refer to it is simply 'The Gulf'.

Countries of the Arabian Peninsula, again with the exception of Yemen, also belong to the GCC (Gulf Cooperation Council). In everyday language, it is common to refer to these countries collectively as the GCC. The GCC has aspirations not dissimilar to the European Union in terms of common market and other economic policies.

There are undefined borders between KSA and the UAE, Oman and Yemen. The border between KSA and Qatar was defined in 2001. KSA borders with countries to the north are not in dispute.

The border between Yemen and Oman was defined in 2000.

A border dispute between Kuwait and Iraq was one of the catalysts leading to the Gulf War in 1990–91. The United Nations defined this border in 1992; it officially remains in dispute by Iraq.

The GCC Countries

These comprise Bahrain, KSA, Kuwait, Oman, Qatar, and UAE.

Cultural Influences

The Gulf Countries are culturally influenced by values, traditions and practices of the Indian subcontinent as well as Iran. Yemen has historical ties with the Horn of Africa, in particular Somalia and Djibouti.

Countries of the Levant (Eastern Mediterranean)

Middle Eastern countries that border or nearly border the Mediterranean Sea are also known as the countries of the Levant. From a Western point of view, it is believed that this name derives from the French, as from their perspective, *'soleil levant'* or rising sun, described the countries of the Eastern Mediterranean or the *Moyen-Orient* (Near East). Arabs will often refer to the same area as the *Mashreq*, meaning the region east of Egypt or – again – the land of the rising sun.

Historically, the Levant has included Anatolia in Turkey, parts of Sinai Egypt, Cyprus and sometimes Southeast Europe, including parts of the Balkan Peninsula.

Conventionally, it is agreed that the following countries are part of the modern Levantine Middle East.

Common Name	Official Name
Iraq*	Republic of Iraq
Israel**	State of Israel
Jordan	Hashemite Kingdom of Jordan
Lebanon	Republic of Lebanon
Palestinian Territories***	Palestinian Territories of the West Bank and Gaza Strip
Syria	Syrian Arab Republic

*   Notwithstanding current political and military events, Mesopotamian Iraqis, who live between the Tigris and Euphrates Rivers, share their identity with people from the Levant. From a practical point of view, this would traditionally include Baghdad, especially its middle and upper classes. Others prefer to label Iraq as Mesopotamian, which refers to people living between (or sometimes near) the Tigris and Euphrates Rivers. It is also known as the Cradle of Civilisation.

    However, southern Iraq is populated by people who more closely identify culturally and religiously with other Gulf Arabs; they would not be happy to be considered Levantine. Not identifying with the Levant also holds true for much of the Iraqi population in northern Iraq, where the population is predominately Kurdish.

**   Israel is most certainly geographically a part of the Middle East as well as a part of the Levant. From the perspective of working in the Arab world, including all of the Middle East, it is prudent to handle the entire matter of even referring to Israel with utmost caution.

    Politically, only Jordan and Egypt recognise Israel; all other Middle East countries are either technically at war with Israel, do not recognise its sovereignty, or do not have official diplomatic relations with the country. It may shock some Westerners the first time they look at a map published for consumption in the Middle East that conspicuously ignores the existence of modern Israel. Other maps are still in circulation as if pre-1948 geography is current.

    Many business professionals to the Middle East avoid referring to Israel if at all possible. When pressed, the author has used euphemisms, including 'a neighbouring country', 'next door', 'the 'I' country' or 'another country in the region'.

*** The Palestinian Territories include two separate regions: the West Bank and Gaza. The borders of Gaza have been recognised by Israel and Egypt, its two neighbours. The borders of the West Bank have not yet been finalised – this is a main cause of the recurring violence between Palestinians and Israelis.

The Palestinian Territories' political status has not yet been finalised. Many people in the Middle East will refer to Palestine as a de facto country. Others will refer to individual cities within the Territories, such as Jericho or Ramallah. Others will refer to 'Occupied Palestine' or 'Occupied Jerusalem', including much of the English language print media found throughout Egypt, the Levant and the Gulf. Still others will refer to the Palestinian Authority, which is the government body recognised internationally.

Although this entire topic is a minefield throughout the Middle East, the safest, most politically neutral way to refer to the land is the Palestinian Territories, the West Bank and Gaza, or indeed, an individual city by name as appropriate.

Cultural Influences

Countries of the Levant are culturally influenced by the values, traditions and practices of Europe and the Ottoman Empire.

Countries of North Africa

Now our quest to define the Middle East is getting trickier. The countries in North Africa that are often considered part of the Middle East are the countries with large Arab populations, including Egypt, Sudan, Libya, Tunisia, Algeria, Morocco and Mauritania.

Other countries in North and Sub-Saharan Africa may have significant Muslim populations; however, their ethnic make-up does not include many Arabs. They are a part of the wider Islamic world, but are most definitely not a part of the Middle East.

Conventionally, Egypt is considered part of the Middle East, in spite of its geography. In fact, referring to Egyptians as African would be an insult to most Egyptians. Furthermore, Egypt is regarded as the cultural centre of the Arab world, with much of the cinema, music, literature and other traditional and modern arts emanating from Greater Cairo.

Cultural Values

Egypt is culturally influenced by the values, traditions and practices of Europe and the Ottoman Empire. It also has a long and glorious pre-Islamic history that is a source of Egyptian pride.

Sudan is less certain in its claim to be part of the Middle East. The Arab and Nubian people living in the north of the country, with their historical, religious and ethnic ties with Egypt, are quite clearly considered to be Middle Eastern. This includes the territories in and around the Sudanese capital of Khartoum. Sudan's south is quite distinct from the north, with its predominately Christian and indigenous religious beliefs and ethnically non-Arab populations. This is where sub-Saharan Africa begins. However, Sudan's government is undoubtedly dominated by the customs and traditions of the northern part of the country, and as such, for the purposes of this book, is included in the Middle East.

Traditional Middle East countries of the Nile River

Common Name	Official Name
Egypt (Misr)	Arab Republic of Egypt
Sudan	Republic of Sudan

Other parts of North Africa are certainly part of the Arab world, yet are not conventionally considered to be part of the Middle East. Readers should be aware that many North Africans identify with the indigenous North African cultures of the Berbers or Imazighen. The countries found between the Atlas Mountains and the Mediterranean Sea are known as the *Maghreb*. *Maghreb* means 'west' in Arabic and refers to the land where the sun sets. The undisputed *Maghreb* countries are Morocco, Algeria and Tunisia. Libya and Mauritania are sometimes included in the *Maghreb*, although others disagree. However, all five countries belong to the Arab Maghreb Union and, as such, will be included for the purposes of this book's definition as part of the *Maghreb* but not as part of the traditional Middle East.

Traditional Maghreb Countries

Common Name	Official Name
Algeria	People's Democratic Republic of Algeria
Libya	Socialist People's Libyan Arab Great Jamahiriya
Mauritania	Islamic Republic of Mauritania
Morocco	Kingdom of Morocco
Tunisia	Tunisian Republic

What about Turkey?

Although Turkey has historically and scholastically been considered part of the Levant, there is ongoing debate as to whether it is part of the modern-day Middle East. Geographically, it sits at a crossroads, with 3% of its territory in Europe and the remaining 97% in West Asia. The influence of the Ottoman Empire, centred in Constantinople (modern day Istanbul) and reaching into most of the Levant and Arabian Peninsula (and beyond), affected the region for more than 400 years. Over 99% of its population is Muslim.

However, since the collapse of the Ottoman Empire in 1922, Turkey has been looking steadily towards the West. Beginning with Atatürk, the father of modern Turkey, through to the steady desire of several political leaders to join the European Union, Turkey is clearly distancing itself from its recent past.

In addition, Turks have several other distinctions from the Arab world. They are not ethnically Arabs; they are predominantly Turkic. A minority Kurdish population lives in Turkey as well, with other ethnicities including other Turkic peoples, Jews, Greeks, Armenians and other Christians. The Turkish language is not derived from Arabic or any other Semitic language; it is also Turkic in origin, and has used the Latin alphabet since the time of Atatürk. Turkic people and languages are also found throughout Central Asia, including the countries known as the modern day '-istans'. Turks are much more likely to identify with Central Asians than with Arabs.

For these reasons, this book does not include Turkey in its definition of the Middle East. It is recognised, however, that many business people may wish to include Turkey into its greater Middle East, EMEA (Europe, Middle East and Africa), or MENA (Middle East and North Africa) territories as a matter of practicality, including relatively short, regional travel times, cost effectiveness, time zone synergies, etc.

Common Name	Official Name
Turkey	Republic of Turkey

What about Iran?

Although Iran is not found on the Arabian Peninsula, it does have a long border with the Persian/Arabian Gulf. It is clearly not a part of the Indian subcontinent, nor is it part of what is traditionally defined as Central Asia.

The influence of the Persian Empire, centred in modern day Iran, extended throughout the Levant and beyond, including Southeast Europe and parts of North Africa, and lasted in one form or another for over 2000 years.

Although the Persian Empire did not officially include most of the Gulf Countries, successive migration to these countries has occurred over the centuries, mostly as a result of trade and religion. Bahrain, for example, has a majority *Shi'a* population, mostly because of this migration pattern. It is estimated that the current population of Dubai is up to 20% Iranian, many of whom have settled there in the years after the formation of the Islamic Republic of Iran.

Iranians are an ethnic mix, with a majority claiming Persian roots. Other ethnicities include Armenians, Azeris, and a number of indigenous ethnicities as well as ethnicities shared with Western Afghanistan. Only 3% of Iranians are of Arab origin. Iran also has the largest number of Jews in the region living outside Israel, and has minority Christian, Zoroastrian and Baha'i populations. About 98% of the population is Muslim; 90% of these are *Shi'a*.

The official language of Iran is Persian; many Westerners also know it as Farsi. Persian/Farsi belongs to the Indo-Aryan family of languages. Although it uses a modern variant of the Arabic alphabet, the language is not Semitic and has different historical and linguistic roots.

Considering the above, the reader would be forgiven if they come to the conclusion that Iran is not considered to be a part of the Middle East. But in fact, most people of the region – including Iranians themselves – do identify themselves as belonging to the Middle East!

It is perfectly acceptable for Westerners to include Iran in the greater geography of the Middle East. However, it is imperative that Iranians are never mistaken for Arabs. It is also imperative that Iranians are not assumed to speak Arabic; if they do so, it's because they have learnt it as a foreign language, just like it would be for people whose first language is English or another Western language.

Common Name	Official Name
Iran	Persia (until 1935)
	Iran (1935 – 1979), Pahlavi Dynasty
	Islamic Republic of Iran (1979 – present)

SUMMARY

As a result of the above analysis, this book has defined the following countries as part of the Middle East:

Bahrain, Egypt, Iran, Iraq, Israel, Jordan, Lebanon, Kuwait, Oman, Palestinian Territories, Qatar, Saudi Arabia, Sudan, Syria, United Arab Emirates, Yemen.

What about other Muslim countries?

Some people may consider other Muslim countries as being part of the Middle

East. Whilst many of these countries enjoy good diplomatic and cultural relations with the region, they are most certainly part of their respective geographies and should never be mistaken for the Middle East. Such countries can be found in locations as diverse as Africa, Asia and Europe.

Within the African continent, the *Sahel* makes a reasonably clear delineation between countries that may be associated with the Middle East and countries that clearly belong to Sub-Saharan Africa. The *Sahel* separates the Sahara Desert in the North from the more fertile land to the South.

Majority Muslim countries include Indonesia, Pakistan, Bangladesh, Nigeria, Afghanistan, Malaysia, Uzbekistan, Kazakhstan, Niger, Mali, Senegal, Guinea, Somalia, Azerbaijan, Tajikistan, Kyrgyzstan, Turkmenistan, Chad, Eritrea, Albania, Kosovo, Gambia, Comoros, Djibouti, Brunei and the Maldives.

Just to keep things in perspective, India, although with a vast majority Hindu population, also has the third largest population of Muslims in the world, after Indonesia and Pakistan. In fact, approximately 80% of the world's estimated 1.5 billion Muslims live somewhere other than in the Middle East.

The largest number of Muslims in the Middle East live in Egypt.

MIDDLE EASTERN DEMOGRAPHICS

The reader can easily look up detailed demographics of the Middle East from sources as diverse as the CIA Factbook, a plethora of websites or travel guidebooks. We will focus on information most important to the Western business professional.

It is notoriously difficult to gather statistics about the population of the Middle East. Many countries' populations are very transient. Other countries have not held censuses for decades. Some governments prefer not to release data. In an attempt to be as accurate as possible, we have taken the following figures from a number of reliable sources.

There are approximately 312 million people living in the area we have defined as the Middle East, roughly equivalent to the population of the US.

Country	Population millions	Muslim %	Christian %	Jewish %	Hindu %	Ex-pats*** %
Egypt	80	90%	10%	<1%	<1%	
Iran	71	98%	1-2%	<1%	<1%	
Sudan	37	70%	7%	<1%	<1%	
Iraq	28	97%	2-3%	<1%	<1%	
Saudi Arabia	24	86%**	5-6%	<1%	6-7%	33%
Yemen	21	99%	<1%	<1%	<1%	
Syria	19	90%	10%	<1%	<1%	
Israel	7	15%	2-3%	76%	<1%	
Jordan	6	94%	6%	<1%	<1%	
UAE	4.5	76%	3-4%	<1%	15%	81%
Lebanon	4.0	60%	40%	<1%	<1%	
Palestine*	3.8	94%	4-5%	<1%	<1%	
Kuwait	2.7	85%	7-8%	<1%	7-8%	63%
Oman	2.6	93%	<1%	<1%	3%	23%
Bahrain	1.0	81%	9%	<1%	6-7%	50%
Qatar	0.9	76%	8-9%	<1%	7-8%	80%

*   Palestine refers to the Palestinian Territories of the West Bank and Gaza. Israelis living in these territories are not included in the % Jewish statistics in the table, but would represent 6% of the population.

** Saudi Arabia officially reports a 100% Muslim population as all Saudi nationals must be Muslim according to Saudi law. The figure for other religions is an estimate within ex-pat communities.

*** Ex-pats statistics are included where they exceed 10% of the local population. They do not include immigrants who have made the decision to relocate permanently to another country.

The basics

Who is an Arab?

Arabs are a Semitic people (as are Jews, some Ethiopians and Maltese) who trace their roots to the Arabian Peninsula. Their common language is Arabic, or in the case of Arabs who have emigrated from the region, they can trace their mother tongue back to Arabic. Arabs can be of any religion, although the vast majority are Muslim (88%), Druze (6%) or Christian (6%).

There are approximately 400 million Arabs. People of Arab descent live in nearly every country throughout the world. Significant populations exist in North Africa, parts of Western Europe, parts of North and South America, some countries in West and East Africa and in Australia. A disproportionately high number of Arabs who have emigrated to the West are Christian, especially those in the USA.

What is the difference between a Jew and an Israeli?

Also Semitic, a Jew is someone who believes in Judaism (the world's oldest monotheistic religion) or can trace their roots back to Judaism. Judaism is carried through the mother's lineage. Hebrew is the ancient language of Jews. Nearly extinct as a spoken language as recently as the early twentieth century, it has been successfully revived as a direct result of the Israeli decision to name Hebrew as one of its national languages. The other national language is Arabic.

An Israeli is a citizen of Israel, and can be of any background or religion, although there are many distinctions made for Jews living in Israel. Israelis who are born in Israel refer to themselves as *Sabra*, named after a local fruit that is prickly on the outside and sweet on the inside.

About one third of Israelis are foreign-born, including large populations from Ethiopia, Europe, Iran, Iraq, Morocco, North America, Russia and the Former

Soviet Union, South Africa and Yemen. Most of India's small Jewish population has also emigrated to Israel.

For centuries, significant Jewish populations were found throughout the Levant, Iraq, Egypt and Yemen. A very small Jewish community has lived in Bahrain. Most Jewish communities throughout the Middle East have now emigrated to Israel or to the West.

What is the difference between an Iranian and a Persian?

An Iranian is a citizen of Iran. In the West, Iran was known as Persia until 1935. Persian is a language, also known as Farsi. Persian is also an ethnic category; just over 50% of all Iranians are Persian. References to Persian culture continue to be made throughout the world.

WHO ELSE LIVES IN THE MIDDLE EAST?

Indigenous ethnic groups

There are a few ethnic groups in the region who do not have their own homeland. There are also ethnic groups that are found in the Middle East who represent a significant minority of their country's population.

Kurds are a large ethnic group found in Northern Iraq, Northwest Iran and Northern Syria. There are also large numbers of Kurds in Eastern Turkey. It is estimated that there are a total of 30 million Kurds. The Kurdish language shares its roots with other languages spoken in Iran; it is not Arabic, although many Kurds also speak Arabic as an additional language. Most Kurds are *Sunni* Muslim, although they can be of any religion.

About 25% of the Iranian population is Azeri – about 18 million people. These are Turkic people who share the same ethnicity with people from Azerbaijan, and are mostly *Shi'a*.

Assyrians live in the northernmost parts of the Middle East, stretching from Syria, through Iraq and into Iran. They are also known as Chaldeans or Syrian Christians. About one million Assyrians live in the region. Several hundred thousand live in the West. Their influence has also reached the Indian subcontinent, where about six million Indian Christians also belong to the Assyrian Christian church.

Nubians are an ethnic group of people who live in Southern Egypt and Northern Sudan. They had their own kingdom until the late 19th century. There are about 300,000 Nubians living in the region. Many were displaced during the preparations to build the Aswan Dam in the 1950s. Nubians are Muslim, and have largely assimilated into Arab culture. There are distinct Nubian languages and dialects.

Expatriates

Expatriates or ex-pats are foreign nationals who choose to take up residence in another country for a period of time, but who do not intend to (or cannot) reside in their new country permanently.

Ex-pats are distinct from foreign refugees, who often have little or no choice but to emigrate. For the purposes of this book, Palestinians who are living in other countries of the Levant will not be considered ex-pats, as they often fled from their homeland to a neighbouring country due to political or safety reasons.

As a side note, many Palestinians have been granted citizenship in Levantine countries, including large numbers in Jordan (where they are now believed to be the majority of the population) and in Syria. Some Palestinians have also achieved citizenship in Egypt and Lebanon. However, many Palestinians in the Levant also remain stateless.

Palestinians living in the Gulf countries are not eligible for citizenship in their host country. Thus, Palestinians living in the Gulf countries will be considered ex-pats.

There are an estimated 35 million expatriates in the Middle East. Most ex-pats can be found in the Gulf countries. Each country has its own ratio of ex-pats to nationals. However, all Gulf countries 'import' many more expatriate men than women. This is simply a matter of demographics, as the vast majority of ex-pats in each Gulf country have accepted manual labour jobs. Jobs in the building trade, whether on a crane on top of the world's tallest building or as a plumber, are almost exclusively filled by men. Service jobs, the next largest employment sector for ex-pats, are also highly skewed towards men – housemaids and nannies are the main exception. In fact, many jobs considered to be traditionally female in much of the West are often filled by men in the Gulf, including hotel room cleaners.

The gender ratio for Western ex-pats is changing rapidly; whilst more Western men than women continue to accept jobs in the Gulf overall, there are some skilled labour markets welcoming an even number of both genders. Employers in law, banking, healthcare, aviation and many multinational corporations all hire large numbers of educated, ex-pat women.

Ex-pats will find the following GCC country profiles of interest.

Bahrain

The ex-pat population in Bahrain is more diversified than in other Gulf countries, in part due to migration patterns long before Westerners arrived. About 45% of ex-pats are from the Indian subcontinent and the Far East, 27% from other Arab countries and 25% from Iran. About 3% of the ex-pat population in Bahrain is Western including about 10,000 British ex-pats.

Bahrain's economy has moved on from its earlier days. Its main focus is no longer oil, but finance. It is a major centre of finance, and is one of the most important centres of Islamic banking in the world. Many Westerners are working in the financial industry. Others are involved in trade, property and tourism.

There are 1.26 men for every woman in Bahrain.

Kuwait

Kuwaiti citizens are defined as those who can trace their family's residency in Kuwait back to 1920. This must be done through a Kuwaiti father. It should be noted that a large number of native born, local residents in Kuwait, known as *bidoon*, are actually stateless and have fewer rights than other Kuwaiti-born residents. For example, they are excluded from voting. *Bidoon* means 'without' in Arabic. We will explore more about the *bidoon* population in a later chapter.

Until the early 1990s, the largest group of Arab ex-pats in Kuwait were Palestinian, many of whom lived in Kuwait since the creation of the State of Israel in the late 1940s, including the family of the Queen Rania, the current Queen of Jordan. The Palestinians were systematically expelled from the country at the time of the 1991 Gulf War in retaliation for then-Palestinian leader Yasir Arafat's support of Iraq during this conflict. Most of these people migrated to other Gulf countries; some went to Jordan, others to the West.

Egyptians are now the largest group of Arab ex-pats in Kuwait, representing about 25% of the total ex-pat population. Most of the rest are from the Indian subcontinent or the Philippines. About 22,000, less than 1% of the total, are Westerners. Most Westerners living in Kuwait are in the oil business.

There are 1.52 men for every woman in Kuwait.

Oman

There are about 600,000 ex-pats living in Oman. It should be noted that, unlike in the rest of the Gulf, there have been people living in Oman for more than 200 years who originated from communities reaching from East Africa to the Indian subcontinent. These people are not considered ex-pats.

The majority of ex-pats in Oman are from the Indian subcontinent. A large minority are from Egypt, Jordan and the Philippines. About 1% are Westerners. Most Westerners work in the oil or defence industries. Many Westerners hold jobs that facilitate the modernisation of Oman's economy. Property development and tourism opportunities are also beginning to grow in the country.

There are 1.26 men for every woman in Oman.

Qatar

About 720,000 of Qatar's 900,000 residents are ex-pats. Most Arabs, about 40% of all ex-pats, are Egyptian, Jordanian or Palestinian. About 36% of all ex-pats are from the Indian subcontinent. Another 10% are from Iran. The remaining 14% are from the rest of the world, including an estimated 2% who are Western. Westerners work in a variety of businesses, including oil and gas industries. Qatar is also home to a number of Arabic- and English-language satellite broadcasting organisations, including Al Jazeera. The US military currently has a substantial operation in the country.

There are 1.88 men for every woman in Qatar.

Saudi Arabia

There are an estimated 8 million ex-pats in Saudi Arabia (KSA). About 20% of Saudi ex-pats are Arabs, with the over 1 million Egyptians, 250,000 Palestinians, 150,000 Lebanese, and a large number of Syrians.

Another 55% of the ex-pat population are from the Indian subcontinent, with an estimated 1.5 million Indians, 1.5 million Bangladeshis, 1 million Pakistanis, 400,000 Sri Lankans and 350,000 Nepalese.

Another 25% of the ex-pat population are from the Far East, including 1.2 million Filipinos and 600,000 people from Indonesia.

There are about 100,000 Western ex-pats in the Kingdom, including 30,000 Americans and 20,000 British. Westerners represent just over 1% of the total ex-pat population. Most Westerners are working in the oil and defence industries.

There are 1.34 men for every woman in Saudi Arabia.

UAE

As each of the seven Emirates has its own business environment, the ex-pat characteristics of the three most populous Emirates are defined separately.

Abu Dhabi

Of the 4.5 million people who live in the UAE, about 1.6 million of them live in the Emirate of Abu Dhabi, of which Abu Dhabi is the main city. Al Ain is the other city in Abu Dhabi Emirate with a small ex-pat population.

Ex-pats comprise 80% of the total population. Seventy-five percent of these are from the Indian subcontinent, another 20% are other Arabs, and the remaining 5% are from the West and Iran.

About 10% of the world's known oil is in Abu Dhabi. Although this is the main reason for Western ex-pats to work in the Emirate, Abu Dhabi's economy is diversifying into the fields of finance, commerce, property and tourism. Abu Dhabi is differentiating itself from Dubai, its neighbouring Emirate, especially in the development of its tourist industry.

There are 2.03 men for every woman in Abu Dhabi Emirate.

Dubai

Dubai is the name of both the UAE's second largest Emirate and the city of Dubai. Until recently, Dubai was amongst the fastest-growing cities in the world, with an estimated 25% of the world's cranes working on its sandy soil until late 2008. Dubai's reputation for ostentatiousness is not hard to justify, with attention-grabbing structures under construction or nearly complete including the world's tallest building (Burj Khalifa), the Gulf's only indoor ski slope (in the Mall of the Emirates), the Burj al Arab (the world's first seven star hotel) and the Palm Islands, developed by reclaiming land from the sea. However, it has not escaped some of the consequences of the global economic downturn, especially in property development, where the bubble has burst.

About 83% of Dubai's population are ex-pats. Fifty-five percent of these are from the Indian subcontinent or elsewhere in Asia. Twenty percent are other Arabs; an estimated 20% are from Iran. It may surprise most first time visitors from the West that only 3% are Western. Dubai's ex-pat population is continuing to change as ex-pats affected by the global economic downturn lose their jobs. This impacts Western ex-pats as well as labourers from the developing world. Other ex-pats with financial difficulties are also leaving Dubai, sometimes fleeing just ahead of the law. Others move to Dubai, especially if their jobs are in expanding lines of business such as law or medicine.

As a city, Dubai has been trading with its neighbours and beyond for centuries. Dubai has virtually no oil; Westerners work in a diverse range of industries not unlike in the rest of the world. Dubai is a regional centre for many lines of businesses; traditionally, many Western organisations initially set up their Middle East offices in Dubai, servicing other markets from this hub before expanding to other Gulf countries.

Dubai has pioneered the establishment of free trade zones that promote specific lines of business, including Dubai Internet City, Dubai Media City, Dubai Healthcare City and Dubai International Financial Centre. Jebel Ali, the oldest Free Trade Zone in the region, was established in Dubai near the border with Abu Dhabi Emirate in the 1970s. Award winning Emirates Airlines has taken over from Gulf Airlines as one of the region's most prestigious and far reaching carriers.

There are 3 men for every woman in Dubai. The average age is 27.

Sharjah
Sharjah is the UAE's third largest Emirate and the last of the seven Emirates to have a large ex-pat population. Of the 800,000 people who live in Sharjah. About 80% are ex-pats, mostly from the Indian subcontinent. Less than 1% of ex-pats are Westerners.

Sharjah maintains a social code that is much stricter than in the other Emirates, especially compared with Dubai and Abu Dhabi. Modest dress is enforced for both sexes. Alcohol is banned.

There are 2.88 men for every woman in Sharjah.

What jobs do ex-pats do in the Gulf countries?

Western business professionals will quickly observe that political correctness carries little weight in this part of the world, including the way the work force functions.

Although Islam dictates that people are treated with equal respect and fairness, in reality the Arab world operates within a hierarchical system. In a business context, this translates to different values of worth that are determined in great part by a person's nationality. This is an anathema to the modern, Western world, and is a challenge for human resources and legal departments of most Western organisations. It is also a contentious, yet everyday fact of life in the region.

The Gulf countries allow jobs to be filled by a person who most importantly fulfils specific personal characteristics, after which their professional qualifications will be taken into account. This practice is widespread, and can be seen in operation in the Appointments Sections of newspapers as well as on internet websites advertising to fill vacant positions. Although there are signs this practice may be softening, it will be prevalent for some time to come.

Selection is often done by the use of coded language. Employers who are looking for someone of a particular national origin, age or gender have many techniques at their disposal. For example, a position may be advertised as suitable for candidates who are fluent Arabic speakers (read: Arabs only), must hold a degree or qualifications from a Western educational institution (read: Westerners only) or who are legally resident through their spouse's work visa (read: women only). Other employers will place advertisements that blatantly specify their criteria, including age ranges, religion and marital status.

As a general rule of thumb, the hierarchy of nationalities in the Gulf works – unofficially, but realistically – as shown in the table on the next page. (If you are working in the Levant, Levantine Arabs will almost certainly swap their position with Gulf Arabs.)

Status	Nationality	Sub group sequence
High	Arab Nationalities	1. Gulf Arabs 2. Levantine Arabs 3. Maghreb Arabs
	Westerners	1. British 2. Western Europeans, North Americans, Antipodeans, South Africans 3. Russians 4. other Eastern Europeans
	'Honorary' Westerners	1. Turks and Iranians 2. Japanese and Koreans 3. some Chinese
	Indian subcontinent	1. some educated Indians and Pakistanis, especially Muslims, sometimes Christians 2. other educated Indians
	Indian subcontinent	1. less educated Indians and Pakistanis 2. uneducated Indians and Pakistanis
	'Service Economy' Countries	Afghanistan, Bangladesh, Philippines, Sri Lanka, other Asian countries
Low	African subcontinent	All other countries south of the Sahel except African nationals of European or sometimes Indian descent

Note

Nationals of a particular country who are ethnic minorities of that country may have mixed experiences of where they fit in the hierarchy. In general, they will enjoy the same status as other nationals in a professional environment. They may suffer in public as well as dealing with bureaucracy (sometimes starting at passport control), at least until it becomes obvious that they belong to the nationality indicated on their passport.

For example, the author worked in a particular line of business in the early 1990s dominated by Western ex-pats. Amongst the reasonably tight group was a Canadian man of Filipino origin. Although he was accepted as a Canadian in his business role, he was forever being refused entry to Dubai's clubs and pubs, especially if he arrived alone.

Westerners can expect to work with Arab nationals in government positions and other Arab ex-pats in the private sector, often in senior positions. Christian Arabs, who are often Lebanese, are regularly sought for key positions as they are usually multilingual, and are seen as being able to do tasks that may be objectionable for observant Muslims.

Westerners usually work in corporate environments and lately in some property and tourist sectors. Iranians also enjoy high status positions, often owning their own businesses and trading throughout the region. Many other Iranians, especially those educated in the West, will work in the same jobs as Westerners.

People from the Indian subcontinent (defined as Indians and Pakistanis in this context) fall into more than one category. Many are office managers or hold other middle management positions in Arab run companies. Many companies are Indian run; these organisations will usually have an almost exclusively Indian staff, although the organisation may be owned and sponsored by an Arab national. (Sponsors are described in further detail in the Ready for Business chapter.) Other Indians are small business owners or traders, working the long hours this requires as in any other part of the world. Most positions within the IT industry, especially technical positions, are almost all held by Indians. Senior management may be either Indian or Western, mostly depending on the organisation's ownership.

However, the majority of people from the Indian subcontinent are in either the service sector or are labourers. People in the service sector will have an excellent command of English, and will be well educated if they are directly customer facing (hotel reception staff, waiters, retail sales clerks, etc.). Drivers will speak enough English to be able to converse with passengers, although their education level will vary. Labourers are usually from remote areas of the subcontinent, generally have very little formal education and are often illiterate. They often come to the Gulf with little or no exposure to the outside world beyond their home village.

Bangladeshis and Sri Lankans, although geographically part of the Indian subcontinent, will most often be employed as drivers, housemaids or nannies.

People from the Philippines fall into a similar category. Other Filipinos work in retail, especially if they are well educated, as their English is invariably of an acceptable standard. Many Filipinos are also employed in bars and restaurants; they are predominantly Christian and, as such, generally have no problem working with alcohol or providing live entertainment such as music.

People from Japan, Korea and China, including Taiwan, are all recent arrivals to the region. The Japanese and Koreans hold jobs similar to Westerners, and hold an 'honorary' Western status in the business world. The Chinese situation is more complex. Chinese who are well educated and speak excellent English will fall into the same category as Japanese and Koreans. Others who own their own small business would be regarded similarly to Indian business owners. Chinese labourers suffer from a lower status, especially if their spoken English is limited.

There are very few residents from Sub-Saharan Africa, with the exception of South Africans and a few Zimbabweans, who are regarded as Westerners as they will almost always be of European or Indian descent. There are also very few residents from South America. Those few who are in the Gulf are often of Arab descent.

'-isation' programmes

The Gulf countries are encouraging their own nationals to take up more positions in the work force, especially in the private sector. Under the leadership of Sheikh Mohammed, Dubai started a programme around the turn of the millennium called 'Emiratisation'. Emiratisation is designed to promote a reduced dependency on foreign workers, a high status on an expanded list of jobs, and to create national pride. Emiratisation also ensures that the reputation of local women is protected, removing a cultural barrier that could have prevented them from joining the work force.

'-isation' programmes have been established throughout the Gulf, and have been adapted to each country's economic and demographic needs. Their success is varied; some countries are doing very well, others are struggling to find qualified nationals who are also willing to work.

Eventually, the impact of '-isation' means that fewer ex-pats should be needed, at least in high status jobs, reducing the number of foreign residents in a region that already has one of the largest population imbalances in the world. Westerners who are involved in recruiting should ensure they are well informed about the latest details of any programmes that could affect their line of business. Many Gulf countries are establishing a quota system that ensures a minimum percentage of employees now joining an organisation are home country nationals.

How easy is it to get to know local Arab nationals?

Throughout the GCC, many Western business professionals never end up working with local nationals, especially if they are working with multinational organisations from the West or, increasingly, India and the Far East. Others may be introduced to a local business partner as a one-off and who otherwise prefers to stay in the background.

Westerners should be aware that it can be difficult to get to know some Gulf nationals on a personal level, most notably those from KSA, Kuwait, Qatar and the UAE, at least in the early days. It is somewhat easier in Bahrain and Oman. Most of the population are much more likely to conduct their social lives around their family, with little room for outsiders, including other Arab nationals. It is possible that this situation may change as various '-isation' programmes take hold, although most conventional wisdom would predict that GCC nationals will continue to keep their private lives separate from their expatriate work colleagues.

Western business professionals who are working in the Levant or Egypt will have many opportunities to get to know local Arab nationals. Although their social lives also revolve around their families, many people from the Levant also socialise outside the home with groups of friends, including women. There is every chance the Westerner could be included in these social circles once a relationship has time to develop.

3

An introduction to Islam

Islam is more then a religion – it is a way of life. It is important that Western business professionals have an elementary knowledge of Islam if they intend to spend any time working in the Middle East.

THE FUNDAMENTALS

Islam is a monotheistic, Abrahamic religion that shares its roots with Judaism and Christianity. The word Islam means submission to *Allah* (God). It comes from the same root as the word *salaam*, which means peace. A Muslim (the preferred spelling and never Mohammedan) is a person who believes in Islam.

Islam follows the teachings of the Prophet Mohammed, who Muslims believe was the final prophet. These teachings are known as the *sunnah* – the traditions and practices of the Prophet. It can also be described as a way of life. The *hadith* refers to the oral traditions regarding the words and deeds of the Prophet. There are some distinctions between the *sunnah* and *hadith* amongst various Muslim groups.

Muslims believe that the *Qur'an* (the preferred spelling to Koran) is the Islamic holy book, revealed over several years to the Prophet Mohammed by the angel Gabriel, initially as a divine revelation during the month of *Ramadan*. It is written in Arabic and usually studied in Arabic, although translations are also used for non-Arabic speakers. Only the Arabic language version is considered to be pure, especially if needed to clarify a point; the translation is never considered correct. The *Qur'an* contains some of the same components as the *Torah* (the Jewish Holy Book) and the Bible (the Christian Holy Book), although they are interpreted in different ways to these texts. Most Muslims believe that Islam and the *Qur'an* are a correction and completion of Jewish and Christian teachings.

The *Qur'an* is used as a source of Islamic Law known as *Shari'a* law. *Shari'a* law is comprehensive, addressing everything from punishment for criminal activity to providing guidance for everyday civil matters.

A mosque (*masjid* in Arabic) is a place of worship for Muslims. General prayers are led by an *imam*. *Imams* are not exact parallels to ministers, priests or rabbis, but are respected community leaders. *Sunni* religious scholars are known as *mufti*. They interpret Islamic law. The *Shi'a* equivalent is an *ayatollah*.

Practising Muslims pray five times per day. These prayers are called *salat*. Prayer times are determined by the movements of the sun, and will vary from day to day and from location to location. They are described in further detail in the Five Pillars of Islam found later in this chapter.

The *azan* is the call to prayer. It is performed by a *muezzin*, who is not a religious scholar but who is considered to be a man (never a woman) of good character, also chosen for the quality of his voice. In the modern world, the *azan* is often pre-recorded. As a side note, Western business professionals who do not wish to be awakened by the first *azan* of the day (held at dawn, as much as 75 minutes before sunrise) should check the location of their hotel room relative to that of the nearest mosque.

Wudu are a proscribed set of ablutions that must be performed prior to prayer, regardless of where a Muslim is praying. Water must be used if available; otherwise, it is possible to use earth, including sand in the desert, or to emulate washing motions if neither is available. There are facilities for *wudu* at all mosques. Shoes must also be removed before entering a mosque and before praying.

Many Muslims pray on a prayer rug called a *sajada*, especially if they are praying away from a mosque. This ensures the ground on which they are praying is clean. Mosque floors are usually carpeted and are considered clean.

The *Ka'aba*, located in Mecca, is the holiest site in Islam. It is believed to have been first built upon by Abraham, and was the site of prayer for the Prophet Mohammed. It is the large, gold-trimmed, black, cube-shaped monolith seen in the media that is often encircled by faithful pilgrims. It is now surrounded by the mosque known as the Masjid al Haram. Muslims around the world face the *Ka'aba* in Mecca when they pray.

It is not uncommon for Westerners to refer to Muslims praying to the East. From most Westerners' geographical point of view, it may roughly describe the general direction of Mecca, but it is not accurate. More importantly, the direction of Mecca can be any of the compass points for those living in the Middle East. For example, someone praying from Dubai would actually be facing nearly due West. Thus, it is better practice to refer to Muslims as praying towards Mecca rather than to reference a compass direction.

Prayers are performed by following a specific set of rituals and reciting specific words. Daily prayers may be performed at a mosque, prayer room at home, or even in transit. Generally, prayers last for about 20 to 30 minutes when praying with others in a mosque. For others praying individually, it may only last for a few minutes. Praying is considered serious business, especially for men.

As in many Jewish congregations, mosques are segregated by gender. Women pray in a separate part of the mosque to men. This may be a separate room, a section of the prayer hall roped off for women, behind men, or in another part of the mosque inaccessible to men. In some cultures, women have no access to their local mosques.

Friday is the holy day throughout the Muslim world. It is expected that Muslims attend mosque during the Friday midday prayer. The Friday midday prayer is called *Jumu'ah* and is the most important prayer of the week. It includes a sermon, led by a *khatib*, who may or may not be the *imam*. The Friday midday prayer can last for 90 minutes.

There are a number of Islamic terms and concepts that have been introduced to the West in recent years and now are used in mainstream Western media. A few in particular are now used with meanings vastly different from their original meaning (and the meaning still used within Muslim communities worldwide):

Jihad means 'struggle' and is applied in everyday Islamic life as an ongoing attempt to live one's life in compliance with *Allah*'s wish. It is considered to be an effort or struggle to live a moral and ethical life. It does not mean a Holy War against the West. There are, however, various interpretations as to what a moral and ethical life within Islam entails.

A *fatwa* is not a death sentence, although a *fatwa* proclaiming the death sentence was issued by the Ayatollah Khomeini against the writer Salman Rushdie upon publication of *The Satanic Verses* in 1989. A *fatwa* is more accurately described as a religious opinion that is meant to guide Muslims in achieving a moral way of life. *Fatawa* (plural) may address everything from recommending the boycott of Danish butter to allowing guide dogs to accompany a blind person into a mosque. *Ulema* (religious scholars) can be found who hold the full range of religious opinion, from the extremist views of the followers of Osama bin Laden to several groups in North America who are supporting various women's rights and equality issues.

A *madrassa* is a place of learning, i.e. a school. A *madrassa* can teach at all levels, from the Western equivalent of primary education through higher education in specialised fields, including mathematics, science, medicine and literature. There are many *madrassas* throughout the world that provide a full curriculum of subjects, leading to a high standard of education.

It is inaccurate to describe all *madrassas* as institutions that espouse radical Islam. However, it is true that there are some *madrassas* that focus on memorisation of the *Qur'an* and sometimes little else. *Madrassas* also hold a diverse range of political thought, often reflecting the political views of their benefactors. Whilst the vast majority of *madrassas* teach tolerance, there are exceptions.

A *talib* is a student. Unfortunately, this word has been hijacked by the fundamentalist political group of former students in Afghanistan known throughout the world as the *Taliban*.

The Five Pillars of Islam

Most mainstream Muslims, including all *Sunnis*, recognise five pillars of Islam. Other groups have additional beliefs as well, including Ibadi, Druze, Ismailis and some *Shi'a*. These groups will be discussed in further detail later in this chapter.

Shahada

Shahada means the profession of the faith that there is only one God and that Mohammed is his prophet. The *shahada* is recited every day by religious Muslims. In English, the recitation is 'There is no God but *Allah*, and Mohammed is his messenger.' The script found on the national flag of Saudi Arabia is the *shahada*. Interestingly, non-Muslims who wish to convert simply do so by reciting the *shahada* in public.

Salat

Salat is formal Muslim prayer. Prayers are performed five times per day by practicing religious Muslims. The *azan* or *adhan* is the call to prayer heard from mosques that announce a prayer time.

- *Fajr* (dawn) – Not to be confused with sunrise, the *fajr* prayer occurs at the first sign of changing light at the end of night. Very religious Muslims believe they need to complete this prayer before sunrise (*shurooq*) begins.
- *Dhuhr* (early afternoon) – *Dhuhr* occurs just after the sun peaks in the sky, and is replaced by *Jumu'ah* on Friday.
- *Asr* (late afternoon) – *Asr* occurs according to a calculation of the size of an object relative to its shadow. From a practical point of view, it is the time when many people can just start to detect a change in the heat of the day.
- *Maghrib* (sunset) – *Maghrib*, as the name suggests, occurs at sunset.
- *Isha* (night) – *Isha* occurs at the end of twilight, when the night sky arrives.

Zakat

Zakat means the giving of alms, which has parallels in the Christian practice of tithing. *Zakat* is calculated by using a formula applied to a person's wealth based on their savings and assets. *Zakat* has other conditions as to when and where it is paid. Western business professionals are most likely to be aware of *zakat* during *Ramadan*, when many acts of charity are visible even to non-Muslims.

Sawm

Sawm means fasting. It is practised during the month of *Ramadan*, which is the ninth lunar month of the Islamic calendar. *Ramadan* is also known as *Ramzan* in Iran and the Indian subcontinent, so do not be surprised to hear this term, especially from Iranians and Pakistanis. *Sawm* lasts for the duration of *Ramadan*, usually 29 or 30 days.

During *Ramadan*, all followers must not eat, drink (including water), smoke, chew gum, or engage in sexual relations from dawn to sunset. They must also strive to think good thoughts and do good deeds.

People who are exempt from *sawm* include anyone where fasting would cause them physical harm: very small children (usually to the age of puberty, but younger in some conservative cultures), infirm elderly people, people with medical conditions such as diabetes, pregnant women and nursing mothers.

Older children who have not yet reached puberty will often start fasting, but are allowed to break the fast as necessary. Menstruating women must not fast during this time. Short-term travellers are also exempt – airlines will be fully catered during *Ramadan*, including Middle East-based carriers. There are rules of compensation for not fasting for most of these exemptions. For example, observers may fast on another day(s) after *Ramadan* is over to make up the 'missed day(s)' not fasting.

Hajj

The *Hajj* is also known as the Pilgrimage to Mecca. It is an act of devotion to *Allah*. Every Muslim who is physically able and has the financial means to do so is obligated to perform *Hajj* at least once in their lifetime. This applies to men and women.

Hajj is held on 8–10 *Dhu al-Hijjah*, the twelfth and last month of the Islamic calendar. Thus, *Hajj* will occur a little over two months after the end of *Ramadan*.

Ihram is the state of being a person experiences whilst performing *Hajj*. A series of rituals will be practised by pilgrims in a set sequence. Many Muslims believe that their past sins are forgiven, but this is not universal. *Ihram* clothing is worn during the pilgrimage. It is usually in the form of two pieces of simple white cloth for men, whilst women will often wear a simple white robe. The purpose of *ihram* clothing is to make all pilgrims of equal status. Westerners may also notice that many men dye their beards with henna upon completion of the *Hajj*, which turns it orange. The same men may also dye their hair with henna; others will ritually shave their hair instead.

Umrah is a pilgrimage to Mecca that takes place at any other time of the year. It is encouraged in Islam, but does not take the place of *Hajj*.

BACKGROUND AND DEMOGRAPHICS

Islam is considered to have begun when the Prophet Mohammed fled from Mecca to Medina in the seventh century. The exact date corresponds to 16th July 622 in the Western calendar. It spread throughout the Arabian Peninsula in just a few years, and through the influence of traders, could be found from Spain to India within 100 years. Islam also became the dominant religion of modern day Malaysia, Indonesia, Brunei, and much of North and East Africa a little later, also introduced by Arab trade.

Today, Muslims can be found in nearly every part of the world. It is estimated that there are up to 1.5 billion Muslims worldwide, representing up to 25% of the world's population. By comparison, it is believed that about 1.9 billion people are Christian or claim a Christian background. There are about 800 million Hindus worldwide. All other religions are much less populous.

Remarkably, only 20% of the world's Muslims live in the Middle East. Another 50% live elsewhere in Asia, including 30% in the Indian subcontinent and 16% in the Far East. About 4% live in the West, mostly in Europe, although Muslim populations are growing in the Americas. Most of the remainder live in Africa.

SUNNIS AND SHI'A

Shortly after the beginning of Islam, the religion split into two main factions, *Sunni* and *Shi'a*. (The term *Shi'ite* has been used in the West for *Shi'a*, but is incorrect.) Between 80% and 85% of the world's Muslims are *Sunni*; most of the rest are *Shi'a*.

Sunnis believe in following the *Sunnah*, the way of life of the Prophet Mohammed. They believe *caliphs* are successors to the Prophet, and should be chosen from the Muslim community, subject to a number of qualifications. A *caliph* is the head of an *ummah* or religious community.

According to *Sunnis*, Abu Bakr was the first *caliph*, followed by Umar, Uthman and Ali. The division between *Sunni* and *Shi'a* is the result of a dispute in the lineage of subsequent *caliphs*; the division was permanently deepened when the third *caliph* Uthman was murdered. His death set off a series of events that led to the eventual split of the Islamic community into the two main sects that exist to this day, reinforced during the events of the Battle of Siffin.

Sunnis live throughout the Middle East. Amongst Muslim populations in the Middle East, they are only in the minority in Iran and Bahrain. Muslims throughout Africa and the Far East are nearly all *Sunni*.

Shi'a believe that Ali should have been the first *caliph*. *Shi'a* do not believe that *caliphs* are the holders of power within Islam. Instead, they believe this power is transferred through the lineage of Ali, the Prophet Mohammed's son in law, whose wife Fatimah was a daughter of the Prophet.

The vast majority of *Shi'a*, about 85%, belong to the sect known as Twelvers, derived from their beliefs back to a group of twelve *Imams*.

Most of the world's *Shi'a* population live in Iran. Elsewhere in the Middle East, there are significant pockets in southern Iraq, the Eastern Province of Saudi Arabia, Bahrain, and southern Lebanon.

Wahhabis (Salafis)

Wahhabis are *Sunni* Muslims who believe in strictly following the teachings of the *Qur'an* and the *hadith*, emulating the way of life found during the first years of Islam during the time of the Prophet Mohammed. It is considered by *Wahhabis* to be the purest form of Islam. Many other Muslims disagree, including many other *Sunnis*.

Unlike most followers of Islam, *Wahhabism* cannot be described as tolerant of other religious beliefs, including other Islamic beliefs. It believes that all non-Muslims and Muslims holding other beliefs are *infidels* – someone who has no religious faith. It also believes in absolute, unquestioning adherence to the interpretations of their religious scholars.

Wahhabism is the dominant sect of Islam in Saudi Arabia, and is responsible for the rules, regulations and restrictions found in everyday Saudi life, including those placed on Western business professionals.

Wahhabism is often described as being synonymous with *Salafism*; others make the distinction that *Salafism* is a group of ultra-conservative Islamic sects, of which *Wahhabism* is prominent. Interestingly, *Wahhabis* themselves prefer to be referred to as *Salafis*, and may consider the term *Wahhabi* as derogatory.

Ibadis

Ibadi Muslims are found mostly in Oman, where they form the majority of the population. *Ibadi* Muslims are neither *Sunni* nor *Shi'a*, although they share some of the beliefs of both groups. *Ibadis* have a reputation for moderation and tolerance.

Ismailis

Ismailis are a sect within *Shi'a* Islam, representing about 15% of the *Shi'a* population. They are known in the West mostly because of the name recognition of the Aga Khan IV, considered to be the *Ismailis'* 49th *Imam* – and stepson of the actress Rita Hayworth.

Druze

The *Druze* are a sect that are not considered to be Muslim by many *Shi'a* and especially *Sunni* Muslims, but followers of an offshoot of Islam; others consider *Druze* to be related to *Ismailis*. *Druze* are monotheistic. A person can only be a *Druze* if they are born of *Druze* parents; it is not possible to convert into this religion. It is believed there are no more than one million *Druze* worldwide; most live in the Levant.

4

Islam and business

As a Western business professional, there are a number of Islamic beliefs and practices that will impact on the rhythm of your business day, how you conduct business, and how well you will be accepted by your local business partners, customers and colleagues.

CONCEPT OF RELIGIOUS HIERARCHY

Lack of political correctness goes beyond nationality. Whilst Islam is generally a tolerant religion, with the notable exception of groups like *Wahhabis*, it does not mean that Muslims view all people with equal acceptance in all circumstances, although Islam actually recognises respect and tolerance for all. Practically speaking, there is a definite hierarchy in play within a religious context as well as in terms of nationality.

As a Western business professional, there are times you will benefit from your position in the hierarchy; at other times the same position will work to your disadvantage. Nor is it always obvious when your position within the religious hierarchy is being taken into consideration. Don't expect anyone to inform you when this is happening, either.

Status	Religion	Sub group
High	'People of the Book'	Muslims, sometimes divided further into *Sunni* or *Shi'a* sub groups
	'People of the Book'	Christians*
	'People of the Book'	Jews**
	'Idol Worshipers'	Other non-monotheistic religions, including Hinduism, Sikhism***, Buddhism, Taoism, Shintoism, Zoroastrians/Parsis, Baha'is, Jainism, Confucianism and animist religions
Low	Agnostics and Atheists	If publicly declared ****

* As a Western business professional, it will generally be assumed that you are Christian. No distinction will be made as to whether you are Protestant, Catholic or indeed from any particular sect. The main exception would be a Westerner who is ethnically Asian. In this case, an inquiry as to your religion can be expected, even from someone you have just met. This is so you can be placed in the religious hierarchy. Sometimes, this can be of benefit to the Westerner who is also Muslim. It can also be a disadvantage in other situations. Westerners of African origin are assumed to come from the UK or possibly the US (especially if military) and are generally assumed to be Christian. Do not be surprised if a Middle Eastern colleague asks you directly about a religious topic, asking for your Christian perspective. Often, they are simply trying to build a relationship with you.

** From a historical perspective, Jews have been regarded in much the same way as Christians. Matters are more complicated in the modern world due to the ongoing conflict between Israel and much of the rest of the Middle East. There is a belief amongst quite a few people in the Middle East that all Jews must be Zionist, which causes much of the current negative attitudes towards Jewish people.

On occasion, people from the US may be asked if they are Jewish; this is highly unlikely to occur with other Western nationalities. We will address several issues regarding Judaism and nationality in further detail in a later chapter.

*** Although Sikhism is considered to be a monotheistic religion, it is not an Abrahamic religion, and is thus placed differently in the religious hierarchy.

**** Most people in the Middle East can become distressed if you make a public declaration of your uncertain or complete lack of religious belief. There is actually little distinction made between agnosticism and atheism. From a Muslim's point of view, religion is a person's moral compass. Therefore, if you make a statement that you are agnostic or an atheist, many people may believe you have just stated you have no morals!

This brings about an ethical dilemma for many Western business professionals, who are indeed agnostics or atheists. It is recommended that if you fall into this category, you make a statement to the effect that you come from a Christian background or that you have Christian values. You are (technically) probably not lying, and your Muslim colleague will be able to satisfy their need to place you in the religious hierarchy.

ISLAMIC VALUES

Jihad

Islam is a way of life. *Jihad* is the struggle to adhere to Islamic values. Religious Muslims will refer to their religion in every day life, considering the correct reference for even the most mundane matter. Do not be surprised if someone uses a number of religious expressions in everyday life. For example, when meeting someone, the typical greeting is *as salaam aleikum* (peace be with you). *Al hamdu lilaah*, which is often used when something good has happened, means 'praise be to God'.

Family

Family obligations are of the utmost importance to Muslims. Family is more important than work. Family obligations will often be the reason why someone doesn't meet you on time or cancels your appointment at the last minute.

Family includes members far beyond the Western definition of a nuclear family. It includes the entire extended family, including grandparents, uncles and aunts, cousins, and sometimes non-relatives who have earned a place as an honorary family member. Family can also mean a wider group of people in certain contexts, including tribes, people from the same ancestral village, or specific religious sects.

The largest family in Islam is the *ummah*, which refers to Muslims around the world. Many of the same obligations and sympathies to family can be seen in practice in the Middle East. For example, Sheikh Mohammed declared that New Year's Eve celebrations be cancelled in 2008/09 to show solidarity with Arabs in Gaza, who were suffering from Israeli attacks.

There is a well-defined hierarchy within a Muslim family. Traditionally, men have more status than women. Men are expected to shoulder the responsibilities of the family in public; the woman is responsible for the well-being of the family and the family's private needs. In this regard, her powers are substantial.

Historically, these are no different than many family values found in Western Christian communities, at least until very recently. However, this is changing in many parts of the Middle East, with women venturing out into the world of work and other public arenas. It's also why the Westerner can still observe separate treatment of women in public, both positive and not so positive. For example, women-only queues in places like government buildings are designed to treat women out in public with special respect; on the other hand, many

Muslim men can be observed queue jumping past women in *souqs* (markets) and other environments.

Marital status is important, as is parenthood. Both genders are considered to have obtained a higher social status once they have married. It is expected that all Muslims will marry, regardless of personal or lifestyle preference.

Gay and lesbian Muslims are expected to marry and live an outwardly heterosexual lifestyle. In fact, many people in the Middle East may ignore or even deny that there are any homosexuals amongst their family or their wider community.

Young adults who are still single will almost always remain with their family until they marry. Cohabitation before marriage is unheard of in Muslim (and most Christian) communities throughout the Middle East.

Parents have a higher status than childless couples. Sons are generally valued more than daughters. It is not unusual to see families with several older girls and one young boy.

Children born out of wedlock remain a strong taboo, in part because it complicates the family hierarchy. It would be highly unusual for a Westerner to be aware of this as it would be considered shameful for the family, and thus a topic to be avoided at all costs.

Age also has more status than youth. It is refreshing for older Westerners to receive a bit more respect simply due to their age. The author has also observed more than one Western man deciding to grow his greying beard when working in the region.

Do not be surprised if someone from the Middle East asks you quite personal questions about your own family. From their perspective, it is not being rude. They are simply trying to work out where you fit in the hierarchy. They may also make some comments that would be considered judgmental in the West, although they are not meant to be hurtful. Single people will often be pitied past a certain age if they are not married. Childless, married couples past a certain age will be asked if they are going to have children soon. People with sons in particular will be praised for their good fortune.

For those Westerners who are not married or do not have children, it is advised that you steer conversations towards other family members to show that you have strong family values. A nephew, cousin or an elderly grandparent are all safe options. Referring to your pets as your surrogate children is not recommended, no matter how adorable you think they are.

Finally, family values are just as important to many other cultures you may be working with, especially those from the Indian subcontinent. Keep this in mind when working with these expatriates as well.

Honour

Personal and family reputation is very important. Throughout the Middle East, the action of an individual reflects not only on themselves, but also on their family. Men and women are expected to act in an honourable manner at all times, especially in public, to preserve the good reputation of their family.

There is a high motivation to avoid losing face, as it can sometimes lead to compromising one's honour. Try not to tease or embarrass anyone, even if it is only meant to be in the spirit of good humour. There is no doubt that many people in the Middle East do have a good sense of humour. However, it's better to get to know someone first before using humour, especially sarcasm or irony.

Traditionally, your word and your handshake represent your honour. Many people in the Middle East still subscribe to this practice, although written agreements are now common throughout the region as well. It remains prudent for the Western business professional to be very careful of what they say, even if it is only a casual or throwaway remark. Chances are good that your Middle Eastern counterpart will remember your comment and expect you to honour it, even without a handshake, even after much time has passed.

Family honour is held to an even higher standard by the women of the family, and will be protected at all costs, sometimes even to an extreme degree. This is particularly relevant with issues of sexuality.

Western business professionals should always keep this in mind whenever they are interacting with a Muslim woman. In today's business environment, many young Muslim women are the first female members of their family working outside the home, especially nationals of most Gulf countries. On the other hand, many more women in the Levant have had careers, sometimes for generations. In general, Western business professionals, especially men, are safe by simply following the woman's lead, as she will not violate her own boundaries of honourable behaviour.

Western men in particular should avoid putting a Muslim woman in a situation where they are alone with only one other person, even in an office environment. Try to ensure someone else is always nearby. Keep the office door open. Western women will find that very religious Muslim men will also avoid being alone with them.

A quick word about honour killings. Honour killings, where a woman is killed to 'restore' the honour of her family, often by a male relative, still exists in some communities in some parts of the Middle East. The issue arises when a woman is perceived to be compromising her sexual purity. This can be interpreted in a number of ways within these communities. These may include circumstances that are considered innocent to Westerners, such as gazing too long at an unrelated man or even smiling at a man in public. Many Westerners may incorrectly associate honour killings with Islam. In fact, Islam considers honour killings to be totally un-Islamic and, in fact, sinful. Honour killings are wholly cultural.

The Western business professional is highly unlikely to engage intentionally in any behaviour that could lead to such a reprehensible act. However, any behaviour that could be interpreted as too familiar, including risqué or overly-friendly remarks, should be avoided. This includes off-colour jokes or anything that could be interpreted as sexual. It is also strongly advised that Westerners should avoid discussing honour killings as a political topic of conversation, even if the Westerner is simply trying to become better educated.

Loyalty

There is a code of loyalty amongst Muslims that exists in both social and business environments which will impact on the Western business professional. In the business world, there is much more loyalty within and amongst organisations than is found in the West, including long tenure by employees and companies doing business with other companies simply because they have traded for many years.

This is particularly true in well-established business relationships with Westerners, where trust has been earned and loyalty expected as a result. Your local business partner may expect you to provide them with information or business practices that could be seen as unfair advantages in the West. However, from the perspective of the Middle Eastern colleague, the expectation is simply natural amongst loyal business partners.

Not too many years ago, there was an expectation of exclusivity in most partnership agreements. The demands of the modern business environment have moved on from exclusive relationships, but do not be surprised if your business partners expect you to remain loyal to them even if you are adding new partnerships in the region.

Courtesy

Courtesy is valued in Islam. There are formal greetings and replies that are repeated by Muslims whenever they meet, which reflect the nature of their relationship and their position within social hierarchies.

The Western business professional is not expected to know the intricacies of these greetings, although learning how to say hello and thank you in Arabic is appreciated. Westerners should always acknowledge their colleagues upon meeting them, even if they just saw them a few hours ago; if seated, they should stand. Failure to greet each and every time is considered rude.

It is also important to remain courteous at all times, even if you become frustrated by circumstances. Confrontational behaviour, arguments and shouting are considered to be rude, and will cause someone to lose status and face, including Westerners. Therefore it is very important to control your reaction at all times, even if you would not do so in the West. Patience is essential.

Respect

Islam values tolerance and respect for others. Attitudes and behaviour should be respectful at all times to both family (in its broadest sense) and others.

Hospitality and generosity

Hospitality is important throughout the Muslim world. It comes from the Bedouin tradition of offering shelter to any traveller making the difficult journey in the desert conditions of the Arabian Peninsula. This hospitality also extends to food. The guest's needs were always attended to first, even if it meant that the family went hungry.

Middle Eastern hospitality remains legendary. As a Western business professional, you will be treated as an honoured guest whenever you visit the region. This includes the level of service you will receive in hotels and elsewhere. Your business contacts will extend many courtesies to you as an honoured guest. This will include anything from constant offerings of tea to elaborate dinners held in your honour, especially if you have completed a key stage of business. Do not be surprised when, as a guest, any question you may pose to your host will receive a response such as 'whatever you like, my friend'.

Never refuse any gestures of hospitality or generosity. Even if you have already had twelve cups of tea earlier in the day, accept one more. Try to drink the first cup; you can pretend to sip it if absolutely necessary. It's okay to politely refuse refills, which is done by gently tipping the cup from side to side or by placing your right hand over the top of the cup. Never make a gesture to pay the bill – not even a half-hearted, token gesture – at a restaurant: it offends the sense of hospitality. Never offer to split a bill for the same reason.

Insh'allah

Insh'allah means 'God's will' or 'if God wills it'. It is a reference to the fatalistic attitude of religious Muslims, who believe that worldly events are ultimately determined by *Allah*. Hinduism's belief in *karma* is closely related. In fact, most Asian cultures believe in some form of fatalism.

It is one of the most common expressions heard throughout the Middle East, and one that most Western business professionals will quickly add to their own vocabulary. People who are finishing a meeting will often part with the comment 'we will meet again next week *insh'allah*' or 'tomorrow should be a lovely day *insh'allah*' or even 'our flight is scheduled to land at 10.45 *insh'allah*'.

The Western business professional should not interpret the use of *insh'allah* as dishonest; quite the opposite. It's generally an indication that the speaker intends to do what they say – if nothing else gets in the way or becomes more important. If it does, then it happened because of God's will. The other party should not be offended, and can generally expect the situation to be rectified as soon as God wills it to happen. Most people in the Middle East will include '*insh'allah*' whenever they refer to something in the future.

Arabic language

The official language of Islam is Arabic. It is held in roughly the same regard as Hebrew for Jews and Latin for Christians. Of course, those who speak Arabic are at an advantage in this regard. This would include most people from the Peninsula; others study it as an additional language. Some very religious communities memorise the *Qur'an* in Arabic even if they do not understand the language well enough to use it in everyday life.

Apostasy and proselytising

Westerners who may be keen to convert Muslims to Christianity should be aware that in many conservative Muslim communities, the penalty for apostasy (renouncing one's religion) for someone converting from Islam to another religion, including Christianity, is death. Although Christianity is tolerated throughout the Middle East, with the notable exception of Saudi Arabia, proselytising is illegal throughout the Gulf and discouraged elsewhere.

Traditional Islamic values do not include proselytising, although people who come to the religion of their own free will are welcomed. Western business professionals will not encounter pressure to convert to Islam, although they may receive comments about living according to Muslim values, especially about drinking, sex or the perceived breakdown of the Western family.

ISLAMIC AND CULTURAL TABOOS

In Islam, practices that are allowed are known as *halal*. Practices that are forbidden are known as *haram*. Muslims believe that there must be evidence that something is *haram*. If there isn't any evidence, then it is considered *halal*.

Pork

As in Judaism, pork is not eaten by practising Muslims. Nor are pork products used, such as items made out of pig skin. It has been the author's experience that over more than 30 years, she has never knowingly seen a Muslim eat pork anywhere in the Middle East. Of course, it is possible that some non-observant Muslims may eat pork in the privacy of their homes or whilst travelling abroad.

Other meat and poultry

Meat and poultry that is not *haram* must be slaughtered and prepared in a specific way as outlined in the *Qur'an* and *Sunnah* before a Muslim can consume it. This is why you will see *halal* butchers in neighbourhoods with a lot of Muslim customers even in the West.

No blood can remain in the meat. This preparation has very close parallels to the same practices in Judaism called *kashrut* that makes their food *kosher*, although the specific prayers said at the time of slaughter are different.

Butchers throughout the Middle East will comply with *halal* procedures. Meat that is not *halal* will be clearly labelled and sold in a separate establishment or at a separate counter in a supermarket if it is permitted in the country at all.

Fish with scales are considered *halal*. Other fish are considered by some sects as *halal*, and others as *haram*. Unlike in Judaism, where all shellfish is forbidden, many Muslims permit consumption of some or all shellfish; others don't. However, it's best to err on the side of caution in the company of very religious people and choose scaly fish if you are unsure.

Alcohol

Alcohol consumption is forbidden in Islam. Unlike the pork ban, many

Muslims can be seen drinking alcohol, both in the Middle East and beyond. Others will tolerate alcohol use by non-Muslims in their presence, but will not drink it themselves. Still others do not wish to be in the presence of anyone drinking alcohol. Alcohol-related issues will be discussed in further detail in relevant sections of this book

The left hand

The left hand is considered dirty throughout the Middle East, as it is in most Asian cultures. The left hand has traditionally been used for unclean functions, including removing shoes and for the toilet. This will be an ongoing challenge for left-handed people no matter how long they work in the Middle East, as this left-handed author can emphatically attest.

The left hand should never be used when eating with the hands. Never take food from a communal serving plate or bowl with your left hand, even when using cutlery. Approach buffets with the right hand only. Cutlery for individual use can be held in the left hand, as can pens and sporting equipment.

The left hand should never be used for passing items to another person. This includes food, an item in the office, business cards and gifts. Items should be passed with the right hand, or with both hands when necessary.

The soles of your feet

As experienced by former President Bush in Iraq, the soles of the feet are considered dirty and should never be seen by another person. The reporter who threw his shoes did not choose his 'weapon' by accident. Mr. Bush may or may not have realised the significance at the time, but the entire Muslim world most certainly did.

Western business professionals should not sit with their legs crossed at the knee, as the sole of your foot will inevitably be seen by someone else in the room. Westerners should also be prepared to sit on low cushions or even on the ground in a manner that does not show the bottoms of their feet. This is much trickier than it sounds, and may require quite a bit of dexterity. Bring a wrap or some other item to cover your feet if you cannot otherwise manage a suitable position.

Western business professionals should also be prepared to remove their shoes when entering a mosque or a person's home. In a home, slippers may be offered for indoor wear, but it's always a good idea to make sure the quality of your socks or tights are of sufficient standard.

Pornography

Islam is in agreement with other religions and most moral codes about the unacceptability of pornography. However, the definition of pornography may differ quite significantly from that of the West. Images of women who are not modestly dressed may be considered pornographic. Whilst images of women wearing tight, revealing clothing may be found in Beirut and Dubai, they will not be tolerated in most of the rest of the Middle East.

In Saudi Arabia, images may be considered pornographic or unsuitable that would not get a second look in the West. This can include any image of a man and woman in a social setting where it's obvious they are not related. It can also include innocuous images of Darcy Bussell in pirouette, Claudia Schiffer modelling a watch in a sleeveless blouse, or a photo of a businesswoman wearing a v-neck jumper in *The Economist*. It can also include the Manchester United team shirtless and in shorts.

A small army of censors are employed in Saudi Arabia whose sole job is to monitor and 'correct' pornographic images. In the examples above, the images would probably still be allowed into the Kingdom, but only once black markers have done their work on Darcy's legs, Claudia's arms, the businesswoman's neckline and the players' chests and legs.

Printed material will draw the most attention at customs, although electronic media may be searched as well. Both are less likely than in the past, but it's still best not to give the officials a reason to draw their attention to you.

If you are preparing marketing material for use in the Middle East, especially in Saudi Arabia, it's important to keep all of the above in mind. Also consider your company logo as to its suitability – consider the challenges for Starbucks or Virgin Atlantic.

Other inappropriate images

Many of the most conservative branches of Islam, including *Salafis*, consider images of other living things as *haram*. This includes photographs and other reproductions of people, animals and anything else that can be worshipped. Photographs of women are particularly frowned upon. From a practical point of view, photographs found in your corporation's annual report will be tolerated. More care should be given to photographs used in advertising and presentations.

Public displays of affection between a man and a woman

Whilst not as strictly enforced as in Saudi Arabia, all public displays of affection between a man and a woman should be avoided throughout the Middle East. This includes between people married to each other. Innocent gestures common in the West that should be avoided are hugging, touching any part of the body, holding hands and kissing on the cheeks, although kissing on the cheeks can be acceptable in some social circles in the Levant.

Dogs

Dogs are considered dirty in Islam. Whilst many people will keep guard dogs throughout the Middle East, they are unlikely to have dogs as pets. Western business professionals should keep this in mind if they are inclined to mention their beloved Fido.

Gambling and lotteries

All forms of gambling are *haram* in Islam. However, like with many other issues, the definition of gambling is open to interpretation.

Activities where money is exchanged for the sole purpose of a win based on chance are forbidden. This is most likely to include betting and lotteries. Card games often fall into the same category. Importing playing cards is technically illegal in Iran. It's also a good idea to leave your National Lottery or Euro Millions ticket at home.

Horse racing and camel racing proliferate throughout the Middle East. Interestingly, many religious scholars site various *hadith* that allow 'competitions' with horses and camels. Many Middle East countries will refer to this opinion to justify the acceptance of these sporting events.

Visitors throughout the Gulf will quickly notice the popularity of raffles held in various airports that include automobiles and other expensive items. Many authorities will justify these raffles by claiming they are designed for non-Muslims only. Others will skirt the rules by defining the way prize money is sourced so that it does not violate Islamic law. Although it is indeed the case that many non-Muslims are the main participants, it is not unheard of for customers to include Muslims from the Gulf countries and beyond.

Western business professionals who often rely on contests, prize draws, raffles or similar promotions amongst their marketing activities should be very careful. The basic rule of thumb is to introduce some skill or another factor so that the event is no longer simply a game of chance. It's probably best to steer clear of this technique altogether in Saudi Arabia.

Gold, silk and diamonds for men

Islam forbids men from wearing items that are considered an excessive display of wealth, which includes gold and silk. Some Islamic scholars will also consider these items to be feminine, and thus *haram* for men. There are many opinions as to whether this includes gemstones, especially diamonds.

Visiting most mosques

Rules vary throughout the world as to whether non-Muslims can visit mosques. Most Gulf mosques do not permit non-Muslims entry although some countries may designate a specific mosque available for non-Muslims during a particular time of day, often as part of a tourism programme; this is most likely to be late in the morning, but before the midday prayer. Many mosques in the Levant do, although there may be restrictions at prayer times or on Friday.

Travel to Mecca and Medina for non-Muslims

Western business professionals who are working in Saudi Arabia should be aware of additional restrictions surrounding travel to Mecca and Medina, Islam's two holiest cities located in the West of the country. Only Muslims are allowed into either city. These restrictions are strictly enforced near Mecca, with several road blocks and checkpoints along the way. Roads leading to restricted areas are clearly sign posted, one for the use of Muslims only and the other for non-Muslims. It is possible for non-Muslims to travel to the outskirts of Medina, including the airport, but not to the city centre. Medina's restricted areas are also clearly signposted. It is sensible advice for even the most intrepid traveller not to try to break this taboo, as penalties are severe and enforced.

Things you may find in your hotel room

A *shajada* (prayer rug) is often stored in a closet or drawer. It will measure about 100cm x 60cm. It will often be woven to contain geometric designs or an item found in a mosque. It should be treated with respect or left alone by guests who do not use it for prayer.

A *qibla* is a sign, sticker or other indication used to assist people as to the direction of Mecca. A *qibla* sticker can be found on desks or affixed to the ceiling in hotel rooms, published in *salat* schedules, or even displayed on video screens on airline flights. It may be a simple arrow, or it may be a degree reading on a compass. Like *salat* times, *qibla* information can also be found on many websites, and can be texted to a mobile.

A copy of the *Qur'an* is often found in a desk drawer. This book should be respected in the same way as a Bible, *Torah*, or any other religious holy book.

THE ISLAMIC CALENDAR

The Islamic world has its own calendar; it is known as the *hijra* calendar. The *hijra* starts when the Prophet Mohammed fled Mecca in the seventh century. It corresponds to 16th July 622 in the Western Gregorian calendar.

The *hijra* operates on lunar cycles. There are twelve lunar months in the *hijra* calendar. Days begin and end at sunset, as they do in the Jewish calendar. Each month starts and ends when the new moon is spotted at sunset. Thus, *hijra* months are typically twenty-nine or thirty days long. As a result, the Islamic year is ten to eleven days shorter per year than the Western calendar.

On 18th December 2009, it became year 1431 AH in the Islamic calendar. AH is used in a similar to using AD in the Gregorian calendar; AH comes from the Latin *anno Hegirae* (*Hijra* year).

Months of the year
Muharram
Safar
Rabi' al-Awwal
Rabi' al-Thani
Jumada al-Awwal
Jumasa al-Thani
Rajab
Sha'aban
Ramadan
Shawwal
Dhu al-Qi'dah
Dhu al'Hijjah

Days of the week	
al-ahad	Sunday
al-ithnayn	Monday
ath-thulaathaa'	Tuesday
al-arbia`aa'	Wednesday
al-khamis	Thursday
al-jumu`a	Friday
as-sabt	Saturday

Islamic, national and other holidays

Islamic religious holidays correspond to dates in the Islamic calendar. Because it is not in synchronisation with the Western calendar, Islamic holidays will occur ten to eleven days earlier than in the previous year.

It is not possible with complete precision to predict the date on which an Islamic holiday falls until shortly before the actual date. This is because traditional rituals are used in spite of the availability of more accurate modern technology, as they are believed to more accurately reflect the will of *Allah*.

Ramadan is a case in point. The start of *Ramadan* is observed by the possibility of a physical sighting of the new moon on the 29th day of the 8th month of the Islamic calendar. If it is seen, *Ramadan* begins the following day; if it is not seen, then there is one more full day before *Ramadan* starts. Thus, religious holidays in particular will only be officially declared shortly before the actual dates.

However, Westerners may wish to know precisely when a religious holiday will fall. This creates a dilemma, as the date is determined by *Allah* alone. The solution is usually provided through coded language. In the lead-up to a holiday, your Middle Eastern counterpart is likely to advise you 'it is 99% certain *Ramadan* will start on the 22nd or '*inshallah Eid* will begin this year on the 19th'.

National holidays correspond to dates on the Western calendar. Countries who also observe other religious holidays will recognise the dates of these holidays in accordance to their traditions; such as Christmas (fixed date), Easter or *Diwali* (lunar).

The names and a brief description of Islam's religious holidays that are most likely to impact the Western business professional are as follows:

Islamic New Year is held on *1 Muharram*, the first day of the Islamic calendar. It is a normal working day in most of the Middle East.

Ashura is held on *10 Muharram*, and is an important date for *Shi'as*. It is the day of martyrdom of Ali, an important *Shi'a* figure. This is the holiday where some men self-flagellate. As most countries in the Middle East have a minority *Shi'a* population, this holiday is most often celebrated in private within this community.

Mawlid is the Prophet Mohammed's birthday. *Sunnis* recognise this holiday on *12 Rabi al-awwal*. Businesses will be open, but alcohol is usually unavailable, even in licensed premises.

The entire month of *Ramadan* is a special time in the Islamic calendar. *Ramadan* is discussed in further detail in relevant sections throughout this book.

Eid al Fitr is held on *1–3 Shawwal*. It is a public holiday throughout the Islamic world and immediately follows *Ramadan*. *Eid al Fitr* is a time of feasting and celebration. Many people will buy new clothes to mark the festivities. It is the smaller of the two *Eid* holidays. Although *Eid al Fitr* officially lasts for three days, do not be surprised if celebrations last for up to one week, especially if the dates fall near the weekend.

The *Hajj* is held on *8–10 Dhu al-Hijjah*, and is described throughout this book.

Eid al Adha starts immediately after the *Hajj* is complete, on *10 Dhu al-Hijjah*, and lasts anywhere from three to five days, depending on location. This holiday is known as the Festival of the Sacrifice. Traditionally, a sheep, goat or camel is slaughtered, with the meat distributed between family, friends and the poor. It's also another time when people will wear their finest clothing.

Middle Eastern countries' and territories' national holidays:	
Bahrain	16th December
Egypt	23rd July
Iran	1st April (varies)
Jordan	25th July
Kuwait	25th February
Lebanon	22nd November
Oman	18th November
Palestinian Territories	15th November
Qatar	18th December
Saudi Arabia	23rd September
Sudan	1st January
Syria	8th March
UAE	2nd December
Yemen	14th October

Western business professionals should check to see if there are any additional holidays in the country they are travelling to. Some rulers have a habit of declaring additional public holidays, sometimes at short notice. Days of mourning are also declared with regular frequency, sometimes for an important figure in the region who may or may not be a national of that country.

References to historical events should be considered in the political and geographical context in which they occurred. For example, from the Israeli point of view, they would refer to the events in 1973 as the Yom Kippur War. From the Egyptian point of view, the same events are known as the 6th October War or the *Ramadan* War.

The working week

In the modern world, Western calendar dates are used in day-to-day business. The main exception to this is found in legal documents such as contracts, where the *hijra* calendar is recognised in some countries. There are many websites that will convert dates between the two calendars. Newspapers are usually published with both dates.

Friday is the holy day in Islam.

The Middle East has undergone significant changes to its working week in recent years. Traditionally, much of the Middle East worked a five and a half or even six day week, with Thursday afternoon and Fridays the only non-working days. However, with the impact of globalisation and time zone challenges, a number of countries have changed the definition of their working week. It should also be noted that many retailers are now opening their shops on Friday afternoons, after the end of the midday prayer. This includes shopping malls and supermarkets in most countries, including some in Saudi Arabia.

The table overleaf shows the working days of various Middle Eastern countries.

Bahrain	Sunday – Thursday
Egypt	Sunday – Thursday
Iran*	Saturday – Thursday, sometimes Thursday morning
Jordan	Sunday – Thursday
Kuwait	Sunday – Thursday
Lebanon	Monday – Friday
Oman**	Sunday – Thursday or Saturday – Wednesday, sometimes Thursday morning
Palestinian Territories	Saturday – Wednesday, sometimes Thursday morning
Qatar	Sunday – Thursday
Saudi Arabia	Saturday – Wednesday, sometimes Thursday morning
Sudan ***	Sunday – Thursday
Syria	Sunday – Thursday
UAE	Sunday – Thursday
Yemen	Saturday – Wednesday, sometimes Thursday morning

* Iran's working week is officially Saturday – Thursday. Many corporate offices will work either a five day week, or will close at lunch on Thursdays.

** Oman's working week is in a state of flux. Many corporations work Sunday – Thursday, similar to other countries in the area. Small businesses are more likely to work a five and a half day week, beginning on Saturday. The Omani government works from Saturday – Wednesday.

*** Sudan declared a five day week in January 2008 that applies to businesses and government offices in the Khartoum area. A six day working week may remain in effect elsewhere, with Friday the only non-working day.

Traditional working hours

Traditionally, the Arab world worked split days, taking a break for several hours in the afternoon, not unlike traditional *siestas* in Spain. Some countries which have retained a five and a half day working week continue to work split days. They will start work from relatively early in the morning – usually before 09.00 – until lunchtime. After a three to four hour break, they will work again until mid-evening. Breaks may be shorter in the winter than in the summer. However, this is somewhat dependent on the organisation, line of business and how much they trade with other countries, especially beyond the Middle East. If you are working in one of these countries, it's best to check which type of working day is in effect for each organisation. Split days are most often found in Saudi Arabia and Yemen.

Most of the Middle East, in conjunction with adapting to a five day working week, has now changed to a straight day, working continuously throughout the day, with a Western style break for lunch.

Each country and line of business has their own traditions as to opening hours, along with cultures of 'early arrivers' and 'late stayers', just like in the West. In general, there are many more countries where employees traditionally work late, especially if they are doing business in Europe or North America, where time zone challenges make this necessary. For example, many workers in Dubai may not be at work much before 10.00, but will be working at 19.00 and sometimes even later. In contrast, much of the work force in Jordan can be found at work at 08.00 or 08.30, but are unlikely to be working much beyond 17.00 or 18.00.

Many government offices in much of the Middle East are only open in the mornings, closing for the day at 13.00 or 14.00. Thus, Westerners who work with these organisations may need to realise that their work hours will differ from those of their counterparts in the private and commercial sectors.

Time zones

Time zones vary throughout the Middle East. Some countries advance their clocks by one hour in the summer months; others don't. The following table provides basic information for the business professional. It should be noted that countries that do change their clocks do so on dates that may vary from year to year and with other countries in the region. Some countries have changed their clocks some years and not others.

Country	Time zone	Clocks advanced in summer?
Bahrain	GMT +3	No
Egypt	GMT +2	Yes
Iran	GMT +3½	Yes
Iraq	GMT +3	No
Jordan	GMT +2	Yes
Kuwait	GMT +3	No
Lebanon	GMT +2	Yes
Oman	GMT +4	No
Palestinian Territories	GMT +2	Yes
Qatar	GMT +3	No
Saudi Arabia	GMT +3	No
Sudan	GMT +2	No
Syria	GMT +2	Yes
UAE	GMT +4	No
Yemen	GMT +3	No

Iranian calendar

Iran operates on its own calendar. It is called the Solar *Hejri* Calendar, and as the name implies, is calculated on the sun. It relies heavily on astronomical calculations. The Iranian calendar also incorporates the Islamic calendar.

The most important holiday in the Iranian calendar that will affect Western business professionals working with Iranian people, either in Iran or elsewhere in the Middle East is *Nowruz*, which is Iranian New Year. It starts on the vernal equinox (usually 21st March) and lasts for thirteen days. On 21st March 2010, it became year 1389 AH in the Iranian calendar.

PRAYER TIMES AND BUSINESS

Salat is mandatory for Muslims in Saudi Arabia, which is enforced by the *mutawwa* (religious police) in many areas of the country. All businesses close for the duration of each prayer, including business offices. You will be asked to leave retail shops, which will then be shuttered.

Religious police in many locations, including Riyadh, will be vigilant towards men complying with prayer times, expecting them to find the nearest mosque or prayer room.

In practice, some business may be conducted discretely and quietly during prayer times if the owner is not particularly religious, is of sufficient status in the community, and has rooms in the office that cannot be seen by the general public.

Western businessmen should leave any public venue if they are caught out and about at prayer time in Riyadh. Finding an out of the way, windowless room is a good idea. It's also possible to sit quietly in a restaurant, but the restaurant will be closed as the staff will be off praying. Others simply drive around aimlessly until prayer time is over. Western businesswomen are given a bit more leeway, and have the option to sit quietly in public if faced with the same dilemma, especially in Jeddah or the Eastern Province.

The practice of *salat* elsewhere will vary with the person. Many religious Muslims do not pray in the middle of a working day, but may pray later. Most religious Muslims believe they are permitted to 'make up' *salat* time by praying at a different time, subject to certain conditions. Less religious Muslims may only pray at the Friday midday prayer. Others may pray even less frequently or not at all.

As a Western business professional, it is important to be aware of prayer times, especially in Saudi Arabia and whenever you are working with religious Muslims. Scheduling a meeting during prayer times is never a good idea in these circumstances, and can cause people to wonder if you have the correct level of understanding of and commitment to the region. If you are responsible for organising a day-long event, it's prudent to determine whether you need to accommodate breaks to coordinate with prayer times; this is an essential strategy in Saudi Arabia.

Salat schedules are printed in every English language newspaper throughout the region. *Salat* schedules can also be found in hotels and, of course, on the internet. It is also possible to organise *salat* schedules to be sent by text to your mobile. Keep in mind that prayer times vary by location, even within a country, as well as being at slightly different times from one day to the next.

For those countries and organisations working a split day, it is traditional to return to work at the end of *Asr* prayers. This practice can still be seen in Saudi Arabia and in other traditional work environments.

RAMADAN AND BUSINESS

During *Ramadan*, business hours will be reduced throughout the Middle East. Outside of Saudi Arabia, specific hours will depend on the nature of the business and the number and influence of Muslims within the organisation. Most government offices will close for the day at the time of the midday prayer; others will work until 13.00 or 14.00. Many private businesses will have softer opening hours, with employees drifting into the office late or leaving early or mid-afternoon. Offices in Saudi Arabia will close early regardless of the line of business.

Ramadan is not generally a good time to travel to the Middle East for business, unless the nature of your trip is so important that it can't wait. A good way to look at *Ramadan* is as a time where business should be kept ticking over, but not a time to expect to make important business decisions, implement a new policy or programme, conduct training, or formally establish a new business relationship.

For those Western business professionals who must travel to the region during *Ramadan*, several courtesies are expected. In Saudi Arabia, Westerners must also fast in public, including in offices. Restaurants throughout the Kingdom will be closed, including those in your hotel. You should time room service or a trip to a supermarket to accommodate any food or beverage requirements you may have during the day and consume anything within the privacy of your room only. Never smoke or chew gum in public during daylight hours. Rules on any ex-pat compounds you may visit will be relaxed.

For those Western business professionals who travel elsewhere in the Gulf, some accommodation is made for non-Muslims. Many canteens will put up a screen where non-Muslims can eat or drink. It is polite to consume all food and beverages behind the screen and not in full view of colleagues and visitors who may be fasting. Try not to eat food that has a strong or distinctive smell. It is also insensitive to return to your desk with a coffee, tea or even a glass of water.

Ramadan is more relaxed in Egypt, Jordan, Lebanon and Syria, although fasting is being taken more seriously than a few years ago, with more restaurants remaining closed during the day and many more people observing the fast than before. This is particularly true in Egypt, Jordan and Syria. Lebanon is patchier, with fasting often unnoticeable in predominantly Christian neighbourhoods.

Alcohol is also less available during *Ramadan* throughout the Levant, especially during the day, even in restaurants designated for non-Muslims. Live music performances (in countries where it is permitted) is generally suspended during *Ramadan*.

Visitors should be careful when out and about in public. Whilst carrying a bottle of water is generally a good idea in a hot climate, it can also be insensitive when encountering taxi drivers and others who may be fasting. Be discrete wherever you go. It is also important to dress even more conservatively than usual during *Ramadan*, including Western business professionals and visitors.

During *Ramadan*, the Muslim world often seems to function in reverse time to the rest of the year. The region becomes lethargic and often grumpy during the day, but lively during the night. And as many people tend to stay up throughout much of the night, they may be tired when they arrive in the office the next morning. It's somewhat like suffering from jetlag without travelling anywhere. You should plan the pace of your business accordingly.

Iftars, the meal eaten to break fast at sunset, are often elaborate. *Iftars* can include extended family and friends, who may be breaking their fast at home or in a restaurant. *Iftars* are also held and hosted by charities for the poor in several public venues such as parks and near mosques. *Suhoor* is a meal that most observants eat just before dawn.

Westerners who find themselves in the Middle East during *Ramadan* should try to attend an *iftar* as a way to experience a pleasant part of *Ramadan*. Hotels generally organise elaborate *iftars*. They are also a good way to host a business dinner and help you gain acceptance in the region.

Contrary to logic, many people actually gain weight during *Ramadan*, especially if they are partaking in too many *iftar* celebrations.

Dealing with alcohol in a business environment

Because there are so many attitudes towards the consumption of alcohol within the Middle East, this issue should be handled with extreme caution. Furthermore, there are official or 'public' attitudes that may or may not be the same as exhibited in a safe, private environment, depending on a number of factors, including who else is present, which country you are in, and if it is *Ramadan* or another religious holiday.

Of course, Western business professionals should never try to import alcohol into Kuwait or Saudi Arabia, where it is illegal. People who feel the need to drink alcohol whilst on a business trip to either country should rethink either their attitude towards alcohol, or possibly have another person travel to these countries instead.

Although there are certainly underground venues where alcohol can be found, the penalty for being caught can be severe. Never accept an invitation from someone you don't know very well, especially to an establishment that doesn't 'feel right'.

It gets trickier if you are invited to the home of a national of either country. Western business professionals have testified to the existence of fully stocked wine cellars in opulent homes in Riyadh. Usually, the local person is very well connected, with enough *wasta* (influence) to have ensured that the *muttawa* (Saudi religious police) ignore its existence.

Although official advice would be to decline such an invitation, the realities on the ground are quite different. Most Western business professionals would actually be wise to accept such an invitation – it's a sure-fire way to build a stronger and more trusting relationship. Businesswomen invited to such a home on their own are an obvious exception in a business environment. Discretion should be used if a woman receives an invitation as part of a larger group.

For the remaining countries, it is a matter of determining the correct etiquette in each social setting.

For some Muslims, simply being in the presence of alcohol is offensive. If you are working with anyone who falls into this category, especially if it's someone important, it's best to plan on omitting alcohol from your event. Most likely that person's colleagues will refrain from alcohol as well, at least in the objector's presence.

Other Muslims choose not to drink alcohol themselves, but are neutral or tolerant of others who drink in their presence. Others may have one drink out of courtesy to accompany Westerners who choose to drink; some others may only drink wine with a meal. Some Muslims will abstain from drinking in public but will drink in private, including venues such as private dining rooms in restaurants or in members-only clubs. These are unlikely to be the same people you may see in nightclubs and bars of the more liberal cities in the Gulf. It's a good idea to moderate your own intake of alcohol in all of these circumstances.

On the other hand, you may be just the excuse some Muslims are looking for to engage in a heavy night of binge drinking. Do not be surprised if you find yourself entertaining Saudis and Iranians, in particular, in the most unlikely of venues, especially in Dubai. Bahrain is also a popular destination, especially for Saudis who cross the Causeway between the two countries for the weekend. Egypt's belly dancing and other nightclubs are also popular, although they are tamer than they were in the recent past. Lebanon continues to be well known for its late night party culture, especially in Christian communities.

If you are unsure of your Muslim colleagues' attitudes towards alcohol, you should explore their preferences with discretion. Directly asking them if they would like a beer or to choose from the wine menu is too direct and will cause offence, even for those who intend to drink. This situation changes once you get to know them very well.

In the meantime, an excellent suggestion is to provide them with the drinks menu and ask them what they would like. If they quickly suggest an orange juice of other soft drink, you should not choose an alcoholic beverage. If they hesitate, it's a good idea to let them know you haven't decided yet either, and that you are considering a number of options on the menu. Drinkers may then make a tentative comment about an alcoholic choice, or may be ready to place their order for alcohol. If this occurs, you should order the same beverage. In the case of women, it's acceptable to order a glass of wine instead. Keep in mind that this process should be repeated each time you move from one location to another.

Vineyards are found in the Levant. Those with the best reputation are found in Lebanon, with some vineyards in the Bekaa Valley producing wines that are exported onto the global market.

Vineyards in Jordan are now producing good regional wines. Vineyards in Syria are beginning a revival and are also producing pleasant wines. Most people would agree that there are better choices than to drink locally-produced Egyptian wine.

SHARI'A LAW

Shari'a law is based on the *Qur'an* and *Sunnah* as interpreted by various religious authorities. Thus, the application of *Shari'a* law can vary widely amongst different communities. *Shari'a* law rules on all matters of day-to-day life, including politics, banking, contracts, family issues including marriage, divorce, child custody, death and inheritance, all manner of behaviour from sexuality to diet, from entertainment to human rights issues. It also rules on criminal matters. All Gulf countries are governed by *Shari'a* law to varying degrees. In Saudi Arabia, there is no other recognised law.

Countries in the Levant are governed by a combination of *Shari'a*, Ottoman law, Napoleonic codes, canon law and English common law, sometimes within the same country. Western business professionals working in the Palestinian Territories should have up-to-date knowledge of current Palestinian law, as it continues to be affected by political events in the region.

Shari'a law can have an impact on the Western business professional. It's a good idea to have at least a general awareness for those circumstances that may involve Westerners.

Shari'a law differentiates between Muslims and a hierarchy of non-Muslims, as well as men and women.

For example, in the case of Saudi Arabia, *diyya* (blood money) can be paid in case of accidental death, such as in a fatal road accident. In a simplified explanation, the following rules are applied:

> A Muslim man's worth is twice the worth of a Muslim woman. Other people of the book are worth half that of Muslims. Thus, a Christian man's worth is half a Muslim man, or one Muslim woman. A Christian woman's worth is one quarter that of a Muslim man and half that of a Muslim woman. Hindus' worth is only $1/16$ that of a Muslim, with the same gender ratio applied.

Similar differences affect other legal situations, such as bearing witness and the value of testimony.

Saudi Arabia's interpretation of *Shari'a* law is at the root of many social restrictions that the Western business professional is likely to encounter. This includes the absence of entertainment facilities such as the cinema or live music performances. Of course, it also impacts on the segregation of the sexes in public, and dress codes as well.

For those Western business professionals who anticipate the possibility of a personal social life with a Muslim, *Shari'a* law states that Muslim men can be married to Muslim, Christian, or Jewish women, although there is usually quite a lot of social pressure for the woman to convert to Islam. Muslim women must marry a Muslim man; it is possible for the man to have converted from another religion for this purpose.

Western business professionals should ensure they have a working understanding of *Shari'a* law if they are involved in drawing up a business contract or partnership agreement. They should also be aware that, in the case of a dispute, the only legal documents that would be admitted to a court of law in some countries of the Middle East are those in Arabic and written to the *Hijra* calendar. Make sure you hire a trustworthy translator who also understands your business. Better still, seek legal advice from someone versed in both *Shari'a* law and the laws of your own country.

Many Western business professionals are finding it beneficial to learn more about the impact of *Shari'a* law on a professional level in growing fields including Islamic banking, insurance and mortgage brokerage. For example, Islamic banking is currently growing at 40% per annum worldwide. Your organisation may benefit from expanding into this lucrative line of business.

Shari'a law also impacts on other banking practices of interest to Western business professionals, including the rules of charging interest that may be important to your Middle Eastern counterparts or local customer base. There are also serious considerations that should be taken into account if entering into an agreement that places a Westerner or their organisation into debt. Defaulting on a debt, including something as simple as a bounced cheque, has serious legal and criminal ramifications throughout most of the Middle East.

5

Other religions and business

OTHER RELIGIONS

We have focused on Islam due to the sheer volume of adherents throughout the Middle East. But there are many circumstances in which a Western business professional will be working with colleagues who practise another religion. Basic information about the most common of these religions will be of practical use for the Western business professional. We will address the most important issues that a Western business professional may encounter in everyday life, including religious holidays, that can affect business plans.

Christianity
Overview
Christianity is the second most practised religion in the Middle East. There are about 18 million Christians living in the Middle East, both indigenous and in the region's expatriate communities. About 40% of Christians in the Middle East are Coptic Christians, mostly living in Egypt. Nearly 22% are Roman Catholic. Another 12% are Protestant. Approximately 5% are Maronites, approximately equal to the number of Syrian Orthodox Christians. Most of the remaining 16% of Christians are from various Eastern Orthodox faiths.

Position in religious hierarchy
Christianity is one of the world's three monotheistic religions. From this point of view, it is regarded highly throughout the Middle East, including in most mainstream Muslim communities. Christians are considered to be people of the book, and part of the Abrahamic family.

Christian Arabs

Christianity continues to have an impact on the lives of many modern day natives of the Middle East, particularly in the Levant. Levantine Christians often have a disproportionately high influence in business, so it would not be unusual for the Western business professional to work with Arab Christians throughout the region.

About 360,000 Christians live in Jordan, mostly Eastern Orthodox. Many Jordanian Christians are Palestinians who have made Jordan their home. These numbers are growing, and do not include recent arrivals from Iraq.

There are about 100,000 Christians living in the Palestinian Territories, mostly in the West Bank. This number is decreasing as Christian Palestinians continue to leave for economic, political and safety reasons, now mostly to destinations in the Gulf or the West.

About 200,000 Christians live in Israel, mostly of Arab descent, although there are many Christians living in the religious communities of Jerusalem.

There are nearly 2 million Christians in Syria, with a slight majority being Eastern Orthodox. Many Syrians are Catholic. A substantial minority of Syrian Christians belong to the Syrian Orthodox Church, which is separate from both Western Christianity and Eastern Orthodoxy. These numbers do not include recent arrivals from Iraq.

Lebanon's population is approximately 40% Christian, or about 1.6 million people. Most Lebanese Christians are either Maronite Catholic or Eastern Orthodox, although many practise other forms of Christianity, including Roman Catholicism, Protestantism Armenian and Greek Orthodoxy, Armenian and Syrian Catholicism, Chaldean or Copt. Interestingly, there are about 18 million people of Lebanese descent living all over the world; only four million of them are in Lebanon. Nearly 8 million are in Brazil; there are significant numbers in America, Australia, Argentina and elsewhere in Latin America. Many of the Lebanese diaspora are also Christian.

Iraq's Christian communities have largely disappeared, especially in recent years, as a result of the 2003 invasion of Iraq. Sectarian violence within Iraq that escalated in the mid-2000s was not limited to various Muslim factions. Many Christians were persecuted as well. It is believed that up to four million Iraqis have left Iraq since the mid-2000s, including over 50% of all Iraqi Christians, and that fewer than 400,000 remain. Most have fled to neighbouring countries, especially Syria and Jordan.

Egypt's population is about 10% Christian – nearly 8 million people. Most Egyptians are Copts, which split from Western Christianity and Eastern Orthodoxy in the fifth century. Sudan's population is about 7% Christian, or about 2.5 million people.

There are small numbers of indigenous Christian populations in Bahrain and Iran. Most other countries of the Middle East have no significant Christian nationals, although they host varying numbers of Christian expatriates.

It is important to check if a Christian religious holiday will impact on your business plans when working in the Levant. Some Christian holidays are recognised as country-wide public holidays; others may only be celebrated by the Christian population of that country. It is also important to keep in mind that some Christians follow a different calendar from the Christian calendar familiar to most Westerners. For example, Eastern Orthodox Christmas is 7th January, not 25th December.

Christian Arabs may also be employed in positions that are undesirable to many Muslims. For example, they may be involved in banking practices that are technically un-Islamic, such as charging interest. They may also be involved in trade of alcohol or pork products in countries where they are allowed.

Do not be surprised if your local business partner makes you aware of his Christianity. Many Christians are held in high regard in most Middle Eastern business communities. They may also relate to your presumed Christianity as a way of building trust. As with Arab Muslims, it is generally not a good idea to tell a Christian Arab that you are an atheist or agnostic, although it would not always be as shocking to most Arab Christians as it would be to their Muslim counterparts.

Christian expatriates

There are large numbers of Christians within several ex-pat communities of the Gulf countries. Most Westerners are presumed to be Christian unless their name and/or ethnicity clearly indicate they come from another religious background. It is generally a good idea to allow people to believe you are a Christian if you are Western and your own background fits with the above description.

As previously mentioned, you will generally enjoy a higher status and cause less confusion if you are considered to be a Christian than if you state you are not religious. Many Muslims do not make further enquiries into the sect of Christianity you may adhere to, even the basic differences of Protestantism and Catholicism. Simply acknowledging your Christianity is usually enough.

A majority – but not all – of the Filipino community are also Christian, as a result of conversion during the time of Spanish influence in the Philippines. It is not unusual to see Filipinos employed in jobs that handle alcohol or in entertainment.

Christians can also be found in substantial numbers in some Indian ex-pat communities, notably those from the state of Kerala. They are often Syrian (sometimes Syriac) Christians, tracing their religious roots back to Syria. Many ex-pats from this region of India are well educated and are hired for professional level jobs, especially in the Gulf countries. Many Indians from Goa are also Christian.

Christians are allowed to practise their religion throughout most of the Middle East. Churches exist where practising Christians can worship. These churches are listed in various publications that cater to travellers and tourists in the Middle East, and are generally welcoming of newcomers, including any Western business professional who wishes to worship during their visit to the Middle East.

Although practising Christianity is tolerated, proselytising is not. Thus, Christian evangelists and others who seek to convert the local population will quickly be punished if caught.

The practice of all religions except Islam is banned in Saudi Arabia. This extends to Western business professionals who might be carrying or wearing religious symbols that would be seen as innocuous in any other part of the world. Thus, it is strongly advised that any practising Christian who is about to travel to the Kingdom does so without their Bible or any other Christian literature as well as any jewellery containing a cross or other symbol of Christianity. Christmas items are also banned.

It is rumoured that there are underground churches in Saudi Arabia, both on Western compounds and in Filipino communities. However, anyone caught practising another religion in the Kingdom runs the risk of criminal punishment and/or deportation.

Judaism
Overview
Judaism is the third most practised religion in the Middle East. There are about 6 million Jews living in the Middle East. About 5.5 million now live in Israel. An estimated 400,000 Jews live in the Palestinian Territories, all of whom are now in the West Bank, and are a major source of political contention.

About 30,000 Jews live in Iran, where they have the right to practise their religion. There are very small indigenous Jewish communities in Egypt, Syria, Iraq, Yemen and possibly Bahrain. Also, there are Jews quietly living in some expatriate communities of the Gulf countries, including Bahrain, the UAE, Oman and Qatar. Public synagogues cannot be found anywhere in the Gulf.

Jews are typically categorised as belonging to one of two main groups. *Ashkenazi* can trace their ancestry back to Europe. *Sephardim* trace their ancestry to the Arab world, from Yemen to Morocco, as well as to Spain and Portugal. Most Jews in Turkey are also *Sephardim*.

Anyone born of a Jewish mother is also a Jew; their father's religious affiliation is irrelevant. Most branches of Judaism considers Jews to be Jews all of their lives, even if they declare another religion or no religion. Unlike Islam, where anyone can become a Muslim by recognising and reciting the *shahada*, it is very difficult for someone to convert to Judaism. It is actually discouraged by most denominations of Judaism, thus ensuring that only the truly dedicated become Jewish.

Judaism's holy day is Saturday. As the Jewish day begins at sunset, all religious days begin at sunset of the evening before the holy day. Thus, the Sabbath, known as *Shabbat*, begins on Friday evening at sundown and finishes at sundown on Saturday evening.

Dietary laws

Observant Jews follow a strict set of dietary laws known as *Kashrut*. Foods that comply with these dietary laws are known as *Kosher* (similar to *halal* in Islam). Foods that are noncompliant are considered *treif* (similar to *haram* in Islam). Observant Jews do not eat pork or shellfish. There are slaughtering rituals for meat products that are nearly identical to those found in Islam.

Kosher laws also prevent the mixing of meat and dairy products in the same meal. Thus, a cheeseburger is never *Kosher*, even if the meat and cheese may be if eaten separately at different times. Although wine is acceptable in Judaism, people following *Kosher* diets must not consume wine prepared by gentiles (non-Jews). There are further dietary restrictions during Passover, where leavened food products are also avoided.

In reality, many Jewish people are much more relaxed about following dietary laws than most Muslims. It is not unusual to see non-Orthodox Jews eating pork products and drinking wine from any origin.

Position in religious hierarchy

Judaism is the world's oldest monotheistic religion. From this point of view, it has been highly regarded historically throughout the Middle East, including in most mainstream Muslim communities. The Jewish Holy Book is the *Torah*, which contains the Old Testament. The *Talmud*, which is a written collection of teachings by rabbis that reflect on all aspects of daily life, is also considered an important part of the Jewish code of law. Thus, like Muslims, Jews are considered to be people of the book, and part of the Abrahamic family.

The realities on the ground can be quite different. Whilst the vast majority of Muslims (and the Arab world in general) do not have any problem working with a Jewish person from a Western country, they may have difficulties working with someone who has ties to Israel. The main exceptions will be found in Syria and Lebanon, where religion and politics are not always separated.

Jewish Holy Lands

The most holy place in Judaism is the Temple Mount, specifically the Western wall of the temple constructed by Herod the Great and located in the Old City of Jerusalem. This is known by many Westerners as the Western Wall or the Wailing Wall. Jews pray in the direction of the Western Wall, similar to the Muslim practice of praying towards Mecca.

The Temple Mount is also sacred to Muslims, as this is where it is believed that the Prophet Mohammed ascended to heaven. In addition to the Western Wall, the Temple Mount also contains the al-Aqsa mosque and the Dome of the Rock. The latter is the oldest surviving Islamic structure in the world.

The Temple Mount has suffered from limited access and worse by the governments of Israel, the Palestinian Authority and Jordan prior to the 1967 War. Optimists believe there may be a way of resolving these religious and political conflicts at some point in the future. Pessimists look at Jerusalem and the Temple Mount in particular as nearly impossible issues to reconcile.

Some comparisons between Judaism and Islam

Islam and Judaism are much closer to each other than either religion is to modern Christianity. Many similarities between Judaism and Islam have already been noted. They are both monotheistic, Abrahamic religions. They both believe that their religion is a way of life, with specific behaviours and values that cannot be separated. They have any number of prayer rituals that are recognised by similar actions. They have similar dietary laws.

Judaism's holy language, Hebrew, is a Semitic language that shares its roots with Arabic. Many words are very similar, including *shalom* and *salaam*, the words for peace, an irony not lost on many.

Many religious Jews send their children to *yeshivas*, especially boys. This would be the rough equivalent of a Muslim *madrassa*.

Religious Jews also have a set of rules that define the requirements of modest dress, which apply to both men and women. Orthodox Jews in particular may live a *de facto* gender segregated life, with contact with the opposite sex limited to immediate family members.

Jewish boys, like Muslims, are traditionally and ritualistically circumcised. This ritual is called a *bris* in Judaism and takes place when the infant is eight days old.

Most Jews, even if they are not particularly religious, will observe a right of passage into adulthood. This is called a *bar mitzvah* for boys and a *bat mitzvah* for girls. It is held when the adolescent is thirteen, or in the case of Orthodox Jews, with the boy is thirteen and the girl is twelve. The nearest equivalent in Islam is *khitan* (circumcision) for boys (if it hasn't happened earlier) and starting to wear the veil for girls.

Jews, like Muslims, bury their dead within 24 hours of death.

The Jewish calendar is lunar, with holidays determined by the moon, although there are leap years built in, unlike in Islam.

Hinduism

Overview

Hinduism is the fourth most practised religion in the Middle East, and is found mostly in the Gulf countries. This is almost entirely due to the large number of expatriates from the Indian subcontinent. There are communities of Hindus in Oman, who are Omani, whose ancestors emigrated from India up to several generations ago.

There are an estimated 2.7 million Hindus in the region. About 100,000 live in Bahrain, 200,000 in Kuwait, 300,000 in Oman, 100,000 in Qatar and about one million in each of KSA and the UAE.

Hindus worship multiple gods. They have several main beliefs that are markedly different from monotheistic religions. *Karma* is the belief in the cycle of cause and effect in life, or – simply paraphrased – what goes around comes around. *Samsara* is the belief in the cycle of life, death and reincarnation. *Nirvana* is the release from the cycle of life. The caste system is sometimes known as *varna* and determines how one is expected to live one's life. *Dharma* is the way of living a religiously dutiful life. Hinduism's religious texts are known as the *Vedas*.

Dietary laws

Many Hindus are vegetarians. Vegetarianism can vary amongst Hindus; the details are somewhat dependent on caste, family background, degree of religious piety and exposure to the wider world. The definition of vegetarianism can also vary. Some Hindus will eat fish and consider themselves to be vegetarian; others will not eat eggs or other animal by-products.

Practising Hindus often observe days where they are required to fast. From a Western point of view, this fasting is defined somewhat differently, as the adherent is ritualistically avoiding certain foods, yet is eating others.

It is very safe to assume that nearly all Hindus will not eat beef, as the cow is regarded as sacred. Western business professionals are well advised to avoid inviting Hindu business colleagues to restaurants such as steakhouses. It is also polite not to choose a beef selection from the menu when dining with Hindus, although many Hindus are otherwise relaxed if you choose another meat dish.

Position in religious hierarchy

Since Hinduism is not a monotheistic, Abrahamic religion, nor does it emanate from the Old Testament, most Muslims regard it as an inferior religion of idol worshipers. This attitude can be observed in everyday life, and can be very uncomfortable for equality-minded Western business professionals who witness dismissive and sometimes abusive behaviour towards Hindus. As previously noted, some aspects of *Shari'a* law officially recognise a Hindu's worth as a small, calculated percentage of the life of a Muslim (or Christian or Jew).

Although Hinduism is tolerated in most Middle Eastern countries (but not Saudi Arabia), it is most often practised privately in the home. There are Hindu temples in Bahrain, Kuwait, Oman, Qatar, Yemen and Dubai. Hindu populations throughout the Levant, Egypt and Sudan are negligible. Hinduism has publicly disappeared in Iran after the Islamic Revolution in 1979.

As is the case with Christianity, any Hindu religious icons or practices are illegal in Saudi Arabia. To illustrate, the author is aware of a Hindu family who were living in Riyadh. A small *Ganesh* (elephant god) statue was eventually seen through a kitchen window by a Muslim neighbour who took offence at the existence of the idol in his country. The family was immediately deported, despite having lived peacefully in Saudi Arabia for more than ten years.

For those Western business professionals who are also Hindu, there can be some unpleasant moments in parts of the Middle East. Whilst they will most often be treated like any other Westerner in a business environment, Western Hindus can expect to encounter some blatant discrimination in certain public climates. This may include dealings with Middle Eastern bureaucracy, often starting at passport control queues at the airport. It can also impact on social life, especially for those Western Hindus who attempt to enjoy a night out in clubs and pubs that practise a selective door policy.

Western Hindus may, however, find they often have a distinct advantage when working with business professionals from the Indian subcontinent, especially if they also speak an Indian language.

Hindu holidays

It is important to keep the Hindu religious calendar in mind if you are working with a Hindu organisation or your colleagues are religious Hindus. Hindu holidays are based on the lunar calendar, so dates will change from year to year. However, unlike in the Islamic calendar, holidays will occur within the same few days or weeks from year to year.

It is also important to be aware that Hindu holidays may be of greater significance to someone originating from a particular region of India. Some holidays are only celebrated by certain castes, or by people who revere a particular god or gods. If you are unsure of their significance to a religious business colleague, it is acceptable to respectfully ask them to explain their holiday to you.

Hindu holidays are also known by different names, depending on if they are being referred to in a Hindi-based language (northern India) or a Dravidian-based language (southern India). For example, *Diwali* – familiar to many in the UK with its large, mostly northern Indian population, is known as *Deepavali* in the South of India.

Holiday	Description	Date
Pongal	Harvest Festival	Mid-January, mostly celebrated in Tamil Nadu
Holi	Festival of Colours	Spring full moon in February or March: 2 days
Vishu	Tamil New year	Mid April
Onam	Harvest Festival	Mid September, celebrated in Kerala
Ganesh Chaturthi	Birth of Ganesh	Early September. Lasts over 10 days, where it is possible to see the elephant god being brought into the sea
Diwali	Festival of Lights	Mid October to mid November: 5 days. This is the major holiday for most Hindus
Dirga Puja	Worship of the Goddess Durga	October, major Bengali festival: 6 days
Pancha Ganapati	Winter Solstice Festival	Mid to late December: 5 days

The chart on the previous page lists some of the most important Hindu holidays. The Western business traveller should consult a more comprehensive resource if they require the full list of all Hindu holidays that might affect working with Hindu colleagues.

In many parts of the Middle East, the Hindu ex-pat community may not work during the major holidays, such as *Diwali*; others may return to India during this time. Hindus may work during other religious holidays, celebrating during the evening hours. You may be invited to participate in festivals such as *Holi*, the Festival of Colours.

The Hindu swastika

The Hindu swastika can be a shock to Western eyes when first encountered, usually on the door of an Indian-run office. It strongly resembles the swastika used in Hitler's Germany, although it also contains four dots and the 'legs' are in the reverse direction. Happily, the Hindu swastika actually represents peace and harmony.

Sikhs

Overview

Sikhism is also practised in the Middle East, and is found mostly in the Indian expatriate communities of the Gulf countries.

Sikhs worship in a *gurdwara*, which functions as a place of prayer and also as a community centre. In the Middle East, there are *gurdwaras* in Bahrain, Dubai and Tehran. The *gurdwara* in Kuwait, home to up to 20,000 Sikhs, appears to remain closed.

There are similarities within Sikhism that resemble both Islam and Hinduism.

Like Muslims, Sikhs are monotheistic, although they believe in a Universal God as opposed to the teachings of Abraham. However, as they are Dharmic and not Abrahamic, they are not regarded by people in the Middle East as people of the book. Other Dharmic religions are Hinduism, Jainism and Buddhism.

Like Hindus, Sikhs believe in *karma*, reincarnation and salvation (similar to *nirvana*).

Unlike Hindus, Sikhs believe in the equality of all believers, although this is not precisely true in practice as recent events in Austria have shown. Sikhs also put a very high value on sharing.

Sikhs follow the teachings of the ten Sikh Gurus, originating in the 15th century with Guru Nanak.

Sikhs do not practise religious rituals, including idol worship, circumcision, or pilgrimages. However, observant Sikhs do go through a baptism ceremony called an *amrit*. Like Hindus, Sikhs cremate their dead.

Practicing Sikhs usually adapt the five 'k's. They are symbols that distinguish Sikhs from other religions and include a comb, uncut hair, sword, bangle and a specific style of underwear:

- *kirpan* – sword
- *kangha* – comb
- *kesh* – uncut hair
- *karra* – bangle
- *kacchera* – underwear.

Most Sikh men carry the name Singh. Most Sikh women carry the name Kaur. In the West, this may or may not be the family name.

Men generally wear a turban, also known as a *dastar* or *pagri* to conceal their uncut hair. Sikh turbans sometimes include a chin strap. Men generally have uncut beards as well. Boys often wear a *patka*, which is a cloth that is knotted at the top of the head. It is not unusual to see Sikh men with a variety of other head coverings, including bandanas and even baseball caps. Religious Sikh women often wear a *dupatta* or *chunni*, which is a long scarf. Rarely, they may choose to wear a turban instead.

Dietary laws

Sikhs are not vegetarians, although they only serve vegetarian food in *gurdwaras*. Sikhs are only permitted to eat meat that did not undergo ritual slaughter or preparation. Thus, they must actually avoid *halal* or *kosher* meat. Although there is no specific taboo against eating beef, as most Sikhs trace their roots back to India, many Sikhs avoid eating beef out of respect to their Hindu neighbours.

Sikhs are forbidden to use tobacco products, although it is possible to see non-religious Sikhs who smoke cigarettes. Alcohol consumption is generally taboo; exceptions to this ban are widespread.

Position in religious hierarchy

As Sikhs are not regarded as people of the book, they fall into a lower position within the religious hierarchy of the Middle East. As with Western business professionals who are also Hindu, there can be unpleasant moments in parts of the Middle East for Westerners who are also Sikh as previously described.

Sikh holidays

Sikh holidays will not be officially recognised anywhere in the Middle East, but may be privately observed by Sikhs. Thus, it is important to check if your Sikh colleague is working during a Sikh holiday.

Other religions

There are Zoroastrians, Baha'is, Parsis/Parsees, Jains, Buddhists, Taoists, Confucianists, Shintoists and practitioners of animist and tribal religions amongst ex-pat populations in the Middle East. Zoroastrianism and Baha'is both originate in modern day Iran.

It is beyond the scope of this book to detail these religions, although it is recommended that the Western business professional learns the basics of these religions, especially if they are working with an adherent of any of them.

However, it is important to highlight the fact that Islam regards all of them to be of lesser status than the three monotheistic religions originating from Abraham. Baha'is in particular have had difficulties, in part because very religious Muslims consider this religion to be apostasy. Some practical exceptions are made when working with people from Korea or Japan, who are sometimes regarded as 'honorary Westerners' in spite of their presumed religion.

Atheists and agnostics

As is highlighted elsewhere, atheists and agnostics are strongly encouraged to claim a religion, especially when confronted with a religious question in bureaucratic matters, such as when applying for a business visa to Saudi Arabia.

It is advised that most atheistic and agnostic Western business professionals opt for Christianity, as it is expected and is regarded as the next highest status religion after Islam.

Some Western business professionals with a Jewish background opt for Christianity when faced with religious questions on official documents, especially if they plan to travel to Saudi Arabia (for religious reasons), or to Lebanon or Syria (for political reasons). The author has travelled with an agnostic business colleague with a Jewish background who was fond of declaring himself a Quaker to officialdom whenever he was travelling in the region.

Westerners who have a Muslim name and come from a Muslim background should almost certainly become Muslim in the eyes of the authorities to avoid any risk of the consequences of apostasy.

Non-Muslim religious symbols in Saudi Arabia

It is safe to assume that all non-Muslim religious symbols are banned in Saudi Arabia. Scriptures and other printed materials are especially frowned upon, particularly if the authorities suspect you may intend to proselytise on Saudi soil. Even items that seem innocuous to Westerners may cause offence to some

Saudis. For example, there was a dispute in 2008 over a Swiss football referee planning to use a whistle that included a symbol of his country's flag – the Swiss flag contains a white cross on a red background.

The best advice is to leave anything remotely religious at home. This even includes items that may be considered to be souvenirs, such as the prayer wheel you bought in Tibet, the voodoo doll you bought in West Africa, or your copy of L. Ron Hubbard's book *Dianetics*.

6

Safety and security

Personal safety is a topic that usually arises when someone is considering travelling to the Middle East, especially for the first time. Most Westerners' exposure to the region is through Western media, with its focus on reporting on the Palestinian conflict, threats over Iran's development of nuclear technology, the morality of the Gulf Wars and cultural conflicts such as the 'sex on the beach' couple in Dubai.

It is important to keep things in perspective. Media throughout the world are unlikely to report on the mundane, safe way that millions of people go about their daily lives. 'Lebanese woman, 30, goes to work at her bank job' is not a headline. Consequently, much that is positive about the Middle East remains unreported in the West.

GENERAL POLITICAL STABILITY

It is recommended that all business professionals to the Middle East have a bit of working knowledge as to the general political stability of the countries they plan to visit. Keep things in perspective when making these assessments. It is also important for Western business professionals to consider that democracy is not the only route to political stability.

Whether ruled by a Sheikh, King, or President, the position of the current ruler of all Middle Eastern countries should be respected, regardless of the Western business professional's own personal views. Western business professionals are often surprised by the presence of larger than life portraits of the current (and sometimes past) rulers in nearly every public building and often on huge outdoor billboards throughout the region. Government and private offices, hotels and restaurants follow this practice as well.

Westerners should be cautious about questioning either the taste or the need for the presence of these portraits throughout the region. It's also a good idea to learn the name of the ruler whose portrait is seemingly everywhere. The local population will not make negative comments about their leaders, at least not in public and certainly not unless they know you very well.

It's a good idea to keep informed about current political activity throughout the region. Things can and do change quite quickly. It's possible to access English language publications from every country of the region to keep up with local current affairs, either on the internet or the English language broadcasting services from Middle East-based organisations such as Al Jazeera. This is highly recommended to supplement information gained from mainstream Western media.

The GCC

All GCC countries are run by ruling families.

It is a fair generalisation to say that the ruling family of the UAE (al Nahyan) are well-respected by nationals of their country. This also applies to the ruling family of Dubai (al Maktoum); the other Emirates' ruling families are highly regarded as well, although their overall influence on Emirati affairs has much less impact. The ruling families of both Abu Dhabi and Dubai have named crown princes to ensure an eventual smooth transition of power. Sheikh Zayed was the first ruler of an independent UAE and remains revered.

The Qatari ruling family (al Thani) have formalised rules of succession, which is seen as stabilising. An heir apparent has been named.

The Bahraini ruling family (al Khalifa) have retained their position as figures of authority. They suffered during a *Shi'a–Sunni* dispute in the mid 1990s, with some clerics of the majority *Shi'a* population unhappy with the ruling family. This issue has settled down in recent years and should not be considered a threat to the country's stability, although it remains in the background.

The Kuwaiti ruling family (al Sabah) have a more complicated status. They are highly regarded by most of the local Kuwaiti families that count, i.e. those who have the right to vote. The National Assembly of the Kuwaiti parliament has considerable power in appointing rulers from the royal family; thus, there is no imminent concern for the stability of Kuwait in this regard.

The Omani ruling family (al Said) are in an altogether different situation. An absolute, if benevolent, monarch, the current Sultan has no heir, having only been in one very brief, childless marriage during his lifetime. Nor has he publicly named a successor, as he has instead taken the decision to announce his hereditary preference in a sealed letter to be opened after his death. Thus it is not certain what will happen once the Sultan no longer rules the country, at least for the general public.

The Saudi ruling family (al Saud) are also absolute monarchs, but with a much more mixed reputation than is the case in Oman. Basic law of Government allows that the country continues to be ruled by a succession of sons and grandsons of Abd al Aziz al Saud, the first king of modern Saudi Arabia. There is a Saudi Crown Prince and a Deputy Crown Prince. The Allegiance Institution, composed of the first king's sons and grandsons, decide on succession. As there are a very large number of sons and grandsons, it is unclear as to which direction the monarchy will take in future. It is also unclear in the distant future as to what will happen once the last grandchild of King Abd al Aziz al Saud has died.

The ruling family holds the full range of political views, from those who are pro-Western reformists to those who wish to impose further tenets of *Wahhabism*.

Unlike in the West, there is no tolerance for criticising the ruling families throughout the GCC. This is important to keep in mind, particularly when coming from Europe, where many Europeans have little problem publicly voicing their negative opinions about their own monarchies.

Interestingly, many of the senior members of the Gulf ruling families have been educated at Britain's Royal Military Academy, Sandhurst. Others have attended prestigious universities elsewhere in the UK and USA.

Yemen

Yemen is the only republic found on the Arabian Peninsula. Its constitution was ratified in 1991, shortly after the unification of what was then known as the countries of North Yemen and South Yemen. The country is headed by a President, with a Prime Minister as head of government. The Prime Minister is appointed by the President.

The government appears to be tenuously stable politically at best. Many opposition parties have tried and failed to unseat the President. It also has little influence outside the capital, especially in some tribal and rural areas of the country, as well as in the former British colony of Aden.

Most businesses regard the country as less than stable, as illustrated by the example of a well known Gulf-wide supermarket chain backing out of building its first modern shopping mall in Sana'a, the capital, because it was deemed too unstable for its business model. It is unclear what will happen once the current President is no longer in office.

The Levant
Jordan

The Jordanian royal family, along with the former Iraqi royal family, are Heshemites, tracing their ancestry directly to the Prophet Mohammed. King Abdullah II, the first son of King Hussein, is the current ruler of Jordan, having been named crown prince by the King in the last few days of his life.

From a Western perspective, King Abdullah has a hard act to follow, as King Hussein was seen by many Westerners, especially in later years, as being the main peace broker within the Arab world. King Abdullah is seen as an economic reformer in Jordan.

Jordan is only one of two countries in the Middle East that has brokered peace with Israel. Jordan, with its large Palestinian population, is a safe and stable destination for Western business professionals.

It would not be recommended that negative comments are made about the Jordanian monarchy although, unlike in the Gulf, this may be quietly done in private amongst trusted companions.

Syria

Syria appears to be a dynastic republic, with Bashar al Assad succeeding his father after his father's death in 2000. The current ruler is seen as a reformist, but is undoubtedly much less powerful than his father in controlling the real power behind the government, the Baath Party. Economic reform is much slower in Syria than in neighbouring countries.

Syria still has an inordinate amount of power over Lebanon, although it has abated somewhat in recent years. Syria still has claims on the Golan Heights, annexed unilaterally by Israel in 1967, and remains technically at war with its neighbour, although there have been no military campaigns for years. In spite of these considerations, as well as any number of political policies out of line with the West's interpretation of a republic, it is a stable country.

Lebanon

Lebanon is a republic, and operates under a system called confessionalism, originally based on Lebanon's 1932 census. This means that certain political positions must be filled by a member of a particular ethnic or religious group. The Confessionalist system was designed to put an end to infighting amongst these diverse groups, and was reinforced at the end of the Civil War. Lebanon's President must come from the Christian community, and must be a Maronite Catholic. The Prime Minister must be a *Sunni* Muslim, and is chosen by the President. The Speaker of the Parliament must be a *Shi'a*.

Lebanon has enjoyed a long period of relative stability from the end of the Civil War until 2005, when its former President Rafiq Hariri was assassinated. In the summer of 2006, there was a period of civil unrest following the capture of two Israeli soldiers along Lebanon's border with Israel. A month-long military campaign was launched, followed by a United Nations ceasefire, which remains in force.

The Lebanese business community is vibrant and resilient, and remains open for business. Western business professionals continue to work in Beirut and other major business centres without any significant danger. But it is strongly advised that all Western business professionals assess the political and civil situation for up-to-date information each time they plan to travel to the country, at least for the immediate future.

Israel

Although it is beyond the scope of this book to describe Israeli politics, it is important for Western business professionals to remain well-informed about the current state of political affairs in Israel, as they often impact on attitudes, and sometimes decisions, made elsewhere in the region.

The Palestinian Territories

The Palestinian Territories derive from the end of British rule of what was then known as the British Mandate of Palestine, which refers to the land contained in modern day Israel, the West Bank and Gaza. The Palestinian Territories refer to the West Bank and Gaza, and will be used as such in this book to avoid ongoing contentious political debate. Defining the exact boundaries of the Palestinian Territories is beyond the scope of this book. The Palestinian Territories are not a fully autonomous country. This is, of course, one of the main political events that have been playing out on the world stage in the Middle East since the mid twentieth century.

The Palestinian Authority, also known as the Palestinian National Authority, is the government body officially recognised by most international organisations and many countries, including most Western governments. It came into existence as a result of the 1993 Oslo Accords, and was negotiated between Israel and the Palestinian Liberation Organisation (PLO). The Palestinian Authority does not have full, autonomous control of their own government. Its members are amongst the best educated politicians in the world – mostly from elite institutions in the USA.

To further complicate matters, the West Bank and Gaza are currently under the control of different, opposing political parties. Elections held in 2006 – widely regarded to be free and fair – were won by Hamas. Fatah, the party most closely associated with the PLO, eventually regained control of the West Bank. Hamas remains in power in Gaza.

There are many unresolved issues surrounding the Palestinian Territories and the eventual form of its permanent government. It is fair to say that conventional wisdom dictates that this region will remain politically volatile for the foreseeable future.

Western business professionals can, and do, conduct business throughout the main business centres of the West Bank. However, they must exercise caution and keep abreast of the political climate throughout their visit to the Territories. Western business professionals should not contemplate doing business in Gaza until the political climate changes. The Israeli government control all border crossings into the West Bank and Gaza, and can close them at a moment's notice. *No* exemptions are made for third-country nationals, including Western business travellers.

Egypt

Egypt is a republic with an uneven relationship with democratic practices. The current President, Mohammed Hosni Mubarek, has been in power since 1981, from the time his predecessor, Anwar Sadat, was assassinated. Although multi-party elections have been held several times since then, Egypt's power rests within the political party of the current President and the President himself. President Mubarek comes from a military background; the Egyptian government relies heavily on military support.

Sudan

Sudan is technically a republic. It endured a military coup in 1989, led by Omar al Bashir, who remains in power to this day. The country remains in a state of emergency since a failed coup attempt in 1999.

Iran

Iran is an Islamic Republic, with a complicated power-sharing structure. The current system has only been in place for just over 30 years, since the fall of Shah Reza Pahlavi, the last Shah of Iran in 1979. The President is elected by popular vote every four years, and may be re-elected only once.

The Supreme Leader, who must be a religious cleric, is elected by an Assembly of Experts, comprised of a body of Islamic scholars that wields the true power in the country. The Supreme Leader controls the legal system, determines much of the policy affecting everyday life, and is the head of the military. The Supreme Leader has no limit in office.

Ali Khameni is the current Supreme Leader. Mahmoud Ahmadinejad is the current President, having officially won his second term of office in June 2009, although this victory continues to be subject to much controversy. Many political and social groups exist both within Iran and in the large Iranian diaspora. Until the 2009 elections, most people would have said that there is no particular reason to believe the current Iranian government is unstable. However, with recent events, many are reassessing their position on this matter, as recent political activities have ventured into uncharted territory for the Islamic Republic. It would not be unusual to work with a business partner who disagrees with their current government structure, especially in secularly-orientated communities in Tehran and other large cities from Dubai to Paris to Los Angeles.

THREAT OF TERRORISM

Over the past several years, there has been considerable Western emphasis on the threat of terrorism presented from Islamist organisations. In this regard, the term 'Islamist' means favouring Muslims to the disadvantage of other groups, similar to the terms racist, sexist, etc. used in a similar context.

However, there is no doubt that the threat of terrorism is global. Recent events have taught us that acts of Islamist terrorism can occur anywhere in the world, not just in the West, as people in locations as diverse as Bali, Casablanca,

Islamabad and Mumbai can attest. In addition, non-Islamist terrorism can be witnessed from organisations as diverse as the Branch Dravidians in Texas (not to mention Timothy McVeigh in Oklahoma City), the Aum Shirikyo in Tokyo, the Basque Separatists in Spain, the Provisional IRA in Northern Ireland or the Tamil Tigers in Sri Lanka.

Without any intention of dismissing the seriousness of terrorist activity, it remains conventional wisdom that an individual business person's risk of being caught up in an act of terrorism is no higher in most – but not all – of the Middle East than in the major cities of the West.

The Western business professional should take certain precautions when planning their journey to the Middle East. Many of these precautions are no different from those necessary when travelling to any destination that is new or unfamiliar to the traveller:

- Just because something is different does not mean it is necessarily dangerous – it's usually just different! Try to prepare for your new destination by embracing the differences rather than reacting with fear or anxiety. Focus on the positive opportunities you are about to experience.
- However, balance your anticipation with common sense. Your instinct exists for a reason – listen to it. If it doesn't feel safe, it probably isn't, even if you cannot immediately identify why.
- Look up your country's government website for their official advice on travel to your destination. Keep in mind that this advice may be politically influenced and is often overly-cautious. However, it is usually your government's official policy that often impacts on the validity of your travel insurance. It is also a good idea to balance this information with your destination's official visitors' websites as well as with any local knowledge you can obtain from your own sources. A list of many Western countries' official travel advice websites is supplied in the 'Recommended Reading' section at the end of this book.
- Do your research on how you travel to the Middle East and how you travel within the region once you arrive. Whilst airlines must meet

international safety standards when flying to and from the West and are thus safe, some airlines may not apply the same safety standards when flying to other destinations within the region, such as recent events with Yemenia have demonstrated. Be especially cautious of airlines flying old, often Soviet-era sourced aircraft. Carriers from countries outside both the West and the Middle East should also be carefully researched if you are faced with this option, especially if travelling from destinations in parts of Africa or the former Soviet Union.

■ Choosing a hotel depends on many factors, including cost, location, corporate travel policy and personal preference. International hotel chains take their security seriously, and are continuing to evolve and develop additional measures. Do not be surprised if security practices are more rigorous than what you are familiar with in the West. For example, it is not unusual to pass through airport style metal detectors under the scrutiny of armed guards in hotel entrances from Cairo to Sana'a.

■ There are business circumstances where some Westerners consider the need for additional personal security, especially if they are in a sensitive line of business or are travelling to a remote or volatile location. Some Westerners rely on the services of established security organisations that specialise in providing ground protection to Westerners; others prefer to rely on local security arrangements; some simply take their chances. All have their advantages and disadvantages. Professional advice should be sought when making this decision, as further detail is beyond the scope of this book.

The GCC

In general, a business professional is not increasing their risk by going about their business throughout the GCC countries. The main exception is to avoid some of the poorest regions of Saudi Arabia, including many run down neighbourhoods in Riyadh, where it is not particularly safe for any outsider – including other Saudi nationals – to visit. Most Western business professionals would have no business reason to visit these neighbourhoods and should avoid them.

Yemen

Advice varies for anyone travelling to Yemen. This country has only recently united following a civil war that played out until the 1990s. Although officially united, the government has little jurisdiction or control over vast territories within its borders.

Much of Yemen remains under the control of a number of tribal factions. These tribal groups control the *de facto* safety of anyone travelling into their territories. The main security risk for Westerners has traditionally been becoming the victim of kidnapping when travelling into tribal areas without advance approval. In the event of travelling to the 'wrong place', the kidnappers expected a ransom to be paid upon release of the hostage as a penalty for straying.

Kidnappings in the past have generally resulted in the safe release of hostages after a financial agreement had been reached. However, the situation on the ground has changed recently as different motivations have resulted in high profile fatalities of both Western and non-Western hostages. These have included a group of South Korean business professionals at one of Yemen's most popular tourist venues and a World Heritage Site, as well as several European business professionals and expatriates.

In addition, some Western governments have turned their attention to Yemen in the belief that increased activity from al-Qaeda is taking place on Yemeni soil. Many authorities believe this will increase the danger for Westerners who may wish to do business in the country. Westerners who do travel to Yemen are generally advised not to travel to destinations outside the busiest neighbourhoods of the major cities of Sana'a and Aden; other destinations require permits that allow outsiders to travel to areas controlled not by the government but by tribal leaders. The best general advice for people who travel to Yemen on business is to remain in the city where possible, and to get on-the-ground advice from their embassy (which may be extremely cautious) and their business contacts, if they intend to travel further afield. Official policy from the Westerner's embassy can also affect the validity of travel insurance. As a side note, the island of Socotra remains safe, although it should only be reached by air.

For those Western business professionals who choose to travel to Yemen, consideration should be given as to their personal security options, even if they are only travelling to Sana'a or Aden. Professional advice should be sought and tailored to the traveller's individual needs. Areas frequented by Westerners, including hotels and embassies are heavily fortified.

Travellers to Aden in particular should also be aware of the growing piracy problem in the waters of the region and, indeed, most of the country.

Lebanon, Jordan and Syria

A business professional is generally at no elevated risk of terrorism throughout the Levant, again with a couple of exceptions. Business professionals to Lebanon, Jordan and Syria should expect to conduct their business as usual in all normal business environments. There is a danger if someone attempts to visit refugee camps located in these countries. These dangers are less likely to be acts of terrorism, but of suspicion towards any outsider.

There are currently Iraqi refugee camps in Syria, but they are not located anywhere near where a Westerner would be likely to travel to for business. These camps should not be confused with recent Iraqi populations who have settled in city neighbourhoods such as Damascus or Amman – these neighbourhoods are as safe as the rest of these very safe cities.

Business professionals who work for an American organisation should be aware of a range of economic sanctions imposed on Syria by the US government in 2004. It is unclear at the time of publication when or if this policy will change. This unilateral action is not in relation to a United Nations mandate, nor is it imposed by the European Union or other Western governments.

Palestinian refugee camps have existed since 1948, and are also located far from any likely Western business interests. Again, these camps should not be confused with Palestinian populations settled in city neighbourhoods in Beirut, Damascus or Amman – these neighbourhoods have been settled for generations and in many instances are amongst the wealthiest neighbourhoods of these cities.

There is more risk of danger along the Lebanese border with Israel. It has long been the advice of most Western governments not to travel south of Tyre in Southern Lebanon. In addition, it is a good idea to avoid some neighbourhoods to the south of Beirut, where Hezbollah are active – again, an unlikely area for a Westerner to travel to for business. Central Beirut itself remains safe for Westerners to work in, as are its northern and eastern suburbs. As ever, Western business professionals should always be aware of elections and other political events at the time of travel, as these can be times of tension. It is also possible and often practical for Westerners to travel overland between Beirut, Damascus and Amman. However, as all Westerners require a visa to enter Syria, it is imperative that they secure a multiple entry visa from their country of official residence prior to travel. Most Westerners can obtain visas for travel to Lebanon and Jordan on arrival at the border.

Israel

This information is being provided for those business professionals who may need to transit through Israel on their way to the Palestinian Territories.

Most of Israel is much safer than most Western countries. Security checkpoints and other measures have been installed and are in full operation in nearly every venue where crowds gather, including hotels, shopping malls and most tourist sites. Western business professionals will also quickly become used to the sight of male and female Israeli soldiers carrying their automatic weapons in public throughout the country, including on public transport and in restaurants.

From the Israeli point of view, the 'security wall' still being constructed between Israel and the West Bank – and sometimes well into the West Bank – has been designed as an additional security safeguard.

Public transport remains the biggest security challenge that may affect a Western business professional. For this reason, it is recommended that Westerners consider organising their own transport. Taxis are safe.

Contrary to the message given in much of the Western media, Jewish and Arab neighbourhoods within the undisputed borders of Israel are both safe destinations for Westerners. Israeli towns and cities very close to Gaza can pose a risk, depending on current activity from both the Israelis and Palestinians. This is where it's important to be informed from a reliable source as to what's actually happening on the ground at the time you intend to travel to this specific region of Israel. In recent years, Israeli towns and cities very close to the West Bank have been as safe from terrorist activity as the rest of Israel.

A word about Israeli settlements in the West Bank: these settlements are a main source of contention throughout the Arab and, indeed, Muslim world. Whilst travel to them is technically safe (the Israelis have built special access roads between Israel proper and these settlements that are not open to Palestinians), it is strongly advised that Western business professionals avoid any use of these transport links when conducting Arab businesses in the West Bank.

The Palestinian Territories

For those business professionals considering travel to the Palestinian Territories, Gaza and the West Bank must be regarded separately at the time of publication.

Gaza is currently off limits to all Western business professionals, with the occasional exception of some NGO workers, medical personnel, etc. Most business people from elsewhere in the Middle East cannot travel there, either. It is not known when this situation will change.

The West Bank is open for business. Again, the realities on the ground are quite different from what the Western media is typically reporting. The main cities of Bethlehem, Jenin, Jericho, Nablus and Ramallah are under semi-autonomous control of the Palestinian National Authority, and are generally safe. Hebron remains difficult and is best avoided. However, the business professional must be prepared to put up with many travel inconveniences, including a high number of Israeli controlled road blocks and checkpoints. These cannot be avoided by using the Israeli bypasses, especially if travelling with Palestinian business partners. The situation in the West Bank remains potentially volatile, and could change at a moment's notice, as the

Israelis continue to control all transport links and border crossings throughout the territory.

Egypt

Travel to Egypt is generally safe. There are occasional political demonstrations that should be avoided by all Westerners (as would be the advice in most of the world). Armed military personnel are much more visible in everyday life throughout Egypt than they are in most other countries in the region.

Sudan

Travel to Sudan for those few Western business people who venture to travel there is riskier, and would be downright foolhardy in many regions of the country. It is imperative to seek advice locally for any travel outside Khartoum, as Sudan currently has many conflicts within its borders. Khartoum's business district is reasonably safe.

Iran

In spite of the Western media's proclamations, Iran is also a safe place to travel to, with the general threat of terrorism much lower than in most Western countries. Its economy continues to grow and diversify, with trade partners as varied as Bahrain, China, Japan, South Africa, Turkey and the UAE (especially Dubai).

However, the situation on the ground is less certain in the aftermath of the volatile June 2009 elections. Local knowledge is of paramount importance if your visit coincides with any demonstration or other political public gathering, especially in areas where Western business professionals may frequent, including business districts and upmarket neighbourhoods in North Tehran.

It is also very important for Western business professionals to understand that Iran is currently under a number of economic sanctions, restricting trade with many countries of the West. These include economic sanctions imposed by the Americans in 1996 for all but a few lines of business, and by the United Nations in 2007 for businesses that could be involved in the potential transfer of technology related to Iran's nuclear industry. Most Iranian banks have been affected as well, including branches outside of Iran. For those organisations considering doing business in Iran, it is strongly advised that legal advice is taken prior to making any economic decisions regarding trade with both the private and government sectors.

In conclusion, the best advice is to seek information and advice from a number of sources: your government's official website for travel to the country, local media, your local business contacts and other ex-pats living in the country.

MILITARY CONFLICT AND WAR

There is no doubt that parts of the Middle East have had their fair share of military conflict and war in modern times.

Most of the region remains technically at war with Israel, although there has been no sustained, active military activity beyond Israel's immediate land borders with Lebanon and Syria since the events of 2006. Border skirmishes do not generally affect the majority of the population in Israel, Lebanon, or Syria, who routinely go about their normal business.

The relationship between Israel and its Palestinian neighbours remains cyclic, with the military activities from late 2008 in the Gaza Strip being the latest conflict. It is fair to note that normal business in the Palestinian Territories is often affected, usually when the Israeli authorities restrict access from one city to another in the West Bank, access into, or out of, the Gaza Strip, or access to East Jerusalem.

The Iran-Iraq War, which claimed the lives of over one million young men, has been over for more than 20 years. The conflict known in the West as the First Gulf War of 1991 has been over for nearly as long, with damage to Kuwait fully restored. The continued Western military presence in the region after this conflict finished fermented anti-Western attitudes amongst some in the region that prevail to this day.

It remains unclear how long Iraq will remain off limits to the general business professional wishing to do business in the country after the current conflict, known as the Second Gulf War, ends. The invasion of Iraq, by predominately Western forces, and their continued presence in that country has hardened attitudes amongst many more of the Arab population. On the other hand, Western business professionals are forging business partnerships with organisations which have ties with Iraqi Kurdistan in the north of the country. Travel to this region is relatively safe, although local knowledge is a must, as there remain pockets of danger.

It is beyond the scope of this book to advise on the viability of travel to Greater Baghdad or the south of Iraq for Western business professionals. It is hoped that the author can expand upon the business potential of this country in a future edition of this book.

Although the Civil War ended in Lebanon in 1990, unrest does flair up on occasion, but it has had no significant, sustained impact on the Western business professional.

Civil War ended in Yemen in 1994. However, there is steady fighting, kidnapping and acts of revenge amongst tribal factions throughout most of the country, including tourist attractions and other areas of potential interest to Western business professionals. Socotra Island remains safe to visit, travelling by air; at the time of publication, its sea route is in the middle of the Somali-based piracy activity.

There are also internal conflicts within Sudan, most notably in Darfur and in the south of the country, although neither region is known as a haven for Western business professionals.

At the time of writing, it is unclear if Iran's continued development of nuclear technology and its perception as a threat to the region will escalate into military activity.

In assessing the region's potential for further wars, it is important to keep things in perspective. For example, since the end of the Second World War, the US and the UK have been involved in many more conflicts outside the Middle East than Middle Eastern countries have been in conflict with each other.

As with assessing the threat of terrorism, the best advice is to seek information and opinions from a number of sources: your government's official website for travel to the country, local media, your local business contacts and other ex-pats living in the country. It's also important to understand the terms of your insurance policy.

SAFETY

Coming from a Western country / Western culture

It is safe to travel to the Middle East as a Westerner! In fact, you will be made to feel more welcome in the region than nearly anywhere else in the world.

Hospitality is the operative word throughout the Islamic world. Guests, including Western business people, are given an honourable status that they will retain throughout the time they visit the Middle East, even if it's for years. There may be slight exceptions to this in the most fundamental societies in Saudi Arabia, but not amongst those Saudis with whom you would be doing business.

The other exception is in Yemen, where the current climate is not always hospitable to Americans in particular, especially after the recent bombings immediately outside the American Embassy. The author, an American/British dual national, recently made it clear she was most definitely travelling within Yemen as a British citizen, to the immediate and obvious relief of her Yemeni minder and others encountered during her visit.

It is important to keep in mind that Middle Eastern countries have access to all forms of Western media, from the large number of satellite television channels that have proliferated in recent years to a huge number of internet websites. Most of the Middle East is finding a way to integrate the best traits of the West with their own values and traditions.

Finally, many people from the Middle East have travelled extensively in the West, whether for higher education, tourism, to visit relatives or to escape the worst of the summer heat. As a result, it's fair to say that most people from the Middle East will be more familiar with the West than Westerners will be with the Middle East. Relax and enjoy the hospitality!

LAW AND ORDER

Violent crime

Middle Eastern countries consistently fall at the bottom of the league tables when it comes to violent crime, including assault, murder, rape and robbery, as all of these actions are un-Islamic. In fact, the highest rates of violent crime are most often found in the West, with the USA and South Africa in particular struggling with these problems. Statistically, the chance of a Western business professional becoming involved in a violent, non-politically motivated crime is negligible.

Personal safety issues

Personal safety should not be a worry for business visitors to the Middle East. Muggings, pick-pocketing, and other 'petty' crimes are rare throughout the region. It is not unusual for wallets, purses, handbags or mobile phones and other electronic devices to be left unattended in restaurants (and bars where they exist) whilst using the toilets. Open handbags are a common sight in supermarket trolleys and on retail counters in the shops. In fact, many long-term residents and visitors to the Middle East observe that their personal guard is lowered so much that they feel they are a danger to themselves, once they return to the West.

Burglary is uncommon, although common sense should prevail when leaving a vehicle unattended. Although there is little likelihood that items would be stolen from a hotel guest's room, safes should be used for valuables that are left behind.

A note of caution: although the Middle East remains remarkably safe, it is prudent to assume responsibility for your possessions. Whilst local residents have little motivation to steal for a variety of reasons, and ex-pats are unlikely to risk their residency status, a Western tourist may have a different attitude.

Road traffic

One unavoidable potential danger to Western business professionals is road traffic. Driving throughout the region is of a standard not found in most of the West, including Mediterranean Europe.

The Gulf is particularly fraught with danger, as huge numbers of ex-pats dominate the roads. Drivers from countries as diverse as India, Malaysia, Japan, Sri Lanka, the United Kingdom, South Africa and Pakistan can be found on roads from Kuwait to Oman, all of whom learnt their driving skills in another environment, and most of whom are driving on the 'wrong side of the road'. Some of the Gulf countries have some of the highest traffic fatality rates in the world.

Gulf roads are of excellent quality, which allows drivers to reach high speeds easily. Large, powerful vehicles are often driven by newly-licensed drivers who have no previous experience of either these types of vehicles or these road conditions. This may be the first time they are driving at any appreciable speed, and may not be fully in control of their vehicle. The common practice of the driver speaking on their mobile phone or texting whilst negotiating traffic adds further challenges. Furthermore, it is not unusual to see toddlers standing upright on the front seat of a moving vehicle with no safety constraints whatsoever.

Many Gulf nationals seem to drive as though they are exempt from many of the rules of the road, which in practice is often true. It's also not unusual to see young teenage local boys, clearly younger than the minimum legal driving age, behind the wheel of huge SUVs or expensive sports cars. It is prudent to give these drivers a wide berth wherever possible.

Road conditions often include the presence of pedestrians, some of whom have probably never seen dual carriageways prior to coming to the Gulf, trying to cross a motorway containing traffic travelling at speeds in excess of 120 kph. Sometimes it's a camel or goat, in rural areas.

If you are a pedestrian, never assume that any motorised traffic will stop for you; the concept of zebra and pelican crossings is not expected to catch on anytime soon anywhere in the region. Bicycles are an additional danger in some areas. In dense traffic, you may need to weave your way through or even run across oncoming traffic, especially if there is no traffic light system to provide a break in traffic. If you are unsure how to do this, do not be embarrassed to ask for help from a resident.

The Gulf countries continue to build new roads, and to implement temporary diversions in the midst of ongoing road works. It's not unusual for visitors and residents alike suddenly to find themselves on the wrong road, in a neighbourhood they thought they were familiar with.

Although the Gulf is usually sunny, it does rain on occasion during some winters. Roads that have been dry for months at a time, build up a layer of oil and other residue. When it does rain, these roads become very slippery, causing treacherous conditions. Many local drivers simply do not have enough experience of these driving conditions.

Many drivers also discover – sometimes on the motorway – that their windscreen wipers do not work. The best advice is to avoid travelling on wet roads whenever possible.

There are occasional sandstorms. These cause conditions not dissimilar to fog or whiteouts for those familiar with snow, with the additional irritation of getting sand everywhere, including in your eyes.

Road rage is uncommon but not unheard of. Drivers should note that obscene hand gestures are illegal in much of the Gulf. The authorities actually take this offence quite seriously. If you must vent your anger, it is recommended that you do so once you are no longer in your vehicle – and out of sight of the source of your anger.

If you are involved in a road accident, it's important to understand that the law of most Gulf countries is not to move your vehicle until the police arrive and give you permission to do so, even if you are obstructing traffic to the point that you are the lead story of the traffic report.

Driving conditions in the Levant are quite different, with Jordan generally a relative oasis of calm, although traffic jams are now known in Amman. Syria is generally comfortable for driving outside Damascus and Aleppo. Beirut is densely congested, and best negotiated by taxi or with a car and driver, especially if you have no arrangements made for parking at your destination. It is also recommended that Western visitors to Egypt avoid driving in Cairo due to the city's density and distinct lack of parking facilities. Similarly, it would be nearly impossible for a Westerner to self-drive in the Palestinian Territories; hire cars from both Israel and Jordan are not permitted.

Zero tolerance for drink driving

The legal limit for alcohol in a driver's bloodstream throughout the most Middle Eastern countries is 0 – absolutely none. It is 0.05% in Egypt.

Most people should be sensible enough to avoid drinking and driving on a night out. Problems can arise the morning after the night before, when residual alcohol levels may still be in your bloodstream. If in any doubt, leave the driving to someone else.

Public consumption of alcohol

Alcohol consumption is illegal throughout Kuwait and Saudi Arabia. Strict penalties, including possible prison sentences and deportation, apply for those who are caught in possession of, or consuming, any alcohol at all.

Alcohol consumption in other Gulf countries is highly regulated. Non-Muslim Western business professionals will be able to consume alcohol in most restaurants found in tourist hotels as well as licensed bars, nightclubs and private members facilities. Muslim visitors, even those from Western countries, are officially banned from consuming any alcohol in the Gulf countries, although this is often ignored.

Visitors should take care not to consume alcohol away from these premises.

For example, it's technically illegal to walk from a hotel restaurant to the restroom carrying an alcoholic drink, if the restroom is located in the lobby or other public area. Alcohol should never be consumed outdoors, including parks, beaches or communal courtyards. Alcohol consumed at swimming pools attached to licensed premises is legal.

Public consumption of alcohol should be avoided throughout the Levant, although it is available in many venues. It should be noted that alcohol consumption during *Ramadan* should be even more discrete. Many venues will only serve alcohol after sunset.

Zero tolerance for drug abuse

Recreational drugs are illegal throughout the Middle East. Punishments throughout the Gulf and most of the Levant range from fines followed by deportation, to prison and even the potential use of the death penalty in Saudi Arabia. If you are motivated to use or experiment with recreational drugs, you would be better off doing so in a different part of the world.

PERSONAL HEALTH

The effects of the sun

Business visitors from some Western countries may have little knowledge about proper behaviour in the sun.

Sunscreen should be used by all people who expose their skin to direct sunlight, including their face, hands, the back of their neck, the top of their feet and bald areas on top of the head. Sunburn can happen in as little as fifteen minutes for very fair skinned people, in this part of the world. Westerners with darker skin, regardless of race or ethnic background, should also exercise caution in the Middle Eastern sun.

The local practice of covering most of your skin makes particular sense in this regard. In addition to being modest, Westerners who wear loose clothing are also going a long way towards preventing sunburn and possible sunstroke. Sunscreen is readily available in all Middle Eastern countries with a thriving tourist economy. Travellers to Saudi Arabia, Yemen and Sudan should consider bringing their own supply with them.

Preventing dehydration is also to be taken seriously. You should have access to water at all times, even if the only source is water that has nearly reached boiling point when accidentally left in a vehicle. Bottled water is safe throughout the Middle East; the seal should not be broken. Tap water, although not always palatable, is safe throughout the GCC and the Levant. Tap water must be avoided in Yemen, Egypt and Sudan.

The effects of temperatures reaching 50°C

Most Western business professionals come from climates that never achieve very hot temperatures – let's say the mid-30s would be a rare hot day. Other Western business professionals may come from hotter climates, but may not appreciate how much hotter still it gets in most of the Middle East. Only people familiar with the summer climates of the deserts of Australia and the American Southwest (such as Phoenix – even Texas is not considered hot enough to compare!) will have an idea of what they are about to face in terms of thermometer readings.

Temperatures throughout the GCC can regularly reach the high 40s during the summer, and periodically climb past 50°C. This extreme heat is coupled with high humidity – often in excess of 80% – throughout most of the Gulf. Egypt experiences similar temperatures, especially in Upper Egypt, although humidity is low. Most of the Levant is relatively cool, with temperatures ranging from the low 30s to the mid-40s in parts of southern Jordan.

In addition to the cautions already covered about sun protection and dehydration, there are a number of everyday, practical considerations that should be taken into account by Western business professionals, especially during the height of a Middle Eastern summer.

Many Gulf countries have built car parks and shelters that allow drivers to park their vehicles in the relatively cool shade. Unfortunately, there are times when a driver is forced to park outside, without this protection, especially in very new neighbourhoods where building works are still in progress. Elsewhere in the Middle East, your vehicle is more likely to be left directly on the street or in an exposed car park.

Cars and other motor vehicles that have been parked in direct sunlight are much hotter on the inside than the air temperatures. Many drivers in the region cover the front interior with purpose-built, cardboard 'car sunglasses'; others make do with towels or other fabrics. The interior of a vehicle can reach in excess of 70°C in the peak of summer. If you must enter such a vehicle, it's best to plan ahead and to use some common sense.

Wait a few minutes before entering the car to let it cool down a bit. Open all windows and even one or two doors if this is practical. Most motorists will turn on their air conditioning immediately, leaving the motor to idle for several minutes. This is not very green behaviour, but many people travelling to this part of the world may be temporarily less concerned with being green than when in the West, especially in countries where the price of fuel is a fraction of the price of water.

Be careful of touching metal parts of the car, including the door handles, steering column and the gear lever. Vehicles with leather upholstery are an additional challenge.

Be mindful of what you leave in the car as there are hidden dangers. Fizzy drinks left in a car are not advised. The author can also confirm that it was a very bad idea to leave red nail varnish out in direct sunlight on the front seat of her car, at about 48°C on a mid afternoon in July, in Dubai.

Happily, most taxi drivers will ensure that their vehicle is as comfortable as outside conditions permit, at least in the Gulf. Taxis in the Levant and Egypt are more hit and miss, as the drivers may only switch on the car's air conditioning once they have secured a fare. In addition, the road worthiness of some taxis in the Levant and Egypt are questionable at best, and may not have functioning air conditioning. However, the Western business traveller can be assured that taxis throughout the region will have functioning horns and radios.

Most Western business professionals can avoid the most intense heat of the day by staying indoors. Sometimes, it is not possible to avoid periods of time in the heat and sun. If this is likely to be part of your agenda, it's not a bad idea to carry a change of clothing, particularly a spare blouse or shirt.

Finally, a word about air conditioning. One of the ironies of working in one of the hottest parts of the world is the overuse of air conditioning in most public buildings as well as hotels, office buildings and up-market shopping centres, especially in the Gulf countries. This means you may find yourself carrying a jumper or wrap with you when it's nearly 50°C outside! Ladies, it's another good reason to have a headscarf handy – they make good impromptu outerwear in just such an environment.

Western over-the-counter medications

Another danger that Western business professionals can get caught up in innocently is the importation of over-the-counter medicines that are perfectly legal in their home country, but illegal in their destination country. This includes many popular codeine-based drugs that are used in the West for headaches, coughs and the common cold, including popular brands such as Nurofen Plus and Tixylix. Most Gulf countries publish a full list of banned drugs on their official websites. If in doubt, leave it out of your baggage; medical facilities throughout the Gulf and the Levant are of an excellent standard, and you can get a perfectly legal substitute at your destination.

Prescription drugs should always be carried in their original packaging and accompanied by an official doctor's note. Business professionals may need to comply with additional rules before importing these drugs. It is strongly advised that guidance is sought from the relevant embassy prior to travel. If you cannot get a straight answer from the embassy, you may wish to check with your local business partner or a trusted ex-pat living in the country.

Food and drink

As previously noted, bottled water is recommended throughout the Middle East. Tap water, although not recommended, is safe to drink throughout the GCC and the Levant, although it will have an unpleasant taste in the GCC in particular due to desalinisation. Tap water from Egypt, Sudan and Yemen must be avoided, as well as ice cubes.

Hot drinks are safe to drink when thoroughly boiled even in the latter three countries. Care should be given to milk in these countries; elsewhere in the Middle East, dairy products are safe to consume if properly handled.

Most visitors to the Middle East will find Arabic cuisine a pleasure, including food purchased from street vendors. Again, the main cautions are in Egypt, Sudan and Yemen, where Western visitors are often better off in established restaurants.

OTHER SOCIAL CAUTIONS

Falling foul of religious laws

Each country in the Middle East has its own rules and regulations as to which Islamic laws must be adhered to by visitors, including Western business professionals. Because these rules are vastly different in Saudi Arabia, we will address that country separately.

Throughout the Middle East, the consumption of pork is frowned upon. Pork is totally illegal only in Kuwait and Saudi Arabia, where any attempt to import pork products can attract the authorities. Throughout the remainder of the Gulf, pork is only on the menu in some hotel restaurants, i.e. in more or less the same establishments that are also permitted to serve alcohol. Pork products may also be purchased by non-Muslims in certain supermarkets, although they will only be sold from a separate meat counter that is clearly labelled for non-Muslims only. Pork products can sometimes be found in the Levant, although they are becoming less common in recent years, even in Lebanon.

Making negative comments about Islam is never a good idea. Laws against blasphemy are taken seriously, as is apostasy (the renouncement of a faith) by a Muslim. Anti-Islamic websites are routinely blocked from access throughout the region. Access to anti-Jewish and anti-Zionist websites is an entirely different matter and can be widely accessed in the Middle East.

Most Gulf countries do not permit non-Muslims to enter mosques. Western business professionals who are Muslim do have access, as they would to mosques anywhere in the world. Several Gulf countries do invite non-Muslims to designated mosques as tourists, at specific times that do not clash with prayer times, including mosques in Abu Dhabi, Dubai, Bahrain, Kuwait and Muscat. All visitors, including non-Muslims, must comply with Islamic dress codes as dictated by the authorities responsible for the visitors.

Many more mosques can be visited by non-Muslims in the Levant, but there may still be hours that are off limits. Fridays are usually off limits as well.

In Saudi Arabia, social laws that dictate the country's version of proper public behaviour are officially enforced by the Committee for the Propagation of Virtue and the Prevention of Vice. The religious police who perform these duties are known as the *muttawa* or *mutaween* and are officially endorsed by the Saudi government. It should be noted, however, that their level of activity will vary tremendously within the country. Most Western business visitors will notice them in Riyadh. Drawing attention from the *muttawa* is best avoided by Westerners; they are unpopular amongst many Saudis as well.

The *muttawa* are mostly concerned about the following activities that may impact on your visit to the Kingdom:

- General disrespect of *Shari'a* law.
- Entering public spaces intended for the other gender, including family sections of restaurants, women only floors of shopping malls, and queues.
- Dress code compliance for men and women in public.
- Confiscation of non-Islamic religious symbols and other materials in the Kingdom, including crosses, bibles, Buddhas, Ganeshes, Stars of David and Christmas items.
- Confiscation of un-Islamic media, such as certain CDs and DVDs that contain some targeted Western entertainment.
- Confiscation of any pork or alcohol products.
- Women travelling without their *mahram* (male guardian).
- Unrelated, mixed-gender groups travelling together, including Western businessmen and women.

- Ignoring prayer time rules and behaviour, including closing shops and restaurants.
- Refusing to stop business during prayer time.
- Attempting to travel to Mecca and Medina for non-Muslims.

Sexuality issues

Heterosexual issues

Heterosexual sexual activity is illegal throughout the Gulf countries for everyone except married couples. The reality on the ground varies tremendously from country to country.

Unmarried Western couples travelling to the Gulf countries are unlikely to have any problem if they simply do not draw attention to themselves. This includes checking in together to a hotel room or other accommodation (this is also technically illegal). As most local married couples do not share a last name, Westerners checking into a hotel together do not raise suspicion simply by having different surnames. The main exception is if either Westerner has a Muslim name or otherwise appears to come from a Middle Eastern or Muslim background. In this situation, the couple may experience difficulties, even when both are travelling on Western passports.

Unmarried ex-pat couples commonly cohabit, especially in Dubai, Abu Dhabi, Musact and Bahrain. It's best to allow the general public to think you are married rather than to correct them if you are not. The main exception is in Saudi Arabia, where it would be unsafe to attempt any sexual activity with an unrelated heterosexual partner. In fact, it is difficult to even be in the presence of an unrelated person of the opposite sex in more conservative areas of the country, including much of Riyadh.

As recent events surrounding the British 'sex on the beach' and 'kissing' couples in Dubai have proven, do not push the boundaries of local law. The best rule is to be discrete and to keep any sexual activity confined to private locations. Local authorities are likely to turn a blind eye when two Westerners are involved in a situation where they can officially ignore sexual behaviour. However, if confronted with sexual behaviour that they can no longer ignore, they will save face and arrest the offending couple. The 'rule' in play here is 'Do not force me to see what I do not want to see. If I am forced to see, then I must take action.'

The situation is generally more relaxed for Westerners in the Levant and in Egypt, although it remains prudent to refrain from announcing your marital status to casual acquaintances.

Many Western business professionals may be surprised to learn that public displays of affection by married heterosexual couples are frowned upon throughout the Middle East, and are illegal in Saudi Arabia. Whilst it is possible to see everything from a simple peck on the cheek to hugs and holding hands, especially in popular tourist areas, the best advice is to refrain from this behaviour. Your business partners and other local people will appreciate your restraint and respect for their cultural values.

Homosexual issues

Homosexuality is illegal nearly everywhere in the Middle East. In Jordan, homosexuality is not technically illegal, mostly because the penal code does not specify gender when referencing illegal sexual activity. However, Jordanian society as a whole is a long way from accepting openly-homosexual lifestyles as well.

Many Western business professionals can become confused about homosexuality in the Middle East. It is quite common to see two adult men walking down the street hand in hand, or with one man's arm around the other man's opposite shoulder. Although it is less likely, some women may also act in a similar manner. Both behaviours are simply signs of friendship and do not imply homosexuality. It's unlikely for Middle Eastern men to behave in this manner with Western businessmen (and certainly not with Western businesswomen), although there may be a few Saudis who do so once they get to know you very well.

Many Middle Eastern men will also touch another man's forearm when speaking, including Western businessmen (but not businesswomen). They may also move closer to the other man, to the point that most Westerners would feel their personal space was being intruded upon. Neither is a sign of homosexuality, either, but a way for the man to emphasise his point and to show sincerity. The Western businessman should never recoil or otherwise move away, at least not in an obvious manner, as this would be interpreted as a sign of extreme rudeness by the Middle Eastern man.

Of course, homosexuality does exist unofficially throughout the Middle East. There are thriving underground social scenes from Dubai to Beirut. Many homosexuals live together in ex-pat communities throughout the region, albeit in the closet. Ironically, it's often easier for homosexual couples to cohabitate than unmarried heterosexual couples.

From the point of view of the Western business professional, it is strongly suggested that you consider the laws of the country you are visiting if you are considering any homosexual activity.

Dealing with uncomfortable public behaviour
Staring
In a business environment

Western business professionals of both genders will notice that quite a few people in the Middle East appear to be staring at them. Culturally, there are quite different rules as to what is considered courteous and what might be rude between the Middle East and the West.

Middle Eastern men are likely to hold eye contact with another man more directly and longer than is often comfortable for many Western men. This may be coupled with the Middle Eastern man moving close enough to the other man to the point that he has entered the Westerner's personal space. As previously mentioned, do not react negatively, as this will be interpreted as an insult.

Some Middle Eastern men who are familiar with, and comfortable working with, Western businesswomen may also look directly at a woman, but it would be quite unusual for him to prolong his gaze, and he is very unlikely to move closer to her. Many more local men will actually do the opposite, and will not look at a woman directly at all. Instead, he will divert his eyes away from the woman, looking askance or possibly down towards the ground. This is not meant to be disrespectful of the woman; in fact, it is a sure sign of respect from the man. This same practice is also common amongst men from the Indian subcontinent working with women.

Out in public

Out in public, many women do encounter very prolonged staring, usually from labourers, but rarely from service people or the educated population. Although many Western businesswomen are uncomfortable with this behaviour, they should not feel threatened. Nor does the Western woman's foreign appearance, blonde hair, blue eyes or the like cause staring; Western women from other ethnic backgrounds will encounter similar behaviour as well. It is important to understand that these men generally come from cultures that do not consider staring to be rude. Most often, staring is simply a display of curiosity from a man who may have very limited contact with any women. Most of these men are far away from home, and may not have seen any of their family, including their wives, for up to two or three years at a time. Western businesswomen are in no physical or verbal danger from these men.

Admiring an object

As a side note, it is strongly advised that Westerners do not stare at an object for a prolonged period of time, nor to praise the object. Many people from the Middle East will feel obligated to offer the object to you!

For example, the author was invited to inspect her business partner's recently refurbished office in Cairo. Stopping at a particularly lovely piece of modern art hanging on the wall, her business partner started to remove it, saying 'you must take this, my friend'. Happily the author was able to make an excuse about not having a worthy enough place to display it, explaining she would have a better opportunity to admire the artwork where it already resided.

Private vs public politeness

Whilst people from the Middle East display exemplary manners with people they know, there is often a completely different code of behaviour practised whilst out and about in public amongst total strangers. Do not be surprised by this behaviour, however unpleasant it may be. From the Middle Eastern point of view, a random encounter with another member of the public does not always have an identifiable status or hierarchy to recognise. Instead, Darwinian principles are in play: survival of the fittest!

Rude or obscene comments and gestures

Swearing is highly offensive to most people from the Middle East. This does not mean that people never swear; quite the opposite, as Arabic swear words are amongst the most colourful and descriptive on the planet. In general, swearing is usually used sparingly. It should be avoided by Westerners in any language as a matter of courtesy.

There are a number of sounds and gestures that are meant to be insulting or obscene throughout the Middle East. Some men may make hissing and teeth sucking sounds that women would find uncomfortable, but it must be said that Western women are unlikely to experience this unless they are alone, on foot and dressed immodestly (as perceived by the young men generally involved). If the Western businesswoman does encounter this behaviour, an effective way of stopping this it is to ask the men – in English is fine – if their behaviour is an example of being a good Muslim, or how they would like it if another man made similar noises at their sister, mother or wife. It works.

Obscene, rude or disparaging hand gestures should generally be ignored. Most Western business professionals should not encounter these in a business environment, but it is possible if you cause enough anger with your Middle Eastern colleagues. The most common are biting the right forefinger (wishing evil), making a churning gesture in front of the stomach (liar), lining up the fingers of the left hand with the right index finger (insulting your parentage), pressing the right fist into the left hand (wishing ill will or harm), or displaying the soles of your shoes or feet. Westerners should be careful not to use the OK gesture, as it is considered rude in the Middle East.

Queue jumping

The concept of forming orderly queues is effectively unknown throughout the Middle East. This can be very difficult for Western business professionals to deal with who come from a culture accustomed to queues, especially the British and North Americans. In many situations, the queue appears instead to be a scrum, with the fittest jostling for position to be served before all others. Middle Eastern culture also tends to operate on a system that recognises the person's hierarchy. Thus, there is every possibility that a national and other Middle Easterners will be served before someone else, even if the other person was there first. On the other hand, Westerners will often be served before people from the Indian subcontinent and other parts of the non-Western world.

Men will often be served before women, although there are exceptions in certain locations where women will actually be brought to the front of the group or even served separately from men. If this happens to a Western businesswoman, the correct behaviour is to accept the special treatment so as not to insult the person who assisted you. Other people present will not challenge this.

It is fair to suggest that Western business professionals should choose their battles. Waiting for a shopkeeper to finish greeting his relative before taking your payment for a newspaper is quite different to potentially missing the last flight to London because a local family of 12 suddenly jumped the queue at the airport five minutes before your flight is scheduled to close.

Other personal habits uncomfortable to most Westerners

Although the following are not specifically safety issues, other behaviours can affect the degree of comfort experienced by the Western business professional throughout the Middle East.

Smoking

The realities on the ground for smoking cigarettes will depend on the country visited. In general, many people from the Levant and Egypt are smokers, including many Lebanese and Syrian women. Some countries in the Levant can be considered an open ashtray, with offices, restaurants and public buildings lacking no-smoking zones. In addition, the general public will also ignore the no-smoking rules in many public areas that are designated as no-smoking zones. For example, Syria's recent public smoking ban is deeply unpopular and routinely flouted. Some concessions to non-smokers will be made in upmarket hotels.

Smoking remains acceptable throughout Egypt, Jordan, Lebanon and Yemen. Non-smokers will be particularly challenged to negotiate a restaurant table or other public venue where they can avoid second-hand cigarette smoke.

In the Gulf, smoking is much less prevalent amongst Gulf national populations, with some exceptions for Saudis and Kuwaitis. It would be nearly unheard of to witness a Gulf national woman smoking in public, although Levantine Arab women may do so. There are no-smoking restrictions in place and enforced in the UAE. It is illegal to smoke in public areas in Bahrain. Some restrictions exist in certain establishments in Qatar and Oman with expectations of more to come; less so in Kuwait. In Saudi Arabia, it is fair to say that the smoking policy will probably reflect the personal attitude of the establishment's owner; thus, some offices and other venues will be smoke free, whilst others will be thick with smoke.

The author, who has been accused of being an outspoken non-smoker on more than one occasion, can only give general hints and tips on how to handle situations where the Western business professional does not want to be exposed to second-hand smoke. For example, try to advise a restaurant that you would prefer to sit very far away from other smokers, even if they need to open a separate section of the restaurant. Try to sit outside and upwind from the smokers in the more pleasant months of the year.

Although it would be very difficult to directly ask a business associate not to smoke in your presence, it is possible to advise that business associate that you suffer from asthma and apologise for any difficulties you may have if exposed to second-hand smoke (this works better than the general Western 'allergies' excuse). Some smokers will take the hint; others will ignore it.

Shisha smoking remains popular throughout the Middle East. In some establishments, it is a male-only affair. In others, especially in some upmarket restaurants, women can also be seen enjoying a relaxing smoke. Whereas a

Western business professional can expect further smoking restrictions to be enacted for cigarettes, it is highly unlikely that the region will implement bans on the *hookah* (water pipe).

Crotch touching

Many Middle Eastern men do not consider touching their genitals in public to be rude or offensive. Do not be surprised if you witness 'adjustments' or a vigorous scratch at random moments in public or anywhere else. Other Asian cultures, including the Indian subcontinent have similar views on the matter. Of course, men in some European cultures share this habit as well.

Qat *chewing and spitting*

Qat is a mild narcotic that has been compared to a milder version of a cocaine high. It is a bush grown in Yemen and in parts of East Africa. The leaves are chewed by both Yemeni men (in public) and women (mostly in private), usually in the afternoon and throughout the evening. By late afternoon, it is difficult to dodge the many green puddles left on the ground as chewed *qat* leaves are spit out. It may also be difficult to find a driver in late in the day who is not under the influence of *qat*. It is illegal to use *qat* in most other countries of the Middle East.

General spitting and snorting

Although these habits are not strongly associated with the Middle East, it is possible to witness spitting and snorting amongst other expatriate communities in the Gulf countries. There is an enthusiastic approach to spitting and snorting amongst some men from the Indian subcontinent and from Greater China in particular. Some people from the Indian subcontinent also chew and spit *paan*, which leaves a blood-red stain on the ground.

Miscellaneous tips

Taxis and other ground transport

The quality of taxis varies tremendously from country to country. For example, Dubai Taxis are operated by reliable, honest drivers who use their meters and who generally speak enough English to communicate with English speakers about their travel requirements. Taxis in Abu Dhabi are also of good quality on the whole. Taxis in Bahrain, Kuwait, Oman and Qatar are of acceptable standard, but are much less prevalent than in the UAE. Taxis in Saudi Arabia are generally best avoided by Westerners, and should never be considered by Western businesswomen unless no other form of transport is available.

Keep in mind that all Gulf countries are undergoing a massive transformation, with new neighbourhoods popping up very quickly. Taxi drivers throughout the Gulf do make an honest attempt to know the location of destinations most likely to be required by Western business professionals. However, some buildings may be so new that you are the first fare who has asked to be taken there. Be patient, and always have the mobile number of your contact available for clarification with the driver.

Taxis in the Levant are of a lower standard – they are not generally unsafe, but they may be older vehicles and they may not always be spotlessly clean. Seat belts, regarded as an option at the best of times in the Middle East, may not exist in Levantine taxis, or they may be so dirty that the passenger may not wish to wear them. Most taxi drivers in the Levant will understand you, but may not speak fluent English.

Standard Egyptian taxis are not generally of a very high quality, nor is it certain the driver will be able to speak English or be literate – an additional problem if you require a receipt. Always use the officially-sanctioned taxi ranks at all Middle Eastern airports. Never accept a ride from any taxi tout operating at any airport, and at Cairo airport in particular. At Cairo airport, ensure that you use the official taxi ranks, which are quite a distance from the arrivals hall. Better yet, organise transport through your hotel, which will provide vehicles of an international standard and will magically make the touts disappear.

The price of any taxi journey that does not operate a meter should be negotiated before the passenger gets into the vehicle. Get the correct rate from your hotel, an airport dispatcher, or other reliable and neutral source. Details should be clarified, including any surcharges for handling baggage, airport entrance fees, tolls or parking tariffs.

A final note about seating in taxis: women should never sit in the front seat of a taxi anywhere in the region. The correct protocol is to have the junior-most male sit in the front with the driver if you have more passengers than will fit in the back seat. All-women groups should split up and take an additional taxi if their entire party cannot fit into the back seat.

Hotel transport is reliable throughout the region and is always a good option, including collecting first-time visitors at the airport upon arrival, at least until the Western business professional determines whether they are comfortable relying on taxis.

Many visitors to the Middle East will be greeted by drivers organised by their local business partner. This hospitality should always be accepted; no attempt at payment should ever be made.

Public transport, especially buses and coaches, are not generally taken by Western business professionals throughout the Middle East. It is unclear whether Westerners will use the Dubai Metro as it expands operations.

Baggage

Porters, doormen and security staff will all carry your baggage. It is the expectation throughout the Middle East that Western business professionals have a high status and therefore should not be lifting any object heavier than a woman's handbag. This also applies to a man's briefcase or computer bag as well as their main baggage.

The Westerner should accept this courtesy and allow the service person to do their job as if you don't, you will look undignified to your Middle Eastern colleagues. There is no need to be worried about theft. Your bags will be delivered to your hotel room safely and quickly. Service people will generally treat your baggage with care, with the exception of security screening at airports, where total chaos and disregard for personal property seems to be the norm. Tipping is not necessary unless an extraordinary amount of baggage is involved or the size and weight of your baggage was particularly awkward.

Losing your passport

As is true anywhere in the world, all travellers should be careful not to lose their passport. In fact, you should routinely carry it with you whilst travelling in the Middle East, as many countries require visitors to carry an official form of identification at all times. Your driving licence is *not* considered to be an official document in this regard.

Although it is much less likely that you will have your passport stolen in the Middle East than in most other parts of the world, it is still possible to simply lose or damage your passport at some point in your travels. Therefore, it is strongly recommended that the Western business professional scans the information page of their passport along with any pages containing a visa that was applied for in advance of travel. It's also an excellent idea to scan the details of your medical coverage as well. Then, simply email the scanned copies to yourself, making sure that you send them to an email address that is web based or accessible through a VPN. This will make your life much less complicated if you need to go through the process of applying for a replacement passport whilst out in the Middle East. For some nationalities, it may be the only way you can gain access quickly to your own embassy or consulate, as proof of citizenship is required in many instances.

EUROPEAN UNION
UNITED KINGDOM OF
GREAT BRITAIN
AND NORTHERN IRELAND
DIEU ET MON DROIT
PASSPORT

7

Business travel to and within the Middle East

The reader is invited to read this chapter for practical advice on what to expect whilst travelling to, from and within the Middle East. It is not meant to be an exhaustive manual that replaces your organisation's corporate travel resources. It is particularly important to keep in mind that travel conditions change quickly, especially in the Gulf. New airports and terminals are seemingly built overnight. More airlines arrive on the scene – from the major carriers of Europe and Asia expanding into the region and also from new carriers owned and operated by regionally-based entrepreneurs.

GETTING READY

Health and jabs

Western business professionals should consult with their government's official website for health advice about the countries to which they are travelling. The World Health Organisation website also has useful information.

Iran, Yemen and Sudan are the only countries in the Middle East that fall within the malarial zone. Even so, malaria is absent in all major cities in Iran, including Tehran, Esfahan and Shiraz. It is also unlikely that most business professionals to Sana'a or Khartoum are at risk of contracting malaria, although many websites will advise taking anti-malarial drugs or other precautions.

Sudan is the only country in the Middle East that falls within the yellow fever zone. Yellow fever jabs are not a condition of entry into Sudan. The risk of yellow fever in Khartoum is negligible for most business professionals.

Western business professionals should ensure they have sufficient medical coverage for travel to all Middle Eastern countries. Medical facilities throughout the GCC are of excellent standard, as are facilities in the major cities of Iran, Jordan and Lebanon. Travellers to Egypt, Sudan, Syria and Yemen may wish to consider evacuation coverage as facilities in these countries are less likely to be acceptable to most Western business professionals.

Toilets, tampons and tummy troubles

First-time visitors to the Middle East who have also never travelled outside of the West may encounter toilets different from those to which they are accustomed. Whilst squat toilets are rare in GCC venues frequented by Westerners, they are still found in less-populated areas of the Levant as well as in some very old office buildings.

Women who are expecting to use squat toilets should seriously consider their choice of clothing. Whilst trousers are often a sensible choice of clothing in the Middle East, they are not very practical when confronted with a squat toilet, especially one that hasn't seen a cleaning brush or bleach for a while. Footwear should also be carefully considered, in part because you will need to have a good sense of balance.

However, sit-down toilets in the Middle East are also different from those found in the West. Firstly, most sewer and septic systems are simply not equipped to accept toilet paper. Forget about disposing tampons, sanitary towels or anything else down the toilet. Instead, a bin for toilet paper, etc. will be found near the toilet, usually placed on the left side when sitting. The Western business professional should follow this convention, as toilets will otherwise quickly become blocked.

Secondly, toilet paper is not always found in Middle Eastern toilets regardless of style. This is because it is traditional to attend to personal cleanliness with the left hand and water. In fact, many people from the region actually consider the use of toilet paper to be unsanitary! If you do not prefer to adapt to Middle Eastern hygiene practices in the toilet, you may want to consider carrying an emergency supply with you at all times.

Thirdly, many toilets in the Middle East do not flush as robustly as they do in the West. Both squat and sit-down toilets may also come equipped with a bucket – not to be confused with the refuse bin. There will also be a tap mounted on the wall of the loo. This bucket should be filled with water that is available from the handily-supplied tap. Simply dump the water down the toilet – gravity will take care of the rest. Repeat as required.

Western businesswomen should carry an emergency supply of tampons or sanitary towels with them to the Middle East, even if you do not expect to need them during your visit. Tampons may not always be available in Yemen or Sudan, or in the more remote villages of the region.

Whilst tampons are generally available throughout the GCC, in most of the Levant and in Egypt, Sod's Law dictates that you will need them on a Friday morning, when all of the shops are closed, including most hotel gift shops. If this does happen to you, it is highly recommended that you find a female employee of your hotel to make a discrete request for assistance.

Most Western business professionals should not have any health problems related to tummy troubles, whilst travelling in the Middle East, if they follow good standards of hygiene and use their common sense. In general, tap water is safe to drink throughout the GCC, although its taste may be unpalatable as much of the water in the region is desalinated. Bottled water is strongly recommended throughout the Levant and Iran, although using the tap for cleaning your teeth is unlikely to make most visitors ill. Tap water is *not* safe to drink throughout Egypt, Sudan and Yemen. Use the usual precautions when drinking bottled water in these countries, especially making sure to check that the seal has not been broken around the cap.

Most Western business professionals do not suffer from an elevated number of tummy upsets in the Levant or GCC. Western business professionals who are prone to tummy troubles due to water or unfamiliar food would be wise to carry their favourite remedy with them into the Middle East, especially if travelling to Sudan or Yemen. Egyptian chemists usually stock over-the-counter medications for the large number of tourists who suffer from tummy troubles.

The weather

It is not always hot in the Middle East! In fact, it gets downright cold in the winter in parts of Lebanon, Syria, Jordan and the West Bank, especially at higher elevations. Jerusalem also gets cold in winter. It snows regularly in Tehran and elsewhere in the north of Iran. It is possible to snow ski in the mountains of Iran and Lebanon. Kuwait can be distinctly cool in the winter months, as can the desert, especially in the interior of Saudi Arabia. The winter months are pleasant in Bahrain, Qatar, the UAE, Oman, Yemen, Egypt and Sudan.

In the summer months, it can easily reach 50°C in the Gulf countries, with high humidity as well. It remains in the mid-30s throughout the night. It is often in excess of 40°C in the Levant, especially along the Mediterranean coast. Cities at higher elevations are often several degrees cooler and usually enjoy lower humidity. Egypt is also hot, with Cairo reaching into the 40s, but with low humidity. Cities along the Red Sea are also very hot and humid.

Most rain falls in the winter months in the Levant. Rainfall in the Gulf, which does not always happen, occurs between December and February. The monsoon affects Yemen and Southern Oman, namely in and around Salalah. The monsoon months are June to September. Visitors should keep in mind that climate change does not discriminate by location. The author can attest to rain in Dubai in April as well as in the winter months.

What to wear

Travellers to the Middle East should dress in modest clothing that will be comfortable to wear at their destination. Western business professionals are advised to look the part, especially if their sponsor or host's driver is collecting them at the airport. It does not leave a good impression to be dressed as a tourist, especially if you are also underdressed. In fact, never underestimate the importance of good dress and grooming throughout the Middle East, as it indicates respect for both yourself and for the local culture.

For business professionals making their journey into Iran or Saudi Arabia, they must arrive at their destination airport in clothing compliant with local laws. In brief, men must not be wearing shorts and must wear a shirt that covers their arms at least to their elbow, and to their wrist in Riyadh. Women must wear clothing that conceals their shape and does not expose any skin other than their face, hands, and tops of their feet. This includes a headscarf throughout Iran and most of Saudi Arabia. Further details are provided in the 'Clothing and Dress Codes', Chapter 8.

Money

Managing money needed for the duration of your business trip is always a personal matter. Western business professionals should be aware that there are many different realities on the ground about money depending on your destination.

Currencies pegged to the US Dollar

Most currencies of the GCC are pegged to the US dollar. Kuwait is an exception, as it has recently uncoupled the Kuwaiti dinar from the dollar. Other GCC countries may reassess their ties if the economic difficulties of the US dollar continue to impact on their own currencies. The Western business professional should ensure they are up-to-date with current economic policies prior to changing money.

> **GCC Currencies and exchange rates**
> 1 US Dollar = 0.37816 Bahraini Dinar
> 1 Bahraini Dinar (BHD) = 2.64438 US Dollar (USD)
> 1 US Dollar = 0.29458 Kuwaiti Dinar *
> 1 Kuwaiti Dinar (KWD) = 3.39466 US Dollar (USD) *
> 1 US Dollar = 0.38616 Omani Rial
> 1 Omani Rial (OMR) = 2.58960 US Dollar (USD)
> 1 US Dollar = 3.64534 Qatari Rial
> 1 Qatari Rial (QAR) = 0.27432 US Dollar (USD)
> 1 US Dollar = 3.75320 Saudi Riyal
> 1 Saudi Riyal (SAR) = 0.26644 US Dollar (USD)
> 1 US Dollar = 3.67383 United Arab Emirati Dirham
> 1 UAE Dirham (AED) = 0.27220 US Dollar (USD)

* No longer pegged to the US dollar. Correct at the time of writing.

In addition, the currencies of Jordan and Lebanon are pegged to the US dollar. Syria, like Kuwait, has uncoupled the Syrian pound from the dollar. Current exchange rates:

Other Dollar-pegged currencies and exchange rates
1 US Dollar = 0.71266 Jordanian Dinar
1 Jordanian Dinar (JOD) = 1.40319 US Dollar (USD)
1 US Dollar = 1,523.20 Lebanese Pound
1 Lebanese Pound (LBP) = 0.0006565 US Dollar (USD)
1 US Dollar = 48.37994 Syrian Pound *
1 Syrian Pound (SYP) = 0.02067 US Dollar (USD) *

* No longer pegged to the US dollar. Correct at the time of publication.

Note

Within Lebanon, many people favour using currencies other than the Lebanese pound, including the US dollar, the Euro, and to a lesser extent, the British pound. Many short-term business professionals to Lebanon do not find the need to convert their currency into Lebanese pounds. Don't be surprised if you receive change in LBP if you are making a small purchase in another currency.

Countries with currency controls

Most Middle Eastern currencies are fully convertible, although there may be limits as to how much cash can be imported or exported. The exceptions are for the currencies of Egypt, Iran, Syria, Sudan and Yemen.

Western business professionals should be careful not to have too much cash in the local currency of these countries at the end of your business trip. Although you may be able to exchange Egyptian and Syrian pounds back to your own currency, it will be difficult to do so outside a major city, and will probably be at a very bad exchange rate. You will probably not be able to exchange local currency at all in Iran, Sudan and Yemen.

The following rates are quoted in US Dollars to remain consistent with the other exchange rates quoted above:

Currency controlled countries' exchange rates

1 US Dollar = 5.62157 Egyptian Pound

1 Egyptian Pound (EGP) = 0.17789 US Dollar (USD)

1 US Dollar = 9,881.11 Iranian Rial

1 Iranian Rial (IRR) = 0.0001012 US Dollar (USD)

1 US Dollar = 2.27830 Sudanese Pound

1 Sudanese Pound (SDG) = 0.43892 US Dollar (USD)

1 US Dollar = 201.746 Yemeni Rial

1 Yemeni Rial (YER) = 0.004957 US Dollar (USD)

Note

Within Iran, the official currency is the rial. However, it is common for Iranians to refer to the toman in many financial transactions. Although the toman is an old currency that has not been in use since the 1930s, the term is currently used to mean 10 rials. Thus, if someone asks for a price of 10,000, you should establish whether they mean 10,000 rial /1000 toman or 10,000 toman /100,000 rial.

Travellers' cheques

Travellers' cheques should be considered a thing of the past; most countries will no longer accept them, even at banks. Thus, it is recommended that Western business professionals do not bring travellers' cheques to the Middle East.

ATMs

It is recommended that Western business professionals use ATMs in any country with good availability. In addition to being safe, withdrawing funds from an ATM abroad often yields a better exchange rate than for cash. Travellers should ensure that their bank does not charge additional fees for using their bank cards abroad as this could negate exchange rate benefits, especially if ATMs are used frequently for relatively small withdrawals.

Good availability

ATMs can be found all over the GCC, and will present no problem for Western business professionals to use. Instructions will be in English and in Arabic. Daily limits, if there are any at all, will probably be more generous than your bank's limits. They will be in good working order, and will be found pretty much everywhere you would expect.

ATMs are easily found in Lebanon, and are found in most areas frequented by business professionals and tourists throughout Egypt and Jordan. ATMs provide instructions in English and Arabic throughout the Levant, and in English, Arabic and French in Lebanon. However, it is possible that some ATMs may not be working or may have run out of cash in some locations. ATMs are also found in major towns and cities throughout the Palestinian Territories. The Palestinian Territories use both Jordanian *dinar* and Israeli *shekels*.

Not-so-good availability

- Iran –ATMs exist in all major cities in Iran. However, due to trade sanctions, most foreign bank cards will not work in Iranian ATMs. It is best to carry enough hard currency to cover all expenses above and beyond your hotel costs for the duration of your trip. You may need to pay for your hotel in cash, as well, if your country is adhering to current trade sanctions, as your credit card may not be accepted if it is issued from your home country. Travelling within Iran with cash is safer than it is in nearly any other country in the world, although common sense should always be used.

- Sudan –Be careful! Sudan has established a new currency, the Sudanese pound (SDG), which replaced the Sudanese *dinar* in 2007. One SDG is worth 100 old *dinars*. There are no ATMs in Sudan. It is assumed that most Western business professionals would be staying in Khartoum, where there are facilities to exchange bank notes. Do not expect this to be easy; nor are you likely to get a good exchange rate. Try not to exchange more money than you think you need, as it is not possible to exchange Sudanese pounds back into hard currency. It's probably best to exchange funds incrementally, in spite of attracting fees for each transaction. Bring enough cash to cover all anticipated expenses, including the cost of your hotel.

■ Syria – ATMs exist in Damascus, but are otherwise in very short supply. There may be some in operation in Aleppo, but they may not accept bank cards issued in another country. It is best to carry enough hard currency to cover all expenses above and beyond your hotel costs for the duration of your trip. Travelling within Syria with cash is safe, although common sense should always be used.

■ Yemen – ATMs exist in Sana'a, although they may not accept your bank card. It is best to carry enough hard currency to cover you for all expenses above and beyond your hotel costs for the duration of your trip. Western business professionals should avoid displaying any cash in public in Yemen, although theft is generally lower than in most countries in the West.

Acceptance of bank cards

The acceptance of credit and debit cards varies throughout the Middle East. GCC countries, on the whole, are more likely to accept bank cards. Jordan, Lebanon and Egypt are reasonably accepting, at least in larger establishments. Iran, the Palestinian Territories, Syria and Yemen are effectively cash economies, with few exceptions. Bank cards are of no use anywhere in Sudan.

Visa and Mastercard are generally accepted in equal measure. Chip and pin has arrived in many locations in the Middle East. Make sure you know your pin number, and make sure it works abroad; check with your bank if in doubt. Cirrus, Plus, Pulse and Maestro are all recognised debit card associations, and are usually accepted in the Middle East wherever credit cards are accepted, but not always. Warn your home bank of your intention to use your cards abroad, otherwise your bank may consider their use outside your home country to be an indication of fraud and thus block any authorisations.

Travellers will struggle to use American Express or Diners Club cards except in Western-owned establishments such as chain hotels. The American card Discover is not accepted in the Middle East.

In general, consider bank card purchases possible for major expenses, such as business class hotels, car hire and meals in most upmarket restaurants that cater to an international clientele. Shopping malls are also likely to accept bank cards.

Smaller merchants who do accept credit cards may be reluctant to accept them if your purchase is under a minimum value. In some countries, they may also try to add a handling fee to cover their merchant fees. Most small businesses throughout the region continue to trade in cash only.

Credit cards issued by American banks will not work anywhere in Iran. This includes overseas branches of American banks. Thus, if you have a bank card issued by Citibank in London, it will not work in Iran. American Express cards issued worldwide are not accepted anywhere in Iran.

Bureaux de change

Reliance on *bureaux de change* in the Middle East is a mixed bag. There will be no problem changing US dollars, euros, British pounds or yen into local currency. Western business professionals coming from Australia, Canada, New Zealand, South Africa or from a European country outside of the Euro zone should consider carrying one of the currencies listed above prior to arriving in the Middle East, although their home currencies should not present a problem in the GCC. Business professionals to Iran may wish to consider bringing a mix of euros and US dollars.

Exchange rates vary. Sometimes it is better to change money in your home country (if they have the currency you want); other times, it's better to wait until you arrive at your destination. Hotel rates are often worse than kiosks or banks, but not always.

Be careful with the quality of the bank notes you plan to exchange, as many *bureaux de change* and merchants will not accept notes that are torn, excessively worn, or written on. Generally, large denomination bank notes in pristine condition are best. It is always recommended that the traveller obtains a receipt for their transaction, especially in a country without hard currency.

As a general rule, most *bureaux de change* in the Middle East will readily exchange hard currencies from neighbouring Middle Eastern countries as well. However, they are less likely to accept non-convertible currencies from the region, including Egyptian and Syrian pounds.

Bureaux de change in Dubai in particular are excellent places to exchange more exotic currencies that you may otherwise be stuck with, especially currencies from countries that have large ex-pat populations in Dubai. This may be your opportunity to get rid of those unwanted Thai *baht*, Indonesian *rupiah*, Indian *rupees* or even South African *rand* that you forgot to reconvert at the end of your holiday when you left Phuket, Bali, Goa or Cape Town. In fact, the only currency you should not try to exchange in Dubai is the Israeli *shekel*.

PERSONAL COMMUNICATION AND TECHNOLOGY

Laptops, data storage and personal entertainment devices

All countries of the Middle East will allow the Western business professional to temporarily import laptops, data storage devices such as external hard drives, CD/DVD players, memory sticks, other removable storage media and iPods. Business professionals to most of the GCC, Lebanon, Jordan and Egypt are unlikely to be stopped for further inspection upon arrival or departure, although it is always a good idea to have proof of purchase from outside the region if your technology is very new-looking.

Western business professionals to Saudi Arabia may be asked to step aside if an airport official is concerned that your media contains material that is un-Islamic. Although this practice has waned in recent years, it's always a good idea not to attract too much attention wherever possible. Thus, try to bring in materials on memory sticks rather than a stack of CDs or DVDs. Carrying a dodgy magazine may prompt a more thorough search, as would the smell of alcohol on your breath.

Mobile phones

All countries in the Middle East work to the GSM 900/1800 standard. This is the same system in use throughout the West, with the notable exceptions of the United States and Canada.

Mobile phones are ubiquitous throughout the Middle East. In fact, they are quite a status symbol, so Western business professionals with very old handsets may want to have a think about the impression their technology may leave with a prospective business partner.

In general, mobile phone coverage is good throughout the Middle East, especially in the main business centres, tourist destinations, and along most road systems. People travelling into the desert cannot expect to get a signal once they are away from the road. Signal quality is generally good, although there have been a number of complaints about inconsistent service from people who are working in Gulf countries near building sites.

New mobile telephone service providers are entering most Middle Eastern markets, with varying reputations and a wide range of roaming charges. It's always a good idea to check with your home service provider before you travel to learn what costs you will encounter when using your mobile phone abroad.

Many Western business professionals who plan to visit the Middle East on a regular basis should consider obtaining either a second mobile phone or at least a local SIM card from each country they will be visiting on a regular basis. Both options provide the business professional with a local or regional mobile telephone number. In addition to greatly reducing roaming charges, which can be very expensive, having a local telephone number shows your commitment to the region. Not only are your local contacts much more likely to call you; it also looks good on a business card.

Although it was difficult in the past to obtain a SIM card without a service contract (and sometimes the need for a residency visa as well), the situation is now more relaxed in most countries. If you run into difficulties, most business partners resident in the region are likely to help you out by obtaining a SIM card for you. If you find this necessary, make sure you work with someone who you can rely on and trust.

The Blackberry and other 3G communications devices

Most mobile telephone service providers throughout the Middle East have enabled 3G technology. Your Blackberry will probably work everywhere, at least in the main cities, except possibly in Iran and Sudan.

Internet access

Internet access is reasonably open in most of the Middle East; much more so than in China for example, where many popular websites used by business professionals are routinely blocked. In general, websites are blocked in the Middle East if they are anti-Islamic, anti-ruling families or anti-government, or are considered to be pornographic as defined by the local authorities. However, some countries may also block websites for reasons that are assumed to be purely commercial. For example, the UAE and Oman have officially restricted access to Skype, although there are ways to work around this.

Unsurprisingly, Saudi Arabia has a more extensive policy in blocking websites considered to be unsuitable for access in the Kingdom. They may include websites that reference alcohol, gambling, a wide range of music and other forms of entertainment, the promotion of religions other than Islam, homosexuality and most political websites.

Syria has a history of repressing many forms of communication. Fax machines required security clearance and a special licence as recently as the mid 1990s. Mobile phones were only allowed in the hands of the general population in the early 2000s. ATMs with connections to the global banking system are still not in common use except in certain areas of Damascus. Internet access is still heavily restricted, even more so than in Saudi Arabia. This may include popular websites that Westerners would assume are benign, including popular chat rooms, reputable news organisations, and some web-based email sites.

Iran also has a robust internet filtering system in place, which operates somewhat depending on the political mood. It should be noted that Iran is also a country with one of the most enthusiastic internet user populations in the world, who are also very clever at circumventing various restrictions officially imposed on them.

For the Western business professional, the use of proxy websites (and robust security) should be considered if access is important when travelling to these more restrictive destinations.

Communication restrictions to and from Israel

Those Western business professionals who work throughout the Middle East will face additional communications challenges when working in the region if they need to communicate with someone who happens to be in Israel, as well as some parts of the Palestinian Territories. This applies from all countries except Egypt and Jordan.

Most Middle Eastern governments will block access to any website that ends in .co.il, which denotes website domains registered in Israel.

It is also not possible to ring any telephone number beginning with the country code 972, which is the country code for Israel, from most other countries in the Middle East. This also applies to any telephone in the Palestinian Territories that does not have a 970 country code; many still have the country code 972.

If you are physically transiting through Israel to the Palestinian Territories, callers located elsewhere in the Middle East will probably not be able to complete a call to your mobile, as roaming services are likely to block such calls, even if your mobile number is from a third country.

For those Western business professionals who find themselves in any of the circumstances above who need to make a restricted communication link, it is recommended that they do so through a third party in their home country. The author suggests organising conference calls initiated in a third country that can connect the other parties located in the Israel and another Middle Eastern country.

Monitoring communications

The author is not in a position to make official comments about the monitoring policies of communications in the Middle East. However, a very good policy is to assume that all of your communications may be monitored by the local authorities, and possibly other interested parties, at any time during your visit to the region. For those Western business professionals who are particularly concerned about this issue, it is strongly recommended that you consider encryption devices and seek the advice of reputable organisations that supply professional standards of security measures.

Mains terminators/electrical plugs

Electricity throughout the Middle East operates on a 50Hz/220–240V system. In general, countries of the Middle East have retained the style of mains terminator originally introduced by their European 'colonisers'. Thus, all GCC countries use the British-style three pin rectangular blade terminator. So do Yemen and Jordan. Sudan uses the old British-style three pin round blade.

Egypt generally uses both British and Continental European terminators. Lebanon and Syria mostly use Continental European terminators, although there may be a combination of other terminator styles in some older buildings. Iran uses Continental European terminators.

Many buildings in the Palestinian Territories use the Israeli terminator. Some buildings also have British and/or Continental European terminators. The Israeli terminator is not used anywhere else in the world.

Surge protectors

Power surges can occur throughout the Middle East. It is strongly advised that all Western business professionals have a plan to protect their electronic devices when travelling to the region. Surge protectors are strongly recommended if you are unsure of the quality of the power supplies you will be using, including in your hotel.

YOUR PASSPORT

There are a few commonsense preparations the Western business professional should consider before travelling to the Middle East. Your passport should have plenty of blank pages, as it will be stamped each time you enter and leave each country in the region. You will need even more room in your passport if you enter countries that require a visa in advance, as the visa will take up additional space.

Most Middle Eastern countries require a passport to be valid for a further six months after the end of the stay. If your passport is getting close to this limit, it's best to renew it before travelling to the region.

Your passport should also be in reasonably good physical condition. Passports that are excessively worn or have pages that are beginning to peel, especially on the page with your photograph, may attract extra attention and could be cause for further investigation at passport control. If the authorities are not satisfied with your passport, you could be refused entry.

Israeli stamps

It is strongly advised that your passport is free from any Israeli stamps; in some countries, any evidence of having travelled to Israel is sufficient to ban your entry. Until recently, as a work-around for those tasked to travel by air through Israel on the way to the Palestinian Territories as well as other destinations in the Middle East, business professionals have asked the Israeli authorities *not* to stamp their entry visa directly into their passport but onto a separate piece of paper instead. However, there is no guarantee that the Israeli authorities will comply with your request. In fact, there is now strong anecdotal evidence that the Israeli authorities are inclined to stamp your passport regardless of any pleas not to do so. If this happens, the Western business traveller has no recourse other than to apply for a new passport prior to travelling to most other destinations in the Middle East.

They must also *not* travel overland between Israel and either Jordan or Egypt, where a stamp from either of these countries showing entry from a shared Israeli border is also considered evidence of travel to Israel. This applies to Egypt's Taba crossing as well as Jordan's crossings at Aqaba and at the Sheikh Hussein Bridge (not to be confused with the King Hussein/Allenby Bridge). There are special circumstances in play at the Allenby Bridge crossing, which are described in further detail in the next chapter.

Many countries, including the UK and US, allow their citizens to carry a second passport that will allow them to enter Israel on a passport separate from the passport they use for other Middle Eastern countries. Dual nationals often choose to use the nationality that is easier to travel on throughout the Middle East, using their other nationality for entry into Israel. The business professional must always keep the two passports separate. Americans who successfully apply for a second passport will receive a document that is only valid for two years; this document should be used for entering Israel as the authorities of most other

Middle Eastern countries will recognise this document as evidence of travel to Israel, negating the purpose of the entire exercise.

Anyone who renews their passport in Israel will also have serious difficulties travelling throughout the rest of the Middle East. It is strongly advised that the traveller applies for a new passport in another location, preferably their home country.

Anyone who was born in Israel will be denied entry to most of the other countries in the Middle East, even if they are a citizen of another country. The author does not have any advice as to how to circumvent this issue. In addition, political events can change the Western business traveller's experience at a moment's notice.

Country	OK to have Israeli stamp?	Can I get in anyway if I have an Israeli stamp?
Bahrain	Maybe	Bahraini border authorities have been known to ignore Israeli stamps in Western passports. An individual border authority may object to an Israeli stamp; if you chose this queue at passport control, you would be out of luck. If it is politically volatile, especially in the Palestinian Territories, they may formally enforce the ban and refuse entry.
Egypt	Yes	Egypt and Israel signed a peace treaty in 1979.
Iran	No	The Iranian border authorities will check each page of your passport to ensure it contains no Israeli stamps. They may also check to ensure you have no entry stamps into Jordan or Egypt that could only have been obtained by making the land crossing from Israel. If found, you will be refused entry. You may also be placed on a blacklist preventing you from future entry into Iran for the remainder of your passport's validity and possibly longer.
Jordan	Yes	Jordan and Israel signed a peace treaty in 1994.
Kuwait	No	There is a strong likelihood that the Kuwaiti border authorities will check each page of your passport to ensure it contains no Israeli stamps. If found, you will be refused entry.

Country	OK to have Israeli stamp?	Can I get in anyway if I have an Israeli stamp?
Lebanon	No	The Lebanese border authorities may check your passport to ensure it contains no Israeli stamps. If so, they will also check to ensure you have no entry stamps into Jordan or Egypt that could only have been obtained by making the land crossing from Israel. If found, you will be refused entry. You may also be placed on a blacklist preventing you from future entry into Lebanon for the remainder of your passport's validity.
Oman	Probably	Although Oman does not formally recognise Israel, there are rumours of possible low-level diplomatic missions between the two countries. Western passport holders are likely to gain entrance with an Israeli stamp. However, in times of political volatility, especially in the Palestinian Territories, they may refuse entry. You would be taking a calculated risk if you travel with an Israeli stamp in your passport.
Palestine	N/A	Israel controls all borders between Israel and the Palestinian Territories.
Qatar	Probably	Although Qatar does not formally recognise Israel, there are rumours of possible low-level diplomatic missions between the two countries. Western passport holders are likely to gain entrance with an Israeli stamp. However, in times of political volatility, especially in the Palestinian Territories, they may refuse entry. You would be taking a calculated risk if you travel with an Israeli stamp in your passport.
Saudi Arabia	No	There is a strong likelihood that the Saudi border authorities will check each page of your passport to ensure it contains no Israeli stamps. This may also be done at the time your passport is presented to the embassy to obtain your visa after receiving your authorisation number. If found, you will be refused entry. You may also be placed on a blacklist preventing you from future entry into Saudi Arabia for the remainder of your passport's validity and possibly longer.

Country	OK to have Israeli stamp?	Can I get in anyway if I have an Israeli stamp?
Sudan	No	The Sudanese border authorities will check each page of your passport to ensure it contains no Israeli stamps. In fact, this will be done at the time you apply for your visa prior to travel. If found, you will be refused entry. You may also be placed on a blacklist preventing you from future entry into Sudan for the remainder of your passport's validity and possibly longer.
Syria	No	The Syrian border authorities will check each page of your passport to ensure it contains no Israeli stamps. In fact, this will be done at the time you apply for your visa prior to travel. They will also check to ensure you have no entry stamps into Jordan or Egypt that could only have been obtained by making the land crossing from Israel. If found, you will be refused entry. You may also be placed on a blacklist preventing you from future entry into Syria for the remainder of your passport's validity and possibly longer.
UAE	Maybe	UAE border authorities have been known to ignore Israeli stamps in Western passports. An individual border authority may object to an Israeli stamp; if you chose this queue at passport control, you would be out of luck. Your chances of successful entry into the UAE with an Israeli stamp are much higher in Dubai, followed by Abu Dhabi. It is not advised to attempt entry into Sharjah if you have an Israeli stamp. If it is politically volatile, especially in the Palestinian Territories, all UAE airports may formally enforce the ban and refuse entry.
Yemen	No	There is a strong likelihood that the Yemeni border authorities will check each page of your passport to ensure it contains no Israeli stamps. If so, you will be refused entry.

As with many other issues in the Middle East, there are formal rules and realities on the ground as to how strictly the 'no Israeli stamp' rule is applied. Finally, it's worth remembering that rules change, often at a moment's notice. It is the author's opinion that rules surrounding the entire Israeli stamp issue are likely to be made more stringent, especially in the aftermath of the assassination in Dubai of Mahmoud al Mabhouh, the prominent Hamas operative believed by most of the Arab world to be the responsibility of Israel's Mossad.

VISA REQUIREMENTS

Do I need a visa before I fly?

It is assumed that business professionals are simply visiting the region on business. Thus, we will be referring to a visit or entry visa for most countries, which can be obtained upon arrival into the country. If a country requires a formal visa for Western business professionals in advance of travel, then we will refer to a *business* visa for these countries.

Those who are planning a secondment or more permanent employment in the region will need to follow a different set of entry requirements, including obtaining a work permit and residency visa. It is not within the scope of this book to offer this level of advice. Check with your employer or with the government department of the country in question for further information. It should also be noted that property owners who have a residency visa related to their property do not automatically have the right to work in that country.

Most Middle Eastern countries take entry formalities very seriously. For example, the penalty for someone found working in Dubai – i.e. employed through a Dubai-based office, even on a short-term secondment – without a visa is a lifetime ban from all seven Emirates of the UAE. This lifetime ban is imposed on the individual involved; you would not even be allowed in again as a tourist on holiday. The employer is also fined a substantial amount; it is currently Dh 50,000 per employee.

Entry requirements for all countries in the Middle East can change with no warning and much confusion. It is strongly advised that each traveller confirms their requirements at the time they intend to travel. To keep things in perspective, most countries, especially in the Gulf, have only been welcoming large numbers of Western business professionals (and tourists) for a few years. Your behaviour and cultural sensitivity can influence future entry requirements for your nationality.

As with the issue of the Israeli stamp, the author believes there is a reasonable possibility that procedures surrounding entry visas for Western passport holders could become stricter in the near future. There is no reason to doubt that Middle Eastern authorities could revert back to the practices in place as recently as the 1990s, where visas had to be obtained in advance of travel to most countries.

In addition, there may be further difficulties for dual nationals as many of the forged passports used in the Dubai assassination were produced from legitimate passports of dual nationals living in Israel.

It is also important to consider that Arab nationals throughout the Middle East (as well as passport holders from the Indian subcontinent) experience a much more complex and unpleasant process whenever they wish to travel to the West – that is, if they are even accepted to start the process at all. The Western business professional should also be sensitive to the relative ease they have in obtaining most visas to the Middle East compared to the reverse situation for their Middle Eastern colleagues.

GCC Countries and Yemen

As a general rule, the GCC countries issue visas on arrival to Western business professionals who hold passports from the early members of the EU (i.e. Western Europe), North America, a small number of wealthy Far East countries, Australia and New Zealand. South Africans require a visa in advance except for Oman. Some are issued for free; others attract a fee. Check with your local embassy of the country you are planning to visit for the current fee. Fee amounts often vary by nationality.

Most visas on arrival are valid for two weeks or for 30 days. British visitors are often granted stays longer than other nationalities; for example, they have historically been granted a stay of 60 days in the UAE and three months in Bahrain, although this has now changed for the most part. All Western business professionals must obtain a visa in advance for travel to Saudi Arabia.

Bahrain: visa on arrival		
Andorra	Iceland	San Marino
Australia	Ireland	Singapore
Austria	Italy	South Korea
Belgium	Japan	Spain
Brunei	Liechtenstein	Sweden
Canada	Luxembourg	Switzerland
Denmark	Malaysia	Thailand
Finland	Monaco	Turkey
France	Netherlands	United Kingdom
Germany	New Zealand	United States
Greece	Norway	Vatican City
Hong Kong	Portugal	

Kuwait: visa on arrival		
Andorra	Hong Kong	Portugal
Australia	Iceland	San Marino
Austria	Ireland	Singapore
Belgium	Italy	South Korea
Brunei	Japan	Spain
Canada	Liechtenstein	Sweden
China	Luxembourg	Switzerland
Denmark	Malaysia	United Kingdom
Finland	Monaco	United States
France	Netherlands	Vatican City
Germany	New Zealand	
Greece	Norway	

Oman: visa on arrival		
Andorra	Iceland	San Marino
Australia	Indonesia	Seychelles
Austria	Ireland	Singapore
Belgium	Italy	South Africa
Brunei	Japan	South Korea
Bulgaria	Latvia	Slovenia
Canada	Liechtenstein	Spain
Croatia	Lithuania	Sweden
Cyprus	Luxembourg	Switzerland
Czech Republic	Macedonia	Taiwan
Denmark	Malaysia	Thailand
Estonia	Moldova	Turkey
Finland	Monaco	United Kingdom
France	Norway	United States
Hong Kong	Portugal	Vatican City
Hungary	Romania	

Qatar: visa on arrival		
Andorra	Hong Kong	Norway
Australia	Iceland	Portugal
Austria	Ireland	San Marino
Belgium	Italy	Singapore
Brunei	Japan	South Korea
Canada	Liechtenstein	Spain
Denmark	Luxembourg	Sweden
Finland	Malaysia	Switzerland
France	Monaco	United Kingdom
Germany	Netherlands	United States
Greece	New Zealand	Vatican City

Saudi Arabia

Business professionals from all Western countries require an official business visa in advance for travel to Saudi Arabia. There are no tourist or visit visas available to a Western business professional.

All Western business professionals

The application process for a business visa is more rigorous than for other countries. The applicant must first obtain an authorisation number that is issued by the Saudi Ministry of Foreign Affairs. This authorisation number will be granted if the Western business professional meets a number of conditions, including the nature of the relationship with their Saudi business partner and their job title. It is wise to ensure that the applicant declares a job title with the highest status possible that does not misrepresent the applicant. Make sure that any professional qualifications such as Engineer or Doctor are noted as this will greatly enhance the traveller's chance of a successful application.

Your Saudi sponsor must provide the traveller with an endorsed letter issued by the Saudi Chamber of Commerce. Once the traveller receives their authorisation number, then they can lodge their business visa application with an authorised agent as designated by the Saudi government in your country of residence. It is no longer possible to submit your completed business visa application directly to the Saudi Embassy, although this has been possible in the past. The endorsed letter must accompany the application, along with the usual photographs and fees.

The Saudi business visa application includes many personal questions that most other countries do not require. These include your religion and sect. It is strongly advised that non-Muslim Western business professionals answer 'Christian' for their religion and 'Protestant' or 'Catholic' for their sect, to enhance their chances of a successful application.

Although there are no religious reasons for the Saudi authorities to reject applications from Jewish travellers from Western countries, the current political climate will reduce the chances of a successful application from these prospective travellers. Similarly, agnostic and atheist business professionals should seriously consider temporarily adopting the likely religion of their ancestors for an increased chance of a successful application. Other non-monotheistic religions, including Hindus and Sikhs, may experience a longer approval process and may suffer increased rejections.

All other personal questions should be completed, including the names of relatives requested who are no longer living. All other instructions should be followed literally, including the requirement to complete the form in black ink.

It is not unusual for successful applicants to receive their visa very shortly before travel to the Kingdom – sometimes within 24 hours of travel. Most Western business*men* are eligible for multiple entry business visas that are typically valid for one year, often longer. Business visas are issued in Arabic only and will contain *Hijra* dates. It is important you translate these dates accurately into the Western calendar to avoid entering or leaving the Kingdom outside dates valid for travel.

Caution

It is especially difficult to obtain a business visa in the lead up to *Hajj*. This is because the Saudi authorities are preparing travel documents and other formalities for up to 2.5 million pilgrims, all of whom will travel to the Kingdom within a specific band of dates in a short period of time. In general, *Hajj* pilgrims' travel requirements will take precedence over your business visa application unless your sponsor has sufficient *wasta*.

Western businesswomen

Saudi Arabia remains one of the most difficult countries in the world for a Western businesswoman to travel to. Most Western businesswomen who are successful in obtaining a business visa in their own right fall into certain categories: they are often professionals in certain medical fields, they are educators, or their business is with other businesswomen. However, things are beginning to change as businesswomen from other lines of business are beginning to travel to Saudi Arabia in slowly, but encouragingly steadily increasing numbers.

The chances for success in obtaining a business visa depend on a number of factors. Of course, if you work for a prestigious organisation that the Saudis want to do business with and you hold a very high job title, you have a much better chance of success. Connections within the Saudi government or connections within an elite Saudi organisation also help. Patience and persistence help; do not give up if your initial application is rejected. Your next application could be successful even if it is identical to your first application.

A businesswoman's personal characteristics will be reviewed more closely than those of her male counterpart. It is much more likely that a woman over the age of 40 will be successful in obtaining a business visa. Some women in particularly important positions, employed in high-status organisations, may be successful if they are over 30. It is nearly impossible for most businesswomen under the age of 30 to obtain a business visa unless they can pull some serious strings within the appropriate Saudi bureaucracy. The businesswoman's nationality will also influence her chances of success – this remains an advantage for British and American passport holders in spite of recent political events elsewhere in the region.

Businesswomen should be prepared for a much longer lead time in processing their application – sometimes weeks. It is not unusual for women to receive additional requests for information or to meet other conditions before their application will be considered. This may include the need to enter and exit the country on a strict timeline, to stay on a Western compound rather than to check into a hotel, or even to attend a cultural awareness course.

Some Saudi sponsors are also reluctant to advise Western businesswomen that their application has been rejected. It can be quite tricky to make the distinction between a delayed application and one that has been officially rejected. If you suspect this is the case, one technique is to ask your Saudi contact whether it's a good idea to reapply or to 'wait'. If they tell you to reapply, you have probably been rejected. If they tell you to wait, then the application is probably still being considered, as they will avoid duplicate applications.

Do not be surprised if you are issued your business visa within a day or two of travel. This is stressful at the best of times, and necessitates flexible, often expensive airfares. For businesswomen who plan to travel to other countries in the region during the same business trip, it is strongly advised that they travel to Saudi Arabia first if they are waiting for their business visa to be approved and collected in their home country. The Saudi authorities are not particularly accommodating if you need to leave for Bahrain or Dubai prior to arrival into the Kingdom. This could leave you visa-less as you set out, or it could leave you with a Saudi visa that has expired before you arrive in the country.

Businesswomen are highly unlikely to receive multiple entry business visas; they should be prepared to repeat this process each time they intend to travel to Saudi Arabia.

UAE: visa on arrival		
Andorra	Hong Kong	Norway
Australia	Iceland	Portugal
Austria	Ireland	San Marino
Belgium	Italy	Singapore
Brunei	Japan	South Korea
Canada	Liechtenstein	Spain
Denmark	Luxembourg	Sweden
Finland	Malaysia	Switzerland
France	Monaco	United Kingdom
Germany	Netherlands	United States
Greece	New Zealand	Vatican City

Yemen: visa on arrival		
Andorra	Hong Kong	Russia
Australia	Hungary	San Marino
Austria	Ireland	Singapore
Belgium	Italy	South Korea
Brunei	Japan	Slovakia
Canada	Liechtenstein	Slovenia
Croatia	Luxembourg	Spain
Cyprus	Malaysia	Sweden
Czech Republic	Malta	Switzerland
Denmark	Monaco	United Kingdom
Finland	Norway	United States
France	Portugal	Vatican City

Business professionals who do not qualify for a visa on arrival to any of the above countries should contact their local embassy for specific advice on their requirements for obtaining a business visa.

Business professionals should note that there have been some recent changes to entry rules throughout the Gulf that do not allow a visitor to return to the same country for 30 days after they leave. No doubt, this rule has been implemented to crack down on the increasing number of illegal residents, as well as for security reasons. At the time of writing, there has been no clarification as to which countries the rules officially apply to.

On a practical level, Western business visitors who are eligible for a visa on arrival will probably be able to re-enter the country at any time they wish, although they may be asked why they have returned to the UAE so quickly after their previous visit. Other passport holders will be held to the rule. This is particularly important to be aware of, as it is not unusual for a business professional to visit several countries on the same business trip, before returning to the first country to fly out of the region. It is strongly advised that all business professionals continue to monitor this situation before finalising their travel plans. It has been the author's experience that the Sharjah airport is most concerned with this issue followed by the airports in Abu Dhabi and Dubai.

Levantine countries

There is quite a variation of entry requirements amongst the countries of the Levant. Jordan will allow all Western countries entry on arrival. Lebanon specifies a long list of Western countries eligible for a visa on arrival; however, South Africa is not included. Check with your local embassy of the country you are planning to visit for the current fee, as these visas are not free of charge for most nationalities for entry into Jordan. Most visas on arrival are valid for 30 days. All Western business professionals must obtain a visa in advance for travel to Syria.

Israel

Entry into Israel will be dealt with later in this chapter.

Jordan

Jordan: visa on arrival
All Western countries, including Canada, the US, the European Union, Australia, New Zealand and South Africa are eligible for a Jordanian visa on arrival.

Lebanon

Lebanon: visa on arrival		
Andorra	Germany	Norway
Argentina	Greece	Panama
Australia	Hong Kong	Peru
Austria	Iceland	Portugal
Belgium	Ireland	San Marino
Brazil	Italy	Singapore
Brunei	Japan	South Korea
Canada	Liechtenstein	Spain
Chile	Luxembourg	Sweden
China	Malaysia	Switzerland
Costa Rica	Malta	United Kingdom
Cyprus	Mexico	United States
Denmark	Monaco	Vatican City
Finland	Netherlands	Venezuela
France	New Zealand	

Palestinian Territories

Entry into the Palestinian territories will be dealt with later in this chapter.

Syria

Business professionals from all Western countries require a visa in advance for travel to Syria. Please note that Syria requires all travellers to apply for their visa in their home country, or in their country of residence if they live abroad. Proof of residence will be required.

Business professionals who reside in a country without a Syrian embassy should contact the Syrian Embassy in the nearest country to determine visa application requirements. It is not officially possible for most Western business professionals to obtain a Syrian visa elsewhere in the Middle East, with the exception of overland travel from Lebanon.

The application process for a Syrian visa is straightforward, requiring the usual application form, photos, letter from your employer and applicable fees. Business professionals should be prepared to answer the following question on the application form: 'Have you visited occupied Palestine?' This, of course, is referring to Israel.

Only applicants who answer 'No' to this question will have their visa application considered for approval. If you have never travelled to Israel, you have nothing to worry about. If you have travelled to Israel in the past, but have no evidence of travel to Israel in your current passport, you also have nothing to worry about if you also answer 'No' to this question. The author will leave it to the reader as to their justification for answering 'No' to this question. Most Western business professionals will receive their visa in about four working days.

American passport holders and those working for an American organisation should confirm the legal position of working in Syria in consideration of American sanctions imposed on this country at the time of publication.

Other Middle Eastern countries
Egypt

Egypt: visa on arrival
All Western countries, including Canada, the US, the Western European countries of the EU, Australia and New Zealand are eligible for an Egyptian visa on arrival. South Africans need a visa in advance of travel.

Sudan

It is possible for Westerners to conduct business in Khartoum, but expect a lot of red tape, including lengthy waits for simple visit visas as well as business visas. Business professionals from all Western countries require a visa in advance for travel to Sudan. The application process includes the usual application form, photos and fees. The Sudanese authorities also require your sponsor to contact the relevant authorities for approval. The process can take up to two months.

Business professionals should seek the advice of their official government websites as well as information on the ground from their local business partners and ex-pats resident in the country, before making their decision to do business in Sudan. As with Syria and Iran, American passport holders and those working for an American organisation should confirm the legal position of working in Sudan in relation to American sanctions currently imposed on this country.

Iran

Caution

There are currently trade sanctions in place that affect many businesses which may wish to do business in Iran. As these sanctions involve the United Nations, they apply to many European countries in addition to America. It is the responsibility of the reader to determine the legality of any business trip they are planning to make to the country. The author can take no responsibility for any traveller who violates any sanction. The following information is for reference purposes only.

Iran has recently instituted a 15-day visa on arrival scheme for certain nationalities. It is a tourist visa. Eligible nationalities reflect political and diplomatic relationships with the Islamic Republic. Thus, some Western nationalities, including the UK and US, are *not* eligible for a visa on arrival. Although this visa was routinely granted to eligible nationalities prior to the June 2009 elections, there have been reports of some travellers being denied entry into Iran upon arrival, especially into Tehran's IKIA airport. These travellers are invariably deported without a reason given by the authorities.

In addition, the Iranian authorities are stricter than in other countries in the region in requiring a business visa, even for some travellers who are making a simple business trip. It is strongly advised that you contact the Iranian embassy in your home country to determine whether your particular trip requires a tourist or a business visa.

Iran: visa on arrival		
Australia	Hungary	Portugal
Austria	India	Romania
Belgium	Ireland	Russia
Bulgaria	Italy	Slovakia
China	Japan	Slovenia
Croatia	Luxembourg	Singapore
Cyprus	Malaysia	South Korea
Denmark	Mexico	Spain
Finland	Netherlands	Sweden
France	New Zealand	Switzerland
Germany	Norway	Ukraine
Greece	Poland	Yugoslavia

Business professionals who do require a business visa should apply for one well in advance of travel to Iran. It is not unusual for the process to take up to one month. The traveller requires an invitation letter from their sponsor, along with the usual photographs and a hefty fee. Women must submit photographs wearing a headscarf that covers their hair and neckline.

Business professionals should also be aware that the entire visa approval process grinds to a halt in the lead up to *Nowruz*. Thus, visa applications should be avoided from the beginning of March until *Nowruz* has ended at the beginning of April.

The Iranian authorities (Ministry of Foreign Affairs or MFA) work on a system outwardly similar to that of Saudi Arabia, where an authorisation number will be issued upon approval. The traveller's passport is then submitted to the Iranian embassy indicated on the original application, where the authorisation number is verified and the visa is then issued. Using a visa service is generally recommended.

Contrary to what many people believe, Americans are allowed to travel to Iran on their American passports. However, it is strongly advised that Americans seek professional advice as to the legality of travelling to Iran on business, as there are may be additional sanctions in place at the time of publication that are specific to Americans.

American business professionals should note that formalities to enter Iran are stricter than for other nationalities. They should plan on about ten weeks to process their visa application, which may or may not be approved. They will also be required to adhere to additional travel restrictions, including an escort, throughout their time in Iran.

WHEN TO GO TO THE MIDDLE EAST

In general, business in the Middle East is more rhythmic than it is in the West. Business hours are shorter during *Ramadan*. This holy month should be considered a time when just enough business will be conducted to keep things ticking over.

Western business professionals should be aware that their colleagues will be working at less than full capacity during *Ramadan*, especially colleagues who are fasting. Some adherents may also be coping with daily nicotine withdrawal symptoms as well.

It is pointless to expect to do business during either *Eid* holiday. People will work during *Hajj*, but pilgrims will be absent from work. Most people work during the Prophet's birthday; other countries recognise it as a public holiday. It is also important to check with your colleagues to ensure that their particular religious sect is not celebrating a holiday important to them.

Summertime can be a tricky time to do business, as many ex-pats leave the Middle East on their annual leave. Many Middle Eastern nationals also leave during the summer for an extended break to escape from the heat, especially from the GCC.

Hotels can also be full during certain times. For the Western business professional, this includes during major religious holidays as well as during major trade shows and other commercial events. In addition, as many Gulf nationals travel to the Levant in the summer, Levantine hotels may have few vacancies and may also be more expensive than at other times of the year. Thus, it is critical to check the situation on the ground at the time you are planning to travel to a particular city.

For example, visitors to Dubai should note whether they are planning to visit the city during the Dubai Air Show or Gitex, which is one of the largest technology trade shows in the world, when all of the city's business-class hotels are usually oversold.

Finally, be aware of the political situation on the ground. Political unrest flares up from time to time throughout most of the Levant. Be aware of elections, as they can also be flashpoints. It is also good to be aware of the situation with the ruling families of the GCC; most of these countries will impose a 40-day mourning period when a ruler dies, both in their own country and out of respect for a ruler from a neighbouring country.

Which airline should I fly with to and from the Middle East?

Western business professionals have a choice of European, Middle Eastern and, increasingly, carriers from the rest of Asia when travelling to destinations in the Middle East, especially to the Gulf countries.

Full service carriers in the Middle East include EgyptAir, Emirates, Etihad, Gulf Air, Iran Air, Kuwait Airways, Middle East Airlines (MEA), Oman Air, Qatar Airways, Royal Jordanian, Saudi Arabian Airlines, Sudan Airways, Syrian Arab Airlines and Yemenia.

Many Middle Eastern carriers enjoy some of the best reputations in the sky, with attentive, luxurious service in premium classes and a tolerable way to fly in economy, at least for routes serving Europe. Most of the Gulf carriers also include ground transport as a benefit of first and business class service at departure and arrival airports. This means the Western business professional will be collected from their home or office at both ends of their journey, thus eliminating the hassle of organising transport to and from the airport. Do not be surprised if your departure and arrival times are at unsocial hours.

Carriers with particularly high reputations include Emirates, Etihad, Oman and Qatar. Kuwait, Saudi Arabian, Sudan and Yemenia are alcohol-free airlines, including on services to Europe.

Middle Eastern carriers based in the Levant have had a long history of serving some North American destinations as well as the main European capitals and business destinations. Service reputations vary from acceptable to 'avoid wherever possible'.

As many of the Gulf-based airlines continue to expand the number of destinations served, it is now possible to fly into the Middle East on some of these carriers from certain airports in North America and/or Australia, including Etihad, Emirates, Kuwait Airways, Qatar Airways and Saudi Arabian Airlines. For those Western business professionals choosing a Gulf airline, they will undoubtedly enjoy an experience superior to that offered on a North American or Australian carrier.

Middle Eastern carriers will often configure their aircraft very differently on routes that cater for a high number of ex-pats coming in from countries that supply a lot of their manual labour, especially on routes to the subcontinent, Indonesia and the Philippines.

Finally, it is strongly advised that Western business professionals consider flexible airfares, as the nature of some business in the Middle East will routinely include the need to stay in the region later than originally planned.

What happens once I arrive?
Gulf countries

Many Gulf airports are busy 24 hours a day. In fact, many Gulf airports are busiest during late evening and the very early hours of the morning, when the air temperature is relatively cooler and aeroplanes can fly heavier. Most other Middle Eastern airports will be busy if several flights arrive at once, but may be reasonably quiet at other times.

Most Gulf airports have separate arrivals queues for passengers who have flown in first or business class. People who have travelled in premium classes of most Gulf-based carriers can also expect complementary ground transport to and from the airport at both ends of your journey.

It is not unusual to take more than an hour to clear passport control during busy times for those travellers who are queuing in the general arrivals queues. Many Gulf airports have a number of arrival services that may be of interest to Western business professionals who fly in economy class. For example, Dubai's Marhaba services or Doha's al Maha scheme also allow passengers to use fast track facilities. These services are relatively inexpensive and can save the traveller quite a lot of time during busy periods.

Many Western business professionals will have their first exposure to hierarchy and nationality in a busy arrivals hall of a Gulf airport. It is not unusual for the airport authorities to pull a Westerner out of the queue, especially if arriving from a non-Western city, and escort them to the front of the queue for processing ahead of others.

It was only a few years ago that most Gulf airports practised a blatant 'queue apartheid' system, where travellers literally formed separate queues designated and signposted by their nationality. The author can distinctly remember the confusion caused at the Dubai airport in the mid-1990s by a South African passport holder of European descent who refused to join the African queue but was turned back from the North American and Europeans queue by an immigration officer, to his distinct distaste.

Western business professionals to Saudi Arabia can almost certainly expect to be escorted to the front of passport control queues once all Arab nationals have been processed and before people from non-Western nationalities. This is especially true for Western women. However, Western passport holders from ethnic minorities may not be selected for this 'courtesy' if it is not clear to the authority that they are in fact a Western passport holder. This often happens in Iranian airports as well.

Many countries charge a fee for nationalities eligible for a visa on arrival, including Bahrain, Iran, Kuwait and Oman. It is possible to pay the fee directly at the immigration desk with a credit or debit card; there is no need to convert funds into local currency for this transaction. The UAE visa remains free to those nationalities eligible for a visa on arrival. There is no visa on arrival scheme in Saudi Arabia. Please keep in mind that this can change at any time.

In recent times, immigration authorities throughout the Gulf have scrutinised passports for very frequent trips to their country in the attempt to determine if the traveller is working locally without the appropriate work and residency visas. Do not be surprised if you are questioned more closely than in the past if this describes your travel pattern in the Middle East. This will not apply to people who hold a residency visa in one Gulf country who are travelling elsewhere in the Gulf. People whose work visas have expired and no longer live in the Gulf may also be questioned as to why they have returned to visit the region.

Western business professionals may be surprised to discover the existence of a well-stocked, reasonably-priced duty free shop in the arrivals hall of most Gulf airports that also have a generous allowance as to how much alcohol can be brought into the country. This does not apply to airports in Kuwait or Saudi Arabia. It is possible for all non-Muslim travellers to purchase alcohol from the duty free shops.

Most Gulf airports will have an additional baggage-screening facility in operation prior to customs clearance. Expect to process all baggage through the scanners, including checked baggage, cabin baggage and your newly-acquired duty free items.

It is unusual for the authorities to select most Westerners for further processing, but it is suggested that you do not give the authorities cause to inspect your baggage. Items that are most likely to give Westerners problems are over-the-counter medications that contain codeine, top shelf magazines and items that are very obviously used as sex toys.

The authorities are much stricter in Saudi Arabia. Although it is less likely than in the past, the authorities may choose Western business professionals to submit to further baggage screening. If you are selected, you can expect to have everything thoroughly checked, including your copy of the Economist, today's complementary in-flight newspaper and the content of your electronic media. It is strongly advised that Western business professionals are prepared for this possibly and leave anything doubtful at home. If you do have a personal item confiscated, make sure that you get a receipt for it at the time the item is removed from your possession. Allow plenty of time for it to be retrieved prior to your departure from the Kingdom. Be prepared for the possibility that the item has mysteriously 'gone missing'. Do not attempt to bring anything containing alcohol or pork into Saudi Arabia; it is simply not worth it. This also applies to any religious material that is not distinctly Muslim.

For a Western businesswoman travelling to Saudi Arabia, there are additional preparations that must be made prior to arrival. She must be dressed in *hijab* upon leaving the aircraft so that she is appropriately dressed in the immigration hall. (See 'Clothing and Dress Codes', Chapter 8, for further detail.) Most Western businesswomen carry their *abaya* (black robe) and headscarf in their cabin baggage to put on shortly before arrival.

Women can expect to be promptly removed from general arrival queues and escorted to the front, to be processed by an authority without further delay. It is possible for a woman to advise the authority that she is travelling with a business associate, who may or may not be invited to join her. If the latter happens, she should have her paperwork processed and wait for her colleague before proceeding further through the airport.

All women *must* be met at the airport by their sponsor or they will not be allowed to exit the airport. It is important for all female travellers to be sure of exactly where and when they will meet their sponsor (or their authorised delegate). She should ensure she has several contact telephone numbers, especially mobile phones, in case there is any confusion and the authorities cannot locate the sponsor in the airport.

Levantine countries and Egypt

Western business professionals who arrive at the airports in Amman and Cairo must purchase their visa prior to approaching passport control. It is important to have the exact fee in the correct currency.

At present, the Jordanian authorities will ask for the fee to be paid in Jordanian *dinars*; you will need to exchange money first before purchasing your visa if you enter the country without JD. Queue for the bank in the arrivals hall prior to queuing at the visa desk – it will save you a lot of time and aggravation.

The Egyptian authorities will accept the usual currencies, including euros, US dollars and Sterling. Egyptian entry visas are purchased at the banks found in the arrivals hall; again, queue here first before proceeding to passport control.

Lebanese visas are currently free to those nationalities eligible for a visa on arrival and who are entering the country by air. Travellers simply queue at passport control, where their visa will be stamped into their passport. Expect a longer process and a visa fee if you are entering Lebanon by road from Syria. There is no visa on arrival scheme in Syria.

Leaving the airport

Finally, a word about what happens when you are ready to leave the airport. First-time visitors to the Middle East often comment that they experience culture shock when they leave the airport and step out into the realities of their destination.

In the Gulf, they are often surrounded by large crowds of people from all over the world. Even if they have been warned about the heat, they cannot be fully prepared for their reaction to their first exposure to 50°C temperatures and high humidity.

First-time visitors may also feel uncomfortable looking and dressing distinctly different from nearly everyone else around them. Western business professionals should not be frightened for their personal safety, even if they find they are being bumped into by a lot of people who are clearly excited to be reunited with friends and relatives they might not have seen for a long time.

Many of these culture shock experiences can be managed by utilising the airport's meet and greet services (for example, the Marhaba services in Dubai). You will have someone with you who will act as a buffer, minimising discomfort from the crowds and from the confusion of sorting out ground transport. They will also look after your baggage safely and at no additional cost, as they will treat you as a guest who is too important to be expected to physically lift their own baggage. It is highly recommended that all first-time business professionals consider using this service if their sponsor cannot meet them at the airport.

For Western business professionals prepared to enter a Gulf country on their own, airport taxis are generally safe, although you should ensure the meter is switched on.

In the Levant, there can be additional factors to consider. Do not accept assistance with your baggage unless you are prepared to pay for this service, know how much it should cost, and follow your baggage to wherever it is being brought. A firm but polite 'no' should work if you do not want any assistance. This advice contrasts with the advice in the Gulf, where this assistance is perfectly safe.

There are any number of taxi touts operating at the airports in the Levant and Egypt that should be avoided, as they are very likely to overcharge you, and may not be operating safe vehicles. For those who need to make their way from the airport on their own, they should ensure they organise transport only from kiosks authorised by the airport authorities. Unlike in the Gulf, non-smokers will instantly notice many Levantine Arabs' fondness of smoking. You may even need to clearly specify that you will only accept a taxi with a non-smoking driver. Do not be surprised if it takes a while to locate such a driver, who may emerge from a group of his laughing colleagues.

Flights within the Middle East

There is still some residual expectation that Western business professionals should travel in either first or business class, especially within the Middle East. This expectation fits into the hierarchy of nationalities and where Westerners are perceived to fit. This is particularly important if you are also travelling with Arab colleagues.

Most of the Gulf's national carriers offer an excellent service on their regional routes. Of course, many people choose a carrier on the basis of whether it is a dry or wet airline, especially if travelling in or out of Kuwait or Saudi Arabia. Surprisingly, some of the Levantine national carriers actually operate a dry service within the Middle East, even if they do serve alcohol on long haul flights into Europe or Asia. The best advice is to check the catering on your particular route on your chosen carrier if this service is important to you.

Westerners flying on Middle Eastern carriers for the first time may be surprised when the aircraft doors shut and the aeroplane pushes back from the gate. Most carriers will broadcast a Muslim prayer before the flight departs. As this is an unfamiliar practice to most Westerners, and certainly not usual practice for most other airlines, it can be quite a shock for the first time visitor. However, it is considered perfectly normal in the Middle East, and should be regarded no differently to the flight attendants' demonstrating safety instructions or other service routines.

In addition to the national carriers, many Middle East-based regional airlines have sprung up in recent years. The main low cost regional carriers and their main hubs are Air Arabia (Sharjah), Bahrain Air (Bahrain), Jazeera (Kuwait) and NAS Sama (KSA). In June 2009, flydubai (Dubai) started operations. All work similarly to budget carriers in Europe, such as EasyJet or Ryanair, with familiar cost savings, baggage restrictions, additional costs for services and reliance on the internet for all transactions.

These are all safe and are suitable and, paradoxically, there is little social stigma if Western business professionals choose to fly on these low cost carriers, especially for a leisure flight within the Middle East. Western business professionals may find flights to other destinations, especially to the Indian subcontinent less appealing, as these carriers are often used by large numbers of manual labourers.

Leaving the Middle East

Leaving the Middle East is also a different experience from that found in most Western airports. Most Middle Eastern airports will have an official posted at the entry of the terminal checking to see that you have a valid ticket for travel. Therefore, it is important to print out your e-ticket, even if there is no other reason to do so, as these officials may not accept your ability to prove you have a booking reference number. As with many other aspects of life in the Middle East, you are less likely to be asked to show your paperwork if you are obviously a Westerner; dressing like a business professional and not a tourist also helps.

All baggage will be screened, including baggage you intend to check into the hold, as soon as you enter the terminal. Airport officials will then affix a security sticker on each of your bags. You are also required to pass through a screening checkpoint. These checkpoints are segregated by gender. Men will be processed by men; women by women.

Women will be relieved to note that the female checkpoints are usually much faster than the male checkpoints due to the sheer volume of men passing through the Middle East in relation to women. Most authorities will manually check you with a hand held scanner. Some women may also be lightly frisked. The Amman airport seems to employ one security guard who is particularly enthusiastic about this part of her job – you have been warned!

Although you may have been separated from your baggage for several minutes, theft is highly unlikely, although your bags may be crushed as the screening operators seem unable or unwilling to stop the belt even though there is no room at the other end to receive any further baggage. It is a very good idea to keep this in mind when you are packing, including your cabin bags.

Once you reach the check-in counter, the clerk will check for your security sticker; if you don't have one, you will be sent back to the screening area to repeat the process. Check-in counters are designated for separate classes of service. Do not be surprised if nationals of the country you are flying from are brought to the head of the queue, especially in first class, even if you arrived first. This is the nationality hierarchy at work once more, this time to the disadvantage of the Westerner.

Passport control queues can also be long and tedious, especially in the middle of the night after a long evening out or in anticipation of your first alcoholic beverage after a longer-than-planned dry period. Most Gulf airports also have a fast track system in place, with premium class passengers and those who have enlisted the help of Marhaba services usually, but not always, suffering shorter queues.

Do not be surprised to see many labourers sleeping on airport floors, even in the Gulf's state-of-the-art airports. On especially crowded evenings, you may literally need to step over an entire row of sleeping men before making your way to your gate.

Western business professionals should seriously consider access to airport lounges, which are part of your first or business class service. Other travellers can purchase lounge access prior to their flight, subject to certain conditions. Most Gulf airport lounges serve lavish meals and a full selection of complementary alcoholic beverages, with the main exceptions of Kuwait and Saudi Arabia. In the Levant, airport lounges are an oasis of relative calm in airports that are often chaotic. Some airport lounges will operate their own boarding facilities, negating the need to return to the gate prior to boarding.

Finally, there are endless opportunities to shop in most Gulf airports. The duty free shopping reputation of Dubai airport has been famous for many years, with ongoing raffles for prestigious cars and luxurious holidays as well as a choice of consumer goods, local handicraft and souvenirs. Most other Gulf airports have emulated Dubai to some extent. Airports in the Levant find it hard to compete, although some are trying.

Westerners should keep in mind that the days of finding a genuine bargain in the Middle East's duty free shops are mostly in the past. On the other hand, you are not in danger of purchasing counterfeit goods, although you should check to ensure that any warranty associated with purchased goods covers export to your home country. You may find good value in the purchase of gold, spices, some locally-grown produce and handicrafts. *Caveat emptor*.

BUSINESS TRAVEL BETWEEN ISRAEL AND THE REST OF THE MIDDLE EAST

Some Western business professionals who are about to work in the Arab Middle East may also be asked to work in Israel. Others travel to Israel, although they are actually working in the Palestinian Territories, as they might find it more convenient than travelling through Jordan.

Either way, this presents a number of unique challenges due to the current political and social climate. Some organisations combine Israel and the rest of the Middle East for budgetary reasons; others will include Israel as part of a European territory or region, for example those also working in Greece or Turkey.

The author does not advocate nor discourage any Western business professional from travelling to Israel on business (or for personal reasons, for that matter), nor from working with either Israelis or people in the Palestinian Territories. However, there are many realities on the ground that should be taken into account before a traveller and their organisation make a decision to combine these regions and expose their employees to the rigorous demands of managing the two destinations. The author is simply making this information available to the reader from a number of sources she has accumulated over the years to assist Western business travellers who make the choice to travel through Israel to the rest of the Middle East on the same business trip.

Restricted countries

Firstly, with the exception of Egypt and Jordan, no other country in the Middle East has formal diplomatic relations with Israel. This makes everyday logistics complicated. There are no direct flights between any other Middle Eastern countries and Israel other than Egypt and Jordan. Many countries will deny entry to any traveller who has evidence of visiting Israel or even intending to visit Israel in their passport or elsewhere, including Western passport holders. This 'evidence' includes notated guidebooks, tourist brochures, Israeli shekels, local Israeli telephone numbers, souvenirs, security stickers, airline tickets to Tel Aviv, etc.

Restricted travellers

Jewish people travelling on Western passports should have no difficulties travelling to the Middle East, although in practice, there can be some difficulties with obtaining a visa for travel to Saudi Arabia if they declare their religion on their visa application. However, Israeli passports are not valid for travel to any countries in the region other than Egypt and Jordan.

Some Jewish people find travel to the Middle East fascinating; others may choose not to travel to the region at all, or at least not to some countries. Many Jewish people will keep their ethnicity and religion concealed from their Middle Eastern contacts; others may share their background with people they get to know very well and trust.

In general, all Western business professionals who have travelled to Israel should consider their audience before ever mentioning this fact anywhere else in the Middle East. You may be putting your business relationship in jeopardy, which will affect not only you, but also your organisation. On the other hand, some Middle Eastern contacts simply accept this as a condition of your employment and will ignore the entire issue.

Restricted communications

Most other Middle Eastern countries also block access to Israeli-based communication, including any telephone number that begins with +972, Israel's country code. Websites ending with .co.il are also restricted. This will present challenges for business professionals who need to contact someone in Israel whilst travelling elsewhere in the Middle East. Generally speaking, the business professional may need to rely on a third party to bridge the communication restrictions, such as having a colleague in a European office set up a conference call between the countries.

Two passports

For those Western business professionals who accept the responsibilities of travelling to all of the Middle East, including Israel, several preparations should be made well in advance of their first trip to Israel.

Most – but not all – Western countries will allow a citizen to hold two passports for valid reasons. Business travel to Israel and elsewhere in the Middle East is generally accepted as a valid reason. The application process generally takes the same amount of time as it does for renewing a regular passport. Once received, most Western passport holders then separate their two passports, using one of them for travel to Israel and the West, keeping the other free for travel to Arab countries and other countries that may have an issue with travel to Israel.

American citizens who successfully apply for a second passport will receive a document with only two years' validity. American passport holders should use their two year validity passport for entry into Israel and their original ten year validity passport for entry into any of the other countries of the Middle East as passports with a validity of two years are a sufficient tip off to countries such as Syria and Lebanon that you have travelled to or intend to travel to Israel; you thus run a significant risk of being denied entry into either of those countries anyway.

Travellers who have two passports should be aware that some Middle Eastern countries deem multiple passports illegal if entering their country, most notably Saudi Arabia. Others will take issue if your Israel-friendly passport is discovered, including deportation. In both instances, the best advice is to keep this passport well hidden or, if you are not going to Israel on this particular trip, leave it at home. Some travellers organise their Israel-friendly passport to be sent to them in a neutral third country where they will be transiting, although this, of course, necessitates access to a trusted contact willing to assist the traveller.

Where do I fly?

Western business professionals who combine a trip to Israel and another destination in the Middle East have certain, well-worn choices when travelling between countries. The most popular are through Amman, Cairo or Larnaca in Cyprus. Istanbul is a good option for others, although this destination may add significant time to your journey.

Separate airline tickets

Separate airlines tickets must be purchased so that there is no through record of your flight in and out of Tel Aviv that can be accessed in the non-Israel-friendly country. This includes e-tickets and other electronic bookings. Otherwise, you are at risk of being deported further along in your journey if a non-friendly country discovers your full itinerary. Leave plenty of time in transit, as flights to and from Israel can be delayed, especially for security reasons.

Israeli passport control upon arrival

Western passport holders do not require a visa for travel to Israel. The Israeli authorities will often, but not always, honour your request not to place an entry stamp directly into your Western passport; thus the need for a second passport as above. There is new evidence that the Israeli authorities are currently taking a harder line about the entire stamp issue, denying requests from Western travellers and stamping their passports in spite of their pleas not to.

Unlike visitors with Israeli stamps in their passport who wish to enter some Middle Eastern countries, Israel allows visitors to enter from all countries regardless of which countries are stamped in their passport. Any stamps you have in your passport from 'hostile' countries are not a reason in themselves for barring entry into Israel. However, you should be prepared for lengthy questioning at the border, if the immigration officer is not satisfied with your explanation for the presence of these stamps. Depending on your answers, this process could take hours, involve being escorted to a separate interview room for further, often rigorous interrogation, and retrieving your checked baggage for thorough inspection, sometimes to the point where luggage is permanently damaged.

All Western business professionals should not be surprised if they are asked a series of questions about their intentions whilst in Israel. It's always best to answer all questions honestly, but without volunteering additional information.

171

Western business professionals who intend to travel to the Palestinian Territories can almost certainly expect additional screening on arrival if they make this known, and may have a reduced chance of successfully entering Israel altogether. Many Western business professionals avoid this issue by only mentioning their hotel in Israel or other contact based outside the Palestinian Territories to avoid further interrogation.

Israel is a pioneer of ethnic profiling, and continues to practise this technique widely for security purposes. Do not be surprised if you are selected for further scrutiny if you are from an ethnic minority, even if you are travelling on a Western passport and you have only ever lived in a Western country. This is also likely to occur if you have a Muslim name or Muslim-sounding name. Western travellers of Arab descent will almost certainly be profiled. Sometimes, this selection will occur between the aeroplane and the main immigration queues.

Israeli airport security upon departure

Western business professionals can expect an additional level of security in Israel, especially when departing the country by air. The authorities will question the traveller very closely, especially if they are travelling to a destination other than that of their own nationality, and especially if it is a regional destination such as Amman, Cairo or Larnaca.

Again, Western business professionals who have stamps from any Arab countries, including Egypt and Jordan, can expect a more thorough security screening process than those who do not present passports with these stamps.

This is also true for stamps originating from other Muslim, non-Arab countries. Do not be surprised if Israeli security treats these with similar suspicion, sometimes not distinguishing between Arabs and Muslims. The author can attest to a rather unpleasant dialogue she heard about when a traveller was challenged over her collection of Malaysian and Indonesian entry stamps: she was asked why she also worked in those Arab countries. When the traveller, possibly with poor judgment, tried to explain that her passport did indeed contain quite a large number of Arab stamps, but that neither the Malaysian nor the Indonesian stamps should be technically considered part of the Arab collection, her geopolitical clarification was most certainly not appreciated.

You may be asked to show your second passport to the Israeli authorities if they discover that your next destination is actually elsewhere in the Middle East and not simply one of the above transit cities. This will probably slow down the process even further. It is therefore a good idea to plan to arrive at the airport at least three hours before your scheduled departure time.

Any Western business professional who is travelling with colleagues will be separated and questioned separately by the authorities. The authorities will ask a series of questions, then consult with each other to ensure your answers match those of your colleagues. Expect this process to take longer than if you are travelling alone.

It is not unusual for the authorities to ask if you have any contacts in Israel. It would be a good idea to provide minimal, but honest, information when answering this question. In general, try to refer back to your hotel or any other contact you may be able to supply within Israel. The authorities may choose to make a quick telephone call to your hotel or contact, which generally reassures them that you are not a security threat. Unfortunately, this scenario may play out at unsocial hours, as many flights depart Tel Aviv in the very early hours of the morning.

Try to have contact telephone numbers memorised or, at least, easily available on a piece of paper. If you need to look it up on your mobile, the authorities may very well ask to see your mobile's contact list, which would of course expose the names and locations of business contacts you may have elsewhere in the Middle East. If this is the case, then you will almost certainly experience a much more rigorous security process that most Western business travellers prefer to avoid.

Western travellers to Israel who are also Jewish will generally have an easier time with Israeli security than non-Jews. American passport holders generally have an easier time than other Westerners, although Americans who are also ethnic minorities may not agree.

It is strongly advised that Westerners do not try to pretend they are Jewish, as the authorities will then ask you very specific questions about your supposed

Judaism that you are unlikely to be able to answer. You will then be deemed a high security risk and will be subjected to additional procedures, which can include a full body search as well as a complete inspection of all of your baggage, including risk to your electronic media.

Removing evidence of travel to Israel

If the business professional has entered Israel first, it is critical that all evidence of travel to Israel is removed no later than at the transit destination. There are no interlinking agreements with any airline carrier in or out of Israel. This means that all baggage must be checked in only as far as the transit destination, collected at the transit airport, and then checked in again to the final destination. This is the time to remove the Israeli security stickers, tags and any other evidence of travel, including duty free bags from Ben Gurion airport, loose *shekels* and anything containing Hebrew script. Don't forget to inspect your cabin baggage and other personal items as well. It's a very good idea to ship any souvenirs or other Israeli products direct to your home prior to leaving Israel.

TRAVELLING TO THE PALESTINIAN TERRITORIES

From Israel

Travel to the West Bank is never straightforward. If you are going to Palestinian cities where you are most likely to be doing business, such as Ramallah, Bethlehem or Jericho, you will need to pass through a series of checkpoints, especially if you are coming from Jerusalem.

With the construction of the 'security wall' (sometimes known as the apartheid wall), travellers must now negotiate permanent physical barriers and present their travel documents to the authorities. The security wall is still being built, so some crossing points may be easier than others.

The Israeli authorities can close checkpoints at any time. If this happens, it is unlikely that they will make an exception for you even though you are travelling on a Western passport. Therefore, you should always have a contingency plan in case you unexpectedly find yourself on the other side of the wall from where you intended to be.

Israeli passport holders are not allowed through some of these checkpoints; it's important to confirm this in advance of any travel to parts of the West Bank under Palestinian control in the unlikely event you are planning to travel with an Israeli colleague. Palestinians living in the West Bank also need permits to travel beyond the wall, including to Jerusalem. These permits are very difficult to obtain, and are often a sore point amongst most Palestinians. Palestinians living within the pre-1967 borders of Israel are considered residents of Israel, yet they carry different identity cards and live by a different set of rules, which may make it hard for them to travel *into* the West Bank.

The Israelis have built a series of roads that bypass the main Palestinian cities. They are designed for Israelis who are travelling to and from Israeli-occupied settlements established in the West Bank. As a Western business professional, you will only have access to these roads if you are travelling with an Israeli. This is also an emotive issue and a flash point throughout the West Bank; you should give serious consideration about your decision to use these roads well in advance of travel to the region.

Western business professionals are currently barred from travel between Israel and Gaza. At the time of publication, there is no real expectation that this situation will change soon. Travellers from the medical profession, NGOs, and others who have received permission to enter Gaza should seek professional advice from their organisation as to how to travel safely to the Territory. There are several land crossings from Israel as well as one from Egypt.

From Jordan

Many Western business professionals who do business in the West Bank prefer to travel from Jordan. The Jordanian authorities continue to regard the West Bank as land permitted to travel to with a Jordanian visa, including those issued to Western passport holders.

Although the distance between Amman and Ramallah is only 70 km (and only a further 16 km to Jerusalem), it is prudent to allow several hours to make this journey, as crossing times are notoriously difficult to predict. It will also be influenced by a number of factors beyond your control, including how many other people are at the crossing and their nationalities, the usual difficulties associated with changing transport on both sides of the border, and the whim of any number of officials you will encounter during the process.

Most Westerners arrive at Amman's Queen Alia International Airport, then make the short road journey to the King Hussein/Allenby Bridge, where they then cross into the West Bank. Jordanian authorities at the King Hussein/Allenby Bridge will only process Western passport holders through this crossing if they are already in possession of a valid Jordanian visa. The visa received at QAIA qualifies. This is also the main crossing valid for Jordanian passport holders and for residents of territories under the control of the Palestinian Authority.

Upon their return, the Jordanian authorities will let Western passport holders back into Jordan, as their Jordanian visa is considered still valid. They will not receive any Jordanian stamps in their passports in either direction, thus keeping it 'pure' for future travel to other non-Israeli friendly countries.

The trick with the King Hussein/Allenby Bridge crossing is to ensure the Israeli authorities do not stamp your passport on the other side of the crossing in either direction. Usually, they will comply with your request, although they are under no obligation to do so. Western business professionals thus run the risk of having their Arab friendly passport 'corrupted' if the Israelis stamp it, in spite of pleas not to do so. In addition, there is a further danger that the Israeli authorities may stamp your passport with the restriction that you are only allowed to travel within the Palestinian Territories and not to Israel proper. Even if this is your only intention, authorities of 'hostile' governments, especially Syria and Lebanon, will consider this stamp as evidence of travel to Israel.

This method of travel from Jordan into the West Bank does not apply to Western passport holders using the land crossing at the Sheikh Hussein/Jordan Bridge in the north of the territory. This crossing will attract mandatory stamps by the Jordanian authorities which, although they are not technically Israeli stamps, will be regarded by other Middle Eastern countries as evidence of travel to Israel. The bottom line is: use a second passport if at all possible.

Western business professionals should be aware of the opening hours of all border crossings between the West Bank and Jordan. In general, they are from early morning to early evening, but this can change at a moment's notice, especially if there is political or social unrest. Again, a contingency plan is advised if you are unavoidably caught up in such an event.

From Egypt

At the time of publication, it is not possible for Western travellers to enter Gaza from Egypt through the Rafah Border Crossing. There are no other crossings between Egypt and the Palestinian Territories.

8

Clothing and dress codes

Throughout the Middle East, and indeed throughout the Muslim world, modest attire is the best way to dress for both men and women and is mandatory in Saudi Arabia and Iran, including for all Westerners. This is not only a fundamental belief of Islam, but is also a sign of respect. Throughout many parts of the Middle East, especially in areas with a large number of tourists, it is possible and sometimes even common to see Westerners dress in a manner that would be considered inappropriate by nearly all of the local population.

Examples of each category of clothing can be found on the internet; see, for example, en.wikipedia.org/wiki/Category:Islamic_dress.

The reader should be aware that many people in the Middle East are dressing more conservatively than hitherto. This trend has accelerated noticeably since the aftermath of the events of September 11th, and applies to both business and social dress code. For example, the author has a photograph taken in 1983 where she is wearing a below-the-knee skirt and a loose, modest neck, but sleeveless blouse in Egypt, all considered to be appropriate at the time. The author would no longer consider the blouse to be appropriate in today's Egypt, especially for a businesswoman.

TRADITIONAL MIDDLE EASTERN WOMEN'S CLOTHING

Hijab

In spite of numerous misuses of the word in the West, *hijab* simply means modest dress. It does not specifically refer to a woman's headscarf, although a head covering is often part of a woman's *hijab* dress style. In the Middle East, it typically means covering one's body everywhere except the face and hands, and to conceal the shape of the body. In much but not all of the Middle East, leeway is given to exposing the lower arms and possibly the ankles. Although many women will cover their hair, others choose to show it. How *hijab* is accomplished is a matter of custom, tradition – and the latest fashion!

Abaya/Balto

The *abaya* is a long-sleeved, black robe that covers a woman's body from the shoulders to the ground, or at least to the feet. It is also loose enough to conceal the woman's other clothing, and will hide a woman's shape. The *abaya* is traditionally worn by women in the Gulf Countries. It is becoming more popular with many Muslim women outside this region, including other parts of the Middle East as well as in areas from the Indian subcontinent to Muslim communities throughout the West. It is known as the *balto* in Yemen. *Abayas/balto* are typically embroidered; very modern styles come with substantial 'bling' that would not have been tolerated even a few years ago.

Chador

The *chador* is a traditional garment of Iran, worn mostly by traditional or very religious women. The *chador* is a simple semi-circle of fabric worn over the head and body. It does not have any fasteners, necessitating the woman to use her hands (or sometimes teeth) to keep the garment closed whilst wearing it. It is safe to assume that a woman who wears the *chador* is a *Shi'a*.

Manteau

Many Iranian women wear a *manteau*, which is an over garment similar to an overcoat in the West. Its name derives from the French word for coat. The small number of Iranian women who belong to other faiths are also very likely to choose the *manteau* when out and about in public. The *manteau* is designed to fit just loose enough at the shoulders to cover clothing worn underneath, falling to a length near the knee (although very modern and stylish versions may end at mid-thigh). The *manteau* is meant to conceal the woman's body shape and is not typically tailored at the waist. Most *manteaux* are worn in dark, dull colours, although this is changing in certain areas of Tehran and other urban, relatively secular areas. Others may push the limits by wearing manteaux that are very tight-fitting at the waist.

Shayla

There are a variety of headscarves worn throughout the Middle East. Most women will notice the *shayla*, which is a simple headscarf, usually associated with the *abaya* and worn throughout the Gulf countries. A *shayla* is rectangular in shape and often matches the *abaya*, usually containing the same embroidery. A *shayla* may be worn with or without a *niqab*.

Niqab

The *niqab* is a face veil that covers all or part of a woman's face. It is solely a cultural choice. Some *niqabs* cover the lower face; others cover the entire face, with slots designed to expose the eyes. Traditional *niqabs* were mask-like. Others were made of stiff material that covers the nose and mouth, almost resembling a bird's beak.

Sometimes, women completely cover their face with fabric sheer enough to see out from but sturdy enough to veil the face from others' view. Modern day *niqab* are typically made of loosely woven black fabric. It fastens at the back of the head (often with Velcro), and is worn under a woman's headscarf.

Traditionally, the *niqab* has been worn by women in the southern Arabian Peninsula, including areas of modern day Yemen, Oman and Saudi Arabia, where they most often cover their lower face with a cloth *niqab*. Westerners are most likely to encounter large numbers of women wearing *niqab* in Riyadh; it is almost universally worn in Yemen as well. Westerners may find it fascinating to observe women in *niqab* going about their daily business, doing everything from talking on their mobile to methodically consuming an ice cream cone.

It should be noted that the *niqab* is a social custom, as the majority of Muslims believe that the *Qur'an* indicates modest dress, but does not dictate covering the face. Western women do not need to wear the *niqab* in any major city in Saudi Arabia, including Riyadh.

Other Islamic dress for women

Many people confuse other terms that relate to modest dress, assuming they are Middle Eastern traditions. Throughout the Muslim world, various cultures have established their own traditions for *hijab* compliance. Here are some of the more common terms heard throughout the West.

Burqa

The *burqa* is an all encompassing garment that includes metres of draped fabric, resembling a tent, with an embroidered cap attached to the top of the garment and a net or grill opening for the woman's face. It is often light blue or purple in colour. This garment is almost exclusively found in Afghanistan and in some areas of Pakistan's FATA (Federally Administered Tribal Areas). Contrary to the misuse of the term in the West, this garment is not associated with any traditional dress anywhere in the Middle East.

Shalwar kameez

The *shalwar* (trousers) and *kameez* (tunic top) may also be known as the 'Punjabi suit', originating not surprisingly in the Punjab of modern day Pakistan and India. Although its origin is far from the Middle East, it is not uncommon to see many women – and indeed men – of Indian, Pakistani or Afghan origin wearing *shalwar kameez* throughout the Middle East. The scarf associated with the *shalwar kameez*, which may or may not be worn over a woman's head, is called a *dupatta*. They come in every colour combination under the sun.

National origin and dress
Women

There are wide variations on national dress for women throughout the Middle East. However, it is important to keep in mind that the following information is provided as a general guideline only. Many women choose to dress as they please; they may or may not conform to a national dress code – or at least not their own!

Women's choice of dress is changing quite noticeably throughout the Middle East, but not necessarily in ways a Westerner would assume.

In general, many women from the Levant are choosing to adapt a more obvious Islamic style of dress than would have been prevalent as recently as ten years ago. Headscarves are appearing on more and more women in Syria, Jordan and the Palestinian Territories, although this is not the case in much of Lebanon, where Christianity and a love of French style continue to have an impact. In Egypt, it is becoming the norm, with women in Western dress and uncovered hair now a noticeable exception.

In the Gulf, women have traditionally worn the *abaya* and *shayla*. Recently, however, many women are choosing to wear less conservative clothing, although it varies quite a lot from country to country. Whilst most national women continue to wear the *abaya*, the garment itself is becoming quite a fashion statement.

In Dubai in particular, it is not unusual to see *abayas* with heavy embroidery and bling encrusted decorations found at the wrists, down the front and on the back of many garments worn particularly by younger women, along with matching headscarves. These women may also wear elaborate hair styles that changes the shape and raises the height of their *shayla*, making an eye catching outline of their head. The author likes to call this look 'Amy Winehouse comes to Dubai'. Some local women in Dubai may forego wearing their headscarf altogether, at least once they reach their destination.

Hijab is enforced in Saudi Arabia. Saudi women wear conservative *abayas*, with modest decoration at the wrists and front of the garment, also in black. Saudi women also wear the *shayla*. *Hijab* is also enforced in Iran, with women choosing to wear a *manteau* or *chador* along religious and social lines. Iranian women must also wear a headscarf if she is not wearing a *chador*. Outside of Iran, Iranian businesswomen often choose to wear Western dress, often no more modest than Westerners themselves. These same women will not wear headscarves. Other Iranian businesswomen may choose to wear modest Western clothing with a headscarf simply knotted at her neckline.

In spite of a general trend toward *hijab*, Western business professionals should not equate conservative dress with limitation to life choices. In fact, many women in the Middle East may justify *hijab* as the only acceptable way to dress when accepting a job or otherwise integrating into public life. In this case, she is actually likely to consider the *hijab* as liberating.

MODEST DRESS FOR WESTERN BUSINESSWOMEN

Many lines of business have their own corporate dress codes, setting rules and guidelines for all of their employees. Dress style that is just right for one line of business may be perceived as too formal for the next business and too casual for another. In general, it's much better to err on the side of caution and formality throughout the Middle East. Local men and women both value polished, well groomed looks, and neat, well tailored business attire. It will often be interpreted that the wearer is serious about her business. It will certainly set you apart from the tourists. It is also a good idea for women with long hair to tie it back in a stylish manner, as this is also seen businesslike.

Western businesswomen have a wide choice of clothing options whilst working in the region. However, the safest way to dress is to respect your host country's expectation by choosing to dress modestly. Your Middle Eastern colleagues may be too polite to say anything if you dress immodestly, but they will remember, wondering how much you and your company are willing to commit to – or even learn about – the region.

From a practical point of view, it's best to consider which regions you are working in, who else you are working with – colleagues and customers, the weather and local conditions on the ground. Working exclusively with other Western ex-pats in a closed, non customer-facing environment in Dubai is quite different to working with the local population in Sharjah.

The general rule is to cover your body from your shoulders to below the knee, and your arms to just above your elbows, although we will explore variations to this rule. Necklines should be modest, with slight V-necks that don't show any cleavage a better choice than U-necks. Clothing should be loose enough so that it doesn't cling tightly to your body.

In most of the Middle East, the author recommends that businesswomen consider wearing trousers and a blouse, or a trouser suit, rather than dresses or skirts. In addition to the benefit of covering your legs, trousers are much more practical when faced with the need to negotiate a building site, broken or non-existent pavements, climbing over high obstructions and walking on sand. Trousers should fall to the ankle in a work environment.

If you do choose to wear a dress or skirt, it is highly advised that the hemline falls below the knee in most locations. The main exceptions are in Dubai, Abu Dhabi, Bahrain and Beirut, where a hemline that falls at the top of the knee is generally ok if the garment isn't also very tight fitting. Keep in mind what happens to your skirt or dress when you sit down – it should never reveal more of your leg sitting than when standing.

The same outdoor conditions described above should also be taken into consideration when making a decision about footwear. As lovely as high heel shoes can be, they aren't very practical in most of the region. Many women wear flat, practical shoes whilst out and about; some then choose to change shoes once they are indoors.

Sleeveless tops that do not show bra straps, have a modest neckline and are not clinging can be worn in some of the more liberal parts of the Middle East, including areas of Dubai, Abu Dhabi, Bahrain, and Beirut, at least in certain environments. Other cities, including Amman, Cairo, Damascus and Jerusalem have become more conservative, where sleeveless blouses are less of a good idea than even a few years ago. Even so, it's always advisable to have something to pop on over this attire if you become uncomfortable with the reaction of those around you.

Keeping a headscarf handy is a good idea throughout the region, as it can be used as a powerful signal to rebuff unwanted attention. It's also good practice to carry one in case of excessive air conditioning, which is a common problem in the Gulf.

From a practical point of view, many Western women may wish to adapt a modified, Westernised version of *hijab* in other circumstances. Travelling to or shopping in very traditional areas of most Middle Eastern cities will generally be more comfortable, including in certain neighbourhoods of the most liberal cities. Travelling alone, particularly to more conservative and/or rural areas of most Middle Eastern countries, may also be easier in modified *hijab*.

In the quest to dress very modestly, it is advised that a Western woman does not wear an *abaya* in any part of the Middle East (with the exception of Saudi Arabia and possibly Yemen). Unlike her male counterpart, it is not illegal for a Western woman to wear Islamic dress anywhere in the Middle East. However, if a Western woman wears an *abaya* or traditional dress of another Middle Eastern country, it is assumed she has married a national of that country.

A final note: all visitors to the Middle East, both women and men, should dress a bit more conservatively during *Ramadan*.

WESTERN BUSINESSWOMEN AND THE VEIL

There are only two countries in the world where a specific dress code is enforced upon all women, including visiting businesswomen. They are Saudi Arabia and Iran. What you wear depends on where you are going.

Saudi Arabia

For those businesswomen about to travel to Saudi Arabia for the first time, they must be prepared to wear the *abaya* immediately upon arrival, whether arriving by air or overland, including over the causeway from Bahrain. If they are arriving in Riyadh, they must wear the *shayla* or headscarf as well. Arrival in Jeddah and the Eastern Province is more lenient in respect of headscarves; it's always a good idea to have one to hand upon arrival, and indeed throughout your stay in the Kingdom.

It is important to note that women seeking dress code advice from expatriate women who lived in Saudi Arabia a long time ago (especially in the 1970s and early 1980s) may receive out-of-date and inappropriate advice. This is because some expatriate women were given some leeway in their choice of dress during that era. In modern day Saudi Arabia, all Western businesswomen should be prepared to wear the *abaya*.

The *muttawa* or religious police have the power to enforce *hijab*, as interpreted by each region of Saudi Arabia. They are particularly active in and around Riyadh as well as other very conservative areas. They have less authority in Jeddah and the Eastern Province.

For women starting their journey from another GCC country, *abayas* can be purchased in any shopping mall or *souq* throughout the Gulf. *Abayas* and *shaylas* will usually be sold with their own box. For women starting their journey from elsewhere in the Middle East, many shops will sell *abayas*, although they may not always be displayed. Ask a friendly shopkeeper; if they don't sell them, they will almost certainly send you to someone else who does.

For women starting their journeys in the West, it's best to check out the shops in neighbourhoods catering to large Arab populations. Of course, it's always possible to purchase *abayas* online, from a number of reputable sources which specialise in Islamic dress.

It is strongly recommended that a woman wears a Saudi-style *abaya*. Styles to avoid include *Shi'a* style *hijab* from Bahrain, very fashionable or trendy *abayas* that are decorated with bold embroidery or beadwork in contrasting colours, Iranian style *chador* and *manteaux*, *shalwar kameez*, or any attempt at a Westernised adaptation of modest dress.

The following hints and tips should help most women make decisions as to which *abaya* will be right for them:

Your *abaya* should be long enough to cover your ankles when walking in your usual business shoes, but not too long to trip over when walking in flat shoes.

Your *abaya* should be roomy enough to easily slip over the most bulky clothes you are likely to be wearing. Be aware that parts of KSA, including Riyadh, the desert and the mountains, can be cool in the winter. You may need to wear a jumper or coat under your veil.

Abayas tend to close in one of two ways. Some either tie or clasp closed at the front centre of the garment, with little or no fabric overlapping. Others will snap closed at the top of one shoulder, with fabric draping over the front so that there is no gaping, even when the body moves. It is strongly recommended that women consider the second style in the interest of freedom of movement, unless the centre-close *abaya* are securely closed to well below the waist. It is much more restrictive to be moving around in public if you are worried about your *abaya* opening immodestly – your hands are much more useful carrying a laptop, mobile phone or Blackberry.

For very frequent travellers to KSA, think about purchasing *abayas* in both summer and winter weight fabrics. You may also want to think about buying a second or spare *abaya* for emergencies. Although *abayas* can generally be worn for several days, if you spill something on them, let the bottom get dirty from the street, trap them in a car door, or catch them on your chair, you may need to wear a different *abaya* at short notice.

Many Westerners are curious as to what a woman wears underneath her *abaya*. The answer is: anything, everything … and sometimes not a lot! Women will have the advantage of learning much more detail about this topic by way of ladies' facilities in public areas, such as restaurants and hotels. The author has seen: aerobics gear, the latest designer fashion from Paris, jeans and t-shirts that would not be out of place in Texas, Western business suits, nightclub attire, *shalwar kameez*, floor length dresses, and a bra, knickers, sandals and nothing else except a smile.

It is the author's opinion that the Western businesswoman dresses professionally underneath her *abaya*, as there is a slight possibility that she might be invited to remove it in very private offices or in her host's home if other women are present. At the very least, she should always be mindful of keeping her lower body covered when walking – trousers or an ankle length skirt or dress are best. The top of the *abaya* will remain closed if a good design has been chosen.

As previously mentioned, *shaylas* or headscarves must be worn in Riyadh and in other very conservative parts of Saudi Arabia. No hair should be showing, including your fringe, although this requirement is no longer as strictly enforced as it has been in the past. If you have a fringe, you may want to bring along some hairclips to keep it tucked away under your headscarf.

In Jeddah, although the *abaya* must be worn, some Western women do not routinely wear a headscarf in some environments, although they will almost certainly be carrying one. In some parts of the Eastern Province, especially facilities related to the oil industry, the dress code is relaxed even further, with very modest Western-style clothing acceptable in certain environments.

Headscarves can be both your best friend and your worst enemy. They resolve the problem of bad hair days. It's very quick to get dressed for work – just as long as you have dry hair.

Middle Eastern women have learnt the art of folding and draping headscarves from an early age. Most Western women will not look as polished unless they have a lot of practice and patience. See if you can get a local woman to help you look your best – many women will be more than happy to oblige. She can also help you drape it in the local style, which you may or may not notice immediately.

Have several safety pins with you to secure your headscarf's folds and at your neckline. It's OK to keep the pins in place if you need to take it off and on several times, as they will help keep its style as originally draped.

Headscarves should be worn ideally for only one day, especially in the summer months, as you will almost certainly find them retaining moisture. It is strongly recommended that you have a much larger supply of headscarves than *abayas*. *Shaylas* can be bought separately as well as part of a matching *abaya* set.

There are a few tricks to help Western women feel feminine in their *abaya* and headscarf. If you have long hair, you might want to wear it gathered on the top of your head, giving a distinct outline under your headscarf. You may also want to consider wearing a bit more eye makeup than usual. On the other hand, don't bother with earrings – they can't be seen and they may become caught in the headscarf.

Women can remove their *abaya* and *shayla* in the privacy of their hotel room, although they should be wearing at least their *abaya* when accepting room service. *Hijab* must be worn in all public areas of hotels, including restaurants. For those women who have access to ex-pat compounds, conventional Western clothing may be worn.

Finally, cost. *Abayas* and *shaylas* vary quite a bit in quality of fabric as well as finish. A good quality *abaya* that a businesswomen would be expected to wear is likely to cost between £50 – £100 in an upmarket shopping mall – less online or in a *souq*. It's very easy to spend more.

Iran

For those businesswomen about to travel to Iran for the first time, they must comply with Iranian dress code immediately upon arrival. Ideally, they should be wearing a *manteau*, although the Iranian authorities will accept modified Western dress that otherwise complies with *hijab*. Headscarves must be worn in public in Iran at all times. Wearing a *chador* is never necessary in an Iranian business environment, although it is required in some tourist destinations that include a visit to certain mosques.

If you are flying in on IranAir, the national airline, you must comply with Islamic dress code from the time you board the aircraft, regardless of your point of embarkation. Other carriers, including carriers based in the Gulf (Emirates, Etihad, Qatar, etc.) aren't bothered.

Manteaux can be purchased online, in most *souqs* in the Gulf, and anywhere in the West with large Iranian populations. Many Western-style raincoats will also do the trick, especially if the belt is left unworn. Most Western women will feel most comfortable wearing a *manteau* that blends in with the local style, especially in Tehran (where she is most likely to be doing business). Colours such as black, grey, tan, and other muted, generally solid colours are advised. Decorations are becoming more acceptable amongst the fashionable set.

The *manteau* should cover a woman's body from the shoulder to at least the mid-thigh. *Manteaux* which fall to just above the knee, whilst more conservative, are also seen as more businesslike. Try not to accentuate the outline of your body, especially if you are working with conservative Iranians.

Attitudes about *hijab* vary much more in Iran than they do in Saudi Arabia, where some version of the *abaya* has been worn since shortly after the inception of Islam. In Iran, most businesswomen, educated women, secular women, and fashion-conscious women were wearing Western dress for several decades, until the time of the Iranian Revolution in 1979. By 1981, *hijab* was mandatory. Do not be surprised if your Iranian business partner apologises for the need for you to comply with current Iranian dress code.

Manteaux should be bought bearing in mind the season and the type of clothing that will be worn underneath them. Tehran, in particular, has one of the most varied climates of any major city in the world, with below-freezing conditions and snow nearby in the winter and temperatures routinely exceeding 40°C in the summer.

Headscarves are worn differently in Iran compared to the Gulf, including Saudi Arabia. They are worn in many different colours and in many different patterns, although red should probably be avoided. This is a marked departure from the conventional black headscarf worn by nearly all Iranian women only a few years ago.

Many women simply tie their headscarf in a loose knot at the neckline, not dissimilar to an English countrywoman. Other women, especially the young and the fashion conscious, will wear them pushed back as far as possible on the crown of the head, where they appear to be in imminent danger of sliding off the head altogether. This will of course provide the opportunity to display remarkably elaborate hairstyles. This style is usually tolerated in most neighbourhoods and business districts the Western businesswoman is likely to visit.

As in Saudi Arabia, women should plan on wearing headscarves for one day only in the summer, possibly a bit longer in the winter. *Manteaux* can be worn for several days if they have not been soiled by food, outside dirt or other conditions.

Women can remove their *manteau* and headscarf in the privacy of their hotel room, although they should be wearing both when accepting room service. *Hijab* must be worn in all public areas of hotels, including restaurants. On the other hand, do not be surprised if you are invited to remove both when visiting a private home in Iran, with the expectation that you will be wearing typical Western clothes underneath. Many Iranians ignore *hijab* in private, including in mixed gender environments.

Decent quality *manteaux*, that a businesswoman would be expected to wear, can start at around £20 if purchased in Iran. As headscarves are typically not matched to her *manteau*, these can be purchased at a range of prices. Western-style scarves can be worn in Iran if they are of the correct size and shape to cover the hair and neck.

Other countries

There is no mandatory Islamic dress code anywhere else in the world that requires Westerners' adherence. In most other Middle Eastern countries, Western businesswomen will be comfortable in appropriate versions of Western dress, although a headscarf may come in handy at times.

The main exception is in Yemen, where Western women will be much more comfortable wearing a headscarf in public, with the option to remove it when entering a Western-friendly office, hotel or restaurant.

TRADITIONAL MIDDLE EASTERN MEN'S CLOTHING

Hijab

As *hijab* simply means modest dress, men are expected to comply with *hijab* dress codes as well. Garments should be loose, not showing the shape of the man's body. Muslim men should not wear gold, silk or diamonds. In fact, one of the ways to tell if a Muslim man is *not* religious is by checking out the metal used in his wedding ring, if he is wearing one. If it is gold, he is probably not religious; if it is silver, he may or may not be.

As it is for women, how *hijab* is accomplished for men is a matter of custom, tradition – and the latest fashion.

Men's robes are most commonly known as the following in each of the Gulf Countries:

- *Dishdash* – Oman, Qatar, UAE
- *Kandura* – also used in the UAE
- *Thobe/Thawb* – Bahrain, KSA, Kuwait

Dishdash, thobe/thawb, kandura

The national dress of men in all of the Gulf Countries includes a floor-length robe that is long sleeved and fastens at the neckline by either buttons or snaps. It may have a collar, or it may be a rounded neck. The neckline may have an embroidered design. Robes are made of fine fabric – usually cotton, or wool in cooler winter climates – and are well pressed and immaculately worn. Some sleeves will be designed for cufflinks, others will button, some are tapered without further adornment.

> **Note**
>
> Western business professionals should note that *Salafis*, most notably *Wahhabis*, will wear their *thobe* shorter than other men – often above the ankles. This characteristic, usually in combination with an ungroomed beard grown to the length of the man's fist is another indication that you are very likely to be working with a strictly observant religious Muslim.

Bisht

The *bisht* is an outer robe, worn over the *thobe*, and is worn either for special occasions or by people with very high status. It is typically black, brown or grey in colour. *Bisht* trimmed in gold or other distinguishing features are often worn by members of the ruling families.

Men's headwear: *Ghutra, shamagh, keffiyeh*

The national dress of men in all of the Gulf countries (with a variation in Oman) includes a headscarf – a square scarf or piece of fabric worn over a man's head. It is typically made of fine cotton, and is folded in a triangle and then draped in any number of ways. Draping styles may denote regional origin, tribal or family affiliation, status, or the latest trend. Most headscarves are worn in one of the following colours:

Ghutra

White *ghutras* are usually worn by men in the Gulf countries, especially in the Kuwait, Bahrain, Kuwait, Qatar and the UAE. Many Saudis may wear a white *ghutra* as well.

Omani men will often tie their *ghutras* in an elaborate fashion, knotting them at the back of the head or along the edge of the folds of fabric.

Shamagh

Red check *shamagh* are usually worn by men who reside near the Red Sea, and live in a country with a ruling family, although this is not a hard and fast rule. They originate in Jordan and are also associated with Bedouins. They are also very popular with most Saudi men. It symbolises that the *Hajj* has been performed by the wearer.

Keffiyeh

Black check *keffiyeh* are usually worn by men of Palestinian origin. It also symbolises that the *Hajj* has been performed by the wearer.

Agal

The *agal* is the double strand of heavy corded fabric that secures the man's headscarf in place. It's usually black in colour and resembles a thick rope. It is worn over any colour *ghutra*.

Islamic skull cap: *taqiyah, kummah*

Men who wear Islamic headscarves will also usually wear a skull cap underneath. It comes in many styles and colours, depending to a great degree on geography and other group affiliations.

Gulf national dress will almost certainly include a white, knitted cap called a *taqiyah*. Nationals of other Middle Eastern countries may wear a variety of colours.

Many Omani men are the notable exception, wearing a distinctive and colourful embroidered *kummah* instead.

Islamic turbans

There is a noticeable variation to men's headwear worn by religious men in Iran and sometimes from *Shi'a* areas of other countries.

Religious men who claim they have descended from the Prophet Mohammed (*pbuh*) or his son-in-law Ali, will wear a black colour turban. Other men who cannot make this claim will wear a white turban.

Prayer beads
Misbaha/tasbih

Many Muslim men carry prayer beads, which are called *misbaha* or *tasbih*. *Tasbih* usually contain 99 beads (there are 99 names for *Allah*), although others may only have 33 beads. *Tasbih* typically have tassels as well. Although they have parallels, it is not advisable to call them worry beads; nor are they rosary beads.

Daggers
Khanjars and jambiya

Khanjars are curved daggers often worn by Omani men. They are known as *jambiya* in Yemen. They are silver, traditionally made with a rhinoceros horn

THE MIDDLE EAST UNVEILED

handle. When worn with an embroidered belt, it can tilt away from the body at an especially phallic angle. It is also found on the Omani flag.

Other Islamic dress for men
Shalwar kameez

Men from Pakistan and Afghanistan will often wear the male version of *shalwar kameez* previously described in women's dress. They will be worn in solid colours, usually tan, beige, brown, or white. Although not of Middle Eastern origin, it is quite common to see men from these countries wearing this style of clothing throughout the Middle East. Men may also wear a waistcoat over their *shalwar kameez.*

National origin and dress
Men

Identifying Middle Eastern dress styles will generally give a good indication of where the man is from. Looking at the combination of robe style and headgear is usually a starting point; however, it is not a certainty. Variations in buttons, tassels and cuffs are also signs of regional variations. Most Iranian men are likely to wear Western style business suits, albeit without neckties, a style developed shortly after the Iranian Revolution.

MODEST DRESS FOR WESTERN BUSINESSMEN

Let's not forget that Western businessmen also have obligations to dress modestly if they wish to show respect to their host culture.

Again, it is recognised that many organisations have their own dress codes. In general, a businessman should opt to wear a business suit if he is not sure what's appropriate when meeting someone in the Middle East for the first time. This should be a conventional, Western suit with matching jacket and trousers.

Neckties should be worn. In spite of the climate, most forms of national dress throughout the Middle East include covering the neck for men, so Westerners are not exempt.

Short-sleeved shirts are acceptable throughout the Middle East, with the exception of Riyadh, where long-sleeved shirts are expected. The man can then roll up the sleeves to just below the elbow if he wishes.

Male grooming is taken seriously throughout the Middle East. It would be appreciated if Western men take special notice of their skin, fingernails and facial hair as well as careful attention to other matters of personal hygiene.

Western men should never wear national dress in public. In fact, wearing *dishdashes*, *thobes*, *bisht* and related headgear is actually illegal for non-Muslims in many Middle Eastern countries. Exceptions may be made for converts to Islam, but it is still realistic to expect to be challenged if you fall into this category and appear to be of a Western or non-Muslim nationality.

MODEST DRESS AND THE HEAT

The best rule of thumb for both genders is to dress in loose clothing in natural fabrics, including cotton, linen and silk (for women). Wearing loose clothing allows the air to circulate around your body – it may not be exactly cool, but it's better than having tight clothing sticking to you when your skin needs room to breathe and perspire.

Paradoxically, exposing large amounts of skin will actually make you feel hotter, as you will be coping with more direct sun on your body. Many Westerners prefer to wear light-coloured clothing; others don't notice any difference regardless of what colours are chosen. However, obviously 'colonial' clothing styles are not recommended and could actually offend. Don't forget sunscreen, even for just a few minutes if you sunburn easily. Sunglasses are a must for most Westerners.

If you are the type of person who perspires a lot, no matter how long you have been exposed to very hot climates, it's an idea to carry a spare blouse, shirt or top if you need to make a change during through the day.

Many first-time visitors to the Middle East are surprised by the winter temperatures in certain countries. It gets cold throughout most of the Levant as well as in the deserts of the upper Arabian Peninsula, and of course in all mountainous areas. It's actually possible to snow ski (naturally, not just in Ski Dubai in the Mall of the Emirates) for at least a couple of months in Iran and Lebanon. Amman, Jerusalem and Ramallah, all at elevation, get snow most winters. Syria and Kuwait can get cold enough for a heavy coat in winter, although Qatar, the UAE, and most of Oman and Yemen remain mild. Bahrain is generally pleasant in winter, as is Egypt.

Make sure you check out the weather for your destination no matter what time of year you are travelling to the Middle East – it can surprise you.

MODEST DRESS WHEN NOT WORKING

It's still best to dress with an eye to modesty when 'off duty'. Trousers can be cropped, showing the ankle, in more casual settings throughout most of the Middle East (Saudi being the main exception). The same rules apply about sleeveless blouses in a casual setting as they do at work. Casual clothing should look neat and clean.

Offensive and controversial slogans will not go down well and could, in some instances, cause the wearer serious trouble. Special care should be given to avoid anything that could offend Islam, your host country's government, most human rights themes, and your souvenir T-shirt displaying the Coca Cola Logo in Hebrew. In addition, the Western trend to wear checked *ghutras* as a scarf or other fashion item should be avoided by Western business professionals throughout the Middle East.

IMMODEST DRESS

Basically, 'immodest' clothing is acceptable in the company of a group made up entirely of Westerners gathering in private, at a venue considered Western-orientated (such as a nightclub or other venue that serves alcohol), or at a venue that is suitable for clothes designed for a particular sport or other physical activity, such as at the health club or on a boat. Care should be given as to what clothing is worn when travelling to and from these venues – yet another example of where a lightweight headscarf or wrap comes in handy.

Beachwear is suitable at Western-orientated resorts, swimming pools and at some beaches. Caution must be given to beach venues, as many beaches are for the use of the local population, where *hijab* compliance is still expected. Other beaches are used for non-bathing purposes, especially along the corniches of the major cities, including fun fairs and other family orientated activities. Some beaches may be designated for the use of one sex only.

It is possible for women to wear Western swimming costumes in Saudi Arabia at certain beach clubs owned by the hotels or other organisations with a members only policy. Women do not have access to swimming pools in Riyadh hotels. Men must use entrances that shield their view from public areas, such as hotel lobbies and restaurants.

Although you will see other Westerners wearing all of the following, it is strongly advised that both women and men refrain from wearing shorts, skimpy sleeveless tops and (for women) any hint of revealing cleavage in any location where it is possible to have a chance encounter with someone local with whom you have a professional relationship. This includes restaurants outside of the tourist hotels and in shopping malls.

In conclusion, your choice of modest dress remains an important way of showing respect for your hosts, and will always be appreciated.

9

Ready for business

It is impossible to cater for the specific business requirements of all people planning to work in the Middle East in one book. For example, the needs of someone working in IT are different from those of someone in the legal profession, a supplier of military technology, a strategist tasked to expand their bank's Islamic product offerings, or in the ever changing building profession.

However, there are common themes, values and practices that should be recognised by all Western business professionals who plan to work in the Middle East. We will address the most important of these issues, focusing on the traditions and practices of the host nationals of the country.

It is also important to keep in mind that many Western business professionals are likely to be working with people from many cultures, especially in the Gulf Countries. Western business professionals should be aware that they may also face business practices that are the norm for other cultures as well, especially those found in the Indian subcontinent, the Far East and the West. Even so, these 'guest' business cultures will operate in a broadly Middle Eastern context within the region.

As a reminder, the focus will remain on the Gulf Countries of the Middle East, with variations pointed out for destinations in the Levant and Egypt. The entire topic of doing business in Israel is beyond the scope of this book.

WORKING WITH YOUR MIDDLE EASTERN COUNTERPARTS

Traditional offices and free trade zones

Traditionally, any office established in the Gulf by a non-Gulf national required a sponsor who is a national of the country where the office is physically located. Of course, it remained of utmost importance that Western business professionals did nothing to upset the sponsor, even if the sponsor showed little interest in being actively involved in the running their organisation. Most, but not all sponsors were men.

Starting with Jebel Ali in Dubai and rapidly expanding throughout the Gulf, there are now a number of free trade zones in nearly all of the Gulf countries (steps are being taken by Saudi Arabia) where foreign nationals can establish an office without the need for a local sponsor. Of course, organisations are much freer to implement policies and practices that are specifically suitable to their line of business. Policies are set by top management who are actively involved in the business (at least to some degree). There are also property ownership and tax advantages to setting up in a free trade zone. However, free trade zones are limited to specific physical locations that may or may not be convenient for you or your prospective customers.

It remains important to keep this distinction in mind if your organisation is starting to work in the Middle East with the aim of eventually setting up a local presence in your own facility. Rules, terms and conditions are changing at a pace that is too fast to detail in this book. Do your homework long before you are ready to make such an important commitment.

Offices in the Levant are nearly all locally owned and operated, although free trade zones are being established in Egypt, Jordan and Lebanon. It remains significantly more difficult to trade independently in Syria.

The office manager

With the proliferation of mobile phones, the office manager's role has been somewhat reduced in that he or she is no longer an exclusive gatekeeper to reaching your Middle Eastern colleague by telephone. However, the office manager remains an important source of office intelligence as to people's whereabouts, general planning issues, as a link to other departments within the organisation such as logistics and accounting and, sometimes most importantly, as an excellent source of gossip and rumour control. It would be a good strategy for all Western business professionals to establish a solid relationship with their Middle Eastern colleague's office manager as soon as possible.

The 'fixer'

Every Middle Eastern office of any significant size will have a 'fixer'. This may be the office manager in a small or newly-established organisation.

From a Western business professional's point of view, the role of the fixer includes dealing with the bureaucracy of their travel and business needs whilst working in the region. A good working relationship with the fixer is of particular use for those Western business professionals who are working in countries that require a business visa in advance of travel, such as Saudi Arabia. The fixer can facilitate (or hinder) other formalities as well. It is a good idea to make their job as easy as possible by ensuring they have all of the information they may require from you well in advance of when you need their services.

Western *wasta*

Wasta can be loosely translated as who you know, your connections, your influence. It is similar in context to *guanxi* in China or *blat* in Russia. Westerners have a version of *wasta* in their 'old boy' network or when calling on frat brothers or alumni associations for assistance, for example. Don't forget to use your own contacts to make business connections or just to learn more about the business climate of the country/region. It's generally a good idea to look up colleagues and contacts you have previously established who are out in the region, even if it is not obvious how they can help you. You may also wish to consider leveraging more formal business resources such as the British Council, which operates in all countries of the Middle East. Most other Western countries will have similar operations available to their nationals.

Fundamental business issues

Without a doubt, it is imperative to understand that the Western business professional will have almost no chance of success without first building a solid relationship with their Middle Eastern business partners. This includes developing trust, which comes over time and is earned by consistent, respectful behaviour. Neither of these important facets of doing business will develop without patience.

BUILDING RELATIONSHIPS

In the West, most business professionals carefully consider many elements of their organisation when planning to establish a new business relationship. These are generally concrete:

- Is the organisation financially stable?
- How long have they been trading?
- Do they have good quality products that are in demand and competitively priced?
- Do they have a healthy market share and a good reputation?
- Is their sales division supported by a good marketing team?
- How professional are their project managers, their technical support group and their customer service organisations?

Throughout the Middle East, all of these elements are important, but only after you have built a relationship with your prospective business partner.

Who is more important than *what*. In the initial stages of doing business in the Middle East, if you are unsuccessful in building a relationship that leads to your partner being comfortable with you – both personally and as a representative of your organisation – no business will get done. This is true whether you are the first person in your organisation hoping to do business with your Middle Eastern counterpart, if you are replacing a predecessor, or if you are expanding your growing business organically.

Building a good relationship with your Middle Eastern business partner goes much further than drinking tea and chatting about how much you like Dubai or Riyadh or Cairo, although you will be doing a lot of this as well. In fact, during the initial stages of getting to know your business partner, it is not unheard of to hold a meeting where all you do is drink tea, have small talk and then agree to meet again soon *insh'allah*. And of course, the only answer to the question 'How do you like Riyadh?' when it's 50°C outside in August and it's *Ramadan* is 'Riyadh is great!'

Do not underestimate the importance of a meeting that seemed to consist of nothing but small talk, especially in the early stages. From your Middle Eastern counterpart's point of view, a comfortable meeting filled with pleasantries is a successful meeting as a positive relationship is beginning to build.

Never moan during small talk, although the topic of traffic may be an exception if referring to jams but not the inferior quality of Middle Eastern drivers.

As previously mentioned, Western business professionals should be aware that they are building a personal relationship as well as an organisational relationship. Thus, it is strongly recommended that your organisation is consistantly sending the same people into the region. Organisations that send Joe one month and Helen the next cause confusion, prevent the formation of a solid personal relationship and are demonstrating no understanding of how business works in the region.

Most Western business people increase their chances of building a good relationship with their local partner by keeping in mind the most important values of the region, and showing their ability to adapt to these traditional cultural values.

COURTESY, GENEROSITY AND HOSPITALITY

Courtesy, generosity and hospitality are all paramount. Never rush meeting and greeting people. Never refuse any gesture of hospitality, even when you are confronted with your twelfth cup of tea in one day.

As an aside, it's also not a good idea to show fussy habits, especially during the getting-to-know-you phase. Accept whatever drink is being offered. If you are given a choice of what you would like to drink, try to choose something that is obviously available and not too much trouble.

Tea will almost always be Arabic tea, which will be served either medium (quite sweet to most Western palates) or sweet (consider your drink to be sugar with a bit of tea in it!). Arabic tea may also be flavoured with herbs and spices, including mint, cardamom or *zahatar* – from the thyme family of herbs – depending on the country. It does not come with milk. Arabic tea is most often served in a clear, decorated glass placed on a saucer.

Coffee is becoming more and more available, although it may be either Arabic style (sweet, and in small cups without handles), Western (think Starbucks or Costa Coffee), or instant, which is usually referred to as Nescafé in the Middle East.

Water is generally OK to request, but not always. Sometimes, you may be offered freshly squeezed fruit juice, which most people find to be a pleasure. Fizzy drinks are not generally offered in most of the Middle East, although you may find them on offer in local offices of American companies.

Courtesy, generosity and hospitality will be extended for the life of your business relationship. Never expect any of these gestures to be skipped in the interest of saving time or getting down to business; it would simply be too rude to contemplate. In fact, if you feel a chill in your relationship with your host, it may be signalled in many ways, but rarely through a lack of fundamental manners.

RESPECTING ISLAM

Always respect Islam. For example, your host may have been late to meet you because he just returned from praying. It would almost certainly be a fatal mistake in the relationship to show displeasure in being made to wait for someone to complete their prayers.

However, showing interest or willingness to learn about Islam can be a good way to build a relationship. Most people will be delighted to explain their way of life to you if you appear to be sincere, genuine in your intentions, and curious to learn more about the religion and its impact on daily life. As Islam is not a proselytising religion, you are not likely to enter into a conversation that leads to an awkward situation where someone wishes to convert you to their religion.

DEALING WITH PERSONAL QUESTIONS

Do not be surprised if your Middle Eastern host asks you personal questions. Many Western business people may be surprised or uncomfortable about personal topics of conversation. However, from the point of view of their Middle Eastern counterpart, they are asking such questions to get to know you better and to establish a better relationship with you.

The Western business professional should be prepared for many value judgments embedded in personal questions. Again, these should not be interpreted as negative, but as a way for your host to place you within the social hierarchy they are familiar with. Thus, you are likely to be asked if you are married, if you have children and something about your presumed Christianity.

Although this topic was briefly raised in the chapter defining Islamic values and family, it is worth expanding on this topic from a business point of view.

How you choose to answer these questions is, of course, up to you. But you must be aware that your response can either advance building your business relationship or can damage it, sometimes irreparably. Let's address a few themes.

Marriage

Very young Western business professionals are not necessarily expected to be married, but if they are not, they may receive questions about when they are planning to marry, with the assumption that marriage is a certain goal for everyone. In general, there may be an expectation that a woman will get married at a slightly younger age than her male counterpart.

If you are young and unmarried, an uncontroversial yet neutral way to answer the marriage question is to comment that 'insh'allah someday I may be lucky enough to marry'. It is polite, indirect and does not cause the Westerner to lose status. It is strongly advised that Westerners who do not plan on marriage for whatever reason do not directly state this, as it can easily confuse many in the Middle East.

If you are older and unmarried, an uncontroversial yet neutral way to answer is to comment that 'I have never been fortunate enough to be married so far. *Insh'allah* it may happen some day'. It is respectful, but probably has just the right content for most people not to enquire further about your marital status.

If you are married, it is generally a good idea to make this known, as it will always be viewed in a positive light and provides you with the expected status.

The one exception to this is for people of the same sex who have been married in a civil partnership. As homosexuality is illegal throughout nearly all of the Middle East, and may challenge the beliefs of even the most Westernised Middle Easterner, great care must be taken in how a gay person should answer this question. Some people choose to claim they are unmarried, some try to mask the gender of their partner, others may reveal their true status only after getting to know someone for a very long time.

Unmarried heterosexuals who are in a long-term relationship often claim to be married in the Middle East, conveniently ignoring their legal status, especially if they occasionally travel to the region with their partner. Whilst the author cannot advocate those who claim what may not be technically true, it is also acknowledged that this tactic generally works well in many environments in the Middle East, especially with people who understand Western attitudes towards marriage, but without directly confronting conventional Middle Eastern sensibilities.

If you are divorced, there is no particular taboo in mentioning this fact, as Islam also recognises divorce. Divorce is increasingly common in the Middle East, as it is in much of the West.

Children

It is usual to be asked about any children you may have, especially if you are a woman. There will be an assumption that you will want to have children, as it would be nearly unheard of for a Middle Eastern national to reject the notion of wanting children, as the family is of paramount importance.

Again, if you have children, it is invariably good to mention this. You can almost predict the next question will then be about their gender. Expect to be praised further if you have a son. It's also not uncommon for someone to wish you luck (or better luck) next time if you only have daughters. Try not to react negatively to any of these comments, regardless of your personal opinions, as being the parent of at least one son is regarded as fulfilment.

If you do have children, but they have been born outside of legal marriage, it is generally best to ignore mentioning this. In fact, your Middle Eastern colleague may assume these children may have come from a previous marriage. If so, it is strongly recommended that this misunderstanding is not corrected.

If you do not have children, but you are young and married, you can expect many questions and comments about when you are likely to start your family, how it is hoped that you have many children, and that it is hoped you have 'your son'. Again, the best response is to be polite, regardless of your personal beliefs. Never announce that you do not want children, especially if you are married, as this can be confusing or even offensive to some people in the Middle East.

Older people who have never had children can be confronted with comments about how sad it must be for them to never have had children. Again, it is not recommended that you correct any beliefs you may hold to the contrary. A response such as 'it must not have been meant to happen' generally works and would not be considered offensive. Many older people without children also find it useful to mention their fondness for nieces and nephews, who are, of course, considered part of their family within the Middle Eastern definition of family.

Religion

As previously mentioned, most people in the Middle East will assume you are Christian if you are coming from a Western country, unless your name or ethnicity is obviously Muslim or clearly originates from somewhere outside of the West. However, you may be asked quite directly if you are a Christian.

If you consider yourself to be a Christian, even nominally, by all means let them know. If you are of another religion, it's generally OK to say so, but be aware that you may be repositioning yourself lower than expected within the religious hierarchy. It may also be confusing if you claim a religion that does not seem congruous with your ethnic background, such as a Scottish Buddhist, or is often considered to be cultist, such as Mormonism.

Again, it is strongly advised that you do not directly state anything that implies you are an agnostic or, especially, an atheist. Not only does this diminish your status in the religious hierarchy, it also may implicitly tell your Muslim counterpart that you have no morals. It is probably better to either let the person continue to assume you are Christian or to advise them that you come from a Christian background if this is the case.

TRUST

Of course, one of the main goals of your Middle Eastern business partner in establishing a relationship with the Western business professional is to determine whether you can be trusted to do business in a manner that is comfortable to your partner. The Middle Eastern business partner does not want to work with someone who cannot adapt to the norms and practices that are in place in the region. Nor do they want to work with someone who may not be dedicated to the region, and thus may not be available or responsive at the very time they need them the most.

There are many ways to earn the trust of your Middle Eastern business partner. Trust only comes once you have established a solid business relationship. In general, trust is best established through face-to-face meetings. Wherever possible, try to be in the region as often as possible, especially in the early days if your organisation does not yet have a physical presence there.

Your personal behaviour can help your partner feel more comfortable in trusting you. For Western businessmen working with other men, strong eye contact and physical proximity, sometimes with touching, especially a forearm, are indications of gaining trust. Western men who are uncomfortable with another man's touch should make every effort not to pull away or otherwise react in a way that could be interpreted as rejecting a friendly gesture. Nor is it a sign of homosexuality.

Western businesswomen should be aware that eye contact and especially physical proximity can make many Middle Eastern men uncomfortable. Eye contact should be brief. Do not be surprised if some Middle Eastern men do not look at you directly at all, especially if they are very religious or culturally traditional. Some very traditional men will instead look to one side of you and towards the ground instead. This is actually a sign of respect.

However, Western businesswomen may not be comfortable speaking to a business colleague whom they can't look directly in the eye. A good compromise is to look at the Middle Eastern man's upper lip. You can still read facial expressions, yet you avoid the discomfort of direct eye contact. This is also a good technique for Western businessmen to use with Middle Eastern businesswomen who may be uncomfortable with too much eye contact from you.

You are more likely to gain trust when you convey a feeling of sincerity. Speaking with confidence and showing respect for your host, Islam and Arab culture in general will invariably go a long way towards establishing trust.

Wherever possible, accept all gestures of hospitality, especially business dinners and other opportunities to socialise with your Middle Eastern colleagues.

Don't be afraid to accept favours in the Middle East. It's another sign of trust building in your relationship. Try to return any favours wherever possible; these can be small gestures, which will not go unnoticed.

Sometimes, your Middle Eastern business partner may test you in your trustworthiness. This can be a minefield, in part because you may not even be aware that you are being tested. The best policy is to always be honest and consistent, especially if you may also be doing business with an acquaintance or even a competitor of your Middle Eastern business partner.

Be very careful about making any negative or disparaging comments about anyone or indeed anything in the region. This can easily lead to a loss of trust, as your partner will logically wonder if something negative or disparaging is being said about them when you are with another client or partner.

Finally, remember that trust is earned over time. It cannot be rushed.

PATIENCE

There is no doubt that most Western business professionals will feel frustrated and possibly even angry at some point during their travels in the Middle East. It may be triggered by something bureaucratic, something misunderstood, a different style or approach to business, or simply an unfortunate side effect of jetlag.

It cannot be stressed strongly enough that the Western business professional must show patience at all times, even if they are in circumstances that from their point of view are patently ridiculous. It should be remembered that your Middle Eastern business partner may simply accept the same situation as God's will and thus normal. Their reaction may be either to relax or to find another way to deal with the situation. If you react with impatience or intolerance, you lose face, status and authority, and can quickly cause your partner to wonder if you are the right person to be working with after all.

Go somewhere to let off steam for a few minutes if you have to, but do it privately. Never lose patience in the Middle East in public, especially in front of your business colleagues.

10
Meeting and greeting

NAMING CONVENTIONS

Arabic names work differently to most Western naming conventions, as they are based on lineage. However, there are variations within the Arab world as well.

Gulf Arabs

Gulf Arab men generally use the naming convention of title, given name, father's given name, family name. It is illustrated in the name of Dubai's ruler, Sheikh Mohammed bin Rashid al Maktoum. Sheikh is his title; it actually means tribal elder, in this case, the 'tribe' is the population of the Emirate of Dubai. Mohammed is his given name. 'bin' is the Arabic word for 'son of'. Rashid is his father's given name. 'al Maktoum' is his family name. The name of the Hereditary (Crown) Prince of Dubai, one of Sheikh Mohammed's sons, is Sheikh Hamdan bin Mohammed al Maktoum, following the same tradition.

Gulf Arab women generally use the same naming convention as men until they marry, i.e. title, given name, father's given name, family name. For example, one of Sheikh Mohammed's daughters is Maitha bint Mohammed bin Rashid al Maktoum. 'bint' is the Arabic word for 'daughter of'. In this example, her name reflects the lineage of both her father and grandfather.

Gulf Arab women who marry make a choice about their name. Many keep it as it is. Others substitute the name of their father with the given name of their husband. However, they traditionally keep their family name after marriage as knowledge of her family lineage remains important. For example, Sheikh Mohammed's second wife is a daughter of the late King Hussein of Jordan. She is known as Sheikha Haya bint al Hussein in Dubai. Interestingly, as she also descends from royalty, she is also known as HRH Princess Haya bint al Hussein in Jordan.

Sheikh Mohammed and Sheikha Haya have a daughter; in a continuation of the Gulf naming convention, she is known as Sheikha Jalila bint Mohammed bin Rashid al Maktoum.

Levantine and Egyptian Arabs

Although Arab names in the Levant also follow lineage, they are not necessarily used in the same way as Gulf Arab names in everyday life. For example, the former Prime Minister of Lebanon's full name was Rafik Bahaa El Deen Al-Hariri; he was usually known as Rafik Hariri.

Many Levantine Arab women, unlike their Gulf counterparts, may take their husband's family name upon marriage. We have an excellent example with Asma al Assad (née Asma Fawaz Akhras), the Syrian President's wife.

Christian Arabs

Christian Arabs follow many of the same naming conventions as their Muslim neighbours, including the tradition of lineage. For example, the former Lebanese President Émile Lahoud's full name is Émile Jamil Lahoud; his father's given name was Jamil.

Kunya names

There is an additional naming convention that is popular amongst many Arabs in the Levant, particularly those of Palestinian descent. Although these people have conventional names in the Arabic style as described above, they may also adopt a *kunya* name. A *kunya* name is in recognition of a child, most often a first-born son. For example, the Palestinian leader Mahmoud Abbas is also known as abu Mazen; his eldest son's given name was Mazen. 'abu' is the Arabic word for 'father of'.

It can be very confusing to the Western business professional when *kunya* names are used in a business setting. You may have just been introduced to a group of people in a meeting, including Mr. Ahmed Zeid. But after formal introductions, you continue to hear someone referenced by the name of 'abu Omar', although you were never introduced to anyone named Omar! However, Mr. Ahmed clearly responds to abu Omar. Abu Omar is Ahmed Zeid's *kunya* name, and in all probability, Omar is his first-born son.

Women may also have a *kunya* name. For example, Mr. Ahmed may have a wife named Mrs. Leila. Leila's *kunya* name would be 'umm Omar'. 'umm' is the Arabic word for 'mother of'.

General hints and tips

It is acceptable to use the terms first name, given name, forename, or *'ism'* (which means personal name) in the Arab world. However, the British practice of using 'Christian name' interchangeably with the above terms is incorrect, even if you are speaking with an Arab Christian. It will be regarded as an insult if you use it to refer to a Muslim.

Arabs traditionally do not give their children the same first name as their parents. Thus, there is no equivalent to John and John Junior as is common in the US.

Many Arabs give their sons and daughters an *ism* that is inspirational. For example, the boy's name Najib means intelligent. The girl's name Rania means queen, and is certainly appropriate for Queen Rania of Jordan!

There are 99 ways to refer to *Allah* in Islam. Often, Muslim parents will choose one of these names for their sons, usually combined with Abdul. Abdul means servant of or slave of, and is often used in conjunction with one of the 99 ways to refer to God or *Allah*. Thus, Abdul Rahman is always referred to by his full *ism*, as simply referring to him as Abdul would be an insult and Rahman inappropriate.

It is acceptable to use the terms last name, family name, surname, or *'nisba'* (which means family name) in the Arab world. The term 'good name' which also means family name, is commonly used in the Gulf and is an imported practice from the Indian subcontinent.

Arab family names usually refer to a place (ancestral origin) or an occupation. For example, Saddam Hussein's full name was Saddam Hussein Abd al-Majid al-Tikriti; it clearly identifies his home village of Tikrit.

Although most women keep their own family name after marriage, children take their father's family name.

Iranian names

Most Iranian names did not include a surname until well into the 20th century, when families often added a name that represented the area of Iran from where they originated. For example, many Iranians now have surnames such as Tehrani or Shirazi. In modern times, Iranian names work similarly to Levantine Arab names, commonly used in the Western style, yet reflecting lineage. Iranian women do not traditionally change their surnames upon marriage.

The late Ayatollah Khomeini's full name, Sayyid Ruhollah Musavi Khomeini, follows the traditional convention. Sayyid is a title, Ruhollah is his given name and Musavi is his father's name. Khomeini is derived from his ancestral village, named Khomein.

Other names

Western business professionals are highly likely to encounter people from other parts of the world, where naming conventions are different from both those in the West and the Arab world. In particular, they should be aware of the main naming conventions of the Indian subcontinent, although knowledge of naming conventions of the Far East is also useful as more people from this region work in the Middle East. It is strongly advised to learn which name is the person's given name and which is the person's family name. They may not occur in the same sequence as in the West.

MEETING AND GREETING

As salaam alaikum

Most Western business professionals will be greeted with 'as salaam alaikum', which literally means 'peace be with you'. The correct response is 'Wa alaikum *salaam'*, 'and peace with you'. Even if everyone in the room speaks fluent English, it is a good idea for Western business professionals to learn these simple greetings, as it is a way of showing respect for the region.

There are actually many different ways to greet people in the Arab world; this is the most formal and polite greeting. You can never go wrong using it. Once you get to know someone well, it is possible to switch to the informal greeting *'marhaba'* in some circumstances. It is not advised when meeting high status or very religious people.

Ahlan wa sahlan

The traditional greeting in the Arab world is to welcome all guests. The greeting above is Arabic for 'welcome', and is usually extended to visitors immediately after saying *'As salaam alaikum'*. *'Ahlan bekum'* is the correct response. A simple *'shokran'*, which means 'thank you' is also an appropriate response.

Visitors who have been away for a period of time, but who have previously established a relationship will be welcomed back. This will include at favoured hotels and restaurants as well as by business associates.

First name or last name?

The traditional way to refer to people in the Arab world is by title and first name. Thus, Mr. David Smith becomes Mr. David. Ms. Sarah Parker becomes Ms. Sarah. It is advised that women specify their preferred title when being introduced if they find this a sensitive issue. Otherwise, the use of a woman's title does not exactly equate to a woman's marital status. Women who do not specify their preferred title are most often referred to as Miss when young and Mrs in later life; the author experienced this transition personally – with mixed emotions – as the years passed working in the region.

For most Westerners, this may initially seem a bit awkward, but it is a tradition that many people quickly become comfortable with. Of course, this practice extends throughout Arab society, as the practice of referring to Dubai's leader as Sheikh Mohammed confirms. Of course, this practice is not unknown in the West, at least with royalty, as the example of Queen Elizabeth confirms.

People from other parts of the world should also be addressed by title and first name. Therefore, it is strongly advised to learn which name is the person's given name and which is the person's family name as naming conventions in many parts of the world do not follow a first name, last name sequence. For example, although Ravi Gupta from Northern India will want to be referred to in the Middle East as Mr. Ravi and not Mr. Gupta; his Southern Indian colleague, Gopal Krishnan Chakyar, will want to be known as Mr. Krishnan. His Chinese business partner Wong Guang will want to be referred to as Mr. Guang.

Hand shakes all around?

There are a number of greeting rituals that are appropriate when Arabs meet, recognising status, family, possible tribal solidarity and other factors. This will involve a series of comments as well as handshakes and/or kisses, depending on how well people know each other. Although it is not expected that you understand these intricacies, it is polite never to interrupt these greetings, no matter how busy your day.

Arabs of the same gender who already know each other generally kiss when meeting. As a Western business professional, you will not be expected to follow this convention, no doubt to the relief of most Western men. Here are the general conventions for meeting people that involves Westerners.

Men shake hands with men. That's the easy bit. Western businessmen will often find that Arab men hold eye contact more directly and for a longer time than is often comfortable in the most Western cultures. Arab men may also retain hand contact for a slightly longer time than in the West, and may also clasp the Westerner's forearm. Arab men may also stand closer to another man than is usual in many Western countries. Although all of this may be uncomfortable for some Western businessmen, it is very important *not* to pull back or exhibit any other body language that could be interpreted as negative. It would be seen as an insult to your Arab host, and will most certainly not promote relationship building and trust.

Western businessmen should always follow an Arab woman's lead when meeting for the first time. Many Arab women, especially younger women who are not particularly religious are happy to shake an unrelated man's hand.

Fewer, older Arab women will shake a Western man's hand, but that may be a matter of habit as much as for the other reasons above. If an Arab woman extends her hand, shake it; it would be very awkward not to do so. However, keep it brief and *never* touch any other part of the woman's body – this advice cannot be emphasised strongly enough as it may be as important to protect the woman's safety as it is for your potential business relationship. Keep a respectful distance; most people from Northern Europe or North America should feel comfortable in their natural personal space. Finally, keep eye contact to a minimum, as this will also be considered respectful.

Western businesswomen should also follow an Arab businesswoman's lead. Most of the above rules above also apply to Western businesswomen. The main exception would be when meeting a religious Arab woman: that woman may have no problem shaking the hand of a Western businesswoman, even if she has chosen not to shake the hand of your Western male counterpart.

Western women can also expect to shake hands with most Arab men, as they will regard you professionally, i.e. as an 'honorary man'. The main exception will be if a Western businesswoman is meeting a very religious Arab man. In this instance, the Arab man will not want to shake your hand because he does not want to make contact with an unrelated woman, i.e. you. Instead, many religious Arab men will greet a woman by placing his right hand over his heart, and will often look down and away from you, avoiding direct eye contact. He will also keep an additional distance from you. Western businesswomen must be careful not to misinterpret these gestures, as they are actually all strong signs of respect.

Handshakes are firm but not bone cracking between men. Western businesswomen should also have a firm handshake with Arab men. Handshakes should be much more gentle when shaking an Arab woman's hand regardless of the Westerner's gender.

It is also important to keep in mind that you are likely to be meeting people from other cultures, especially when working in the Gulf Countries. Similar handshake rules apply to Muslims from other parts of the world, including the Indian subcontinent and the Far East. Many other non-Muslim women from the Indian subcontinent may also not have a long tradition of shaking hands, although many younger, Indian businesswomen will almost certainly do so. Again, it's best for all Westerners to follow a non-Western businesswoman's lead. In general, people from the Indian subcontinent shake hands much more gently than others, even between men. A weak handshake in these cultures is actually seen as a sign of respect. Westerners should never force others to adopt a handshake that is too firm.

You will not be expected to bow to people from the Far East whilst working in the Middle East, even if you might do so in their home countries. It is always good form to stand when meeting others.

Other helpful greeting tips

In most business environments, you can expect your host to introduce you to others in the correct sequence and hierarchy; simply follow their lead. If this is not possible, then try to greet the most senior people first, recognising age and status wherever possible. If a person's professional status is unclear, then greet elders before younger people – this will never be an insult.

Always use a person's title, especially if they have a professional title such as engineer, doctor, or military rank. You will be informed if you are meeting someone from a ruling family and will most certainly be given the correct title and protocol for greeting royalty in advance.

Low-status people such as the teaboy do not expect to be acknowledged; do not make circumstances awkward for the teaboy or indeed anyone in the room by attempting to introduce yourself to someone present solely in a service capacity.

BUSINESS CARDS

Business cards are a must throughout the Middle East. If you do not have a business card, then in effect you have no identity and no status.

Business cards should be printed on high quality paper stock. They should include your full name, job title, contact details including at least your physical address and mobile phone, and your organisation's website and logo. Always include telephone country codes, ideally leading with the + symbol. Include the name of your country at the end of your physical address.

It is always a good idea to have your business cards printed in English on one side and in Arabic on the other side, although it is possible to get away with English-only business cards in Dubai if your business is only with other expatriates. Make sure you work with a translator you can trust and who understands your business, including the correct positioning of your logo – it may not be in the same position in English and in Arabic. If you are not sure, consider approaching a language-learning organisation in the West, or a hotel concierge or business centre whilst in the Middle East.

If at all possible, try to establish a local presence that you can print on your business cards. At a minimum, obtain a local mobile phone number and add it to your Western details. Use a trusted local contact's business address if you can reach an agreement, or enlist the services of a company that provides *ad hoc* office rental space, such as Regus, if you don't think this is a good idea, or if you are worried about this being too big a favour.

In addition, you should always use the highest job title you can possibly get away with that is not a misrepresentation of your position. Middle Eastern business people want to do business with others who have high status and the perception of being able to make decisions quickly. You should keep this in mind when choosing a job title.

Although some of these tactics may seem to be somewhat devious business practices to some Westerners, they actually show your intentions to become committed to the region, and are thus valued by most Middle Eastern business people.

When exchanging business cards, keep in mind that they represent you and your company personally. Whilst it is not necessary to hold them with two hands, always handle them with care.

Offer your card so the recipient can read your details without turning the card around. You should extend the Arabic language side face-up for Arabic speakers, and the English language side face-up for all others. Never pass your business card with the left hand only, as it is symbolic of offering your prospective business partner dirt. It is good form to study business cards you have just received for a period of time somewhat longer than you would in the West.

Always handle other people's business cards with respect. Once you have received everyone's business cards, it is a good idea to keep them laid out on the table in front of you, matching them with the relative position of where each new contact is sitting in sequence. This will be particularly useful if you have just met ten new people and seven of them are named Mohammed. Gather them in sequence when your meeting has finished so you can remember who is who. Whilst it's OK to write notes on a separate piece of paper to minimise confusion, never write on a business card, at least in the presence of their owner.

11

Taboos

Most Western business professionals will go out of their way to avoid causing offence when travelling abroad. What causes offence in the Middle East varies tremendously and can be quite different depending on a person's nationality, age, gender, religiousness, education level and family values. Regional and global politics have an impact as well.

It's also important to keep in mind that, in the Arab world, many people are strongly motivated to remain courteous at all times, especially towards guests (i.e. you), even if you have caused offence. Thus, it is possible to be unaware of a social *faux pas* that you may have made, as most Arabs are unlikely to tell you directly. However, if you are observant, their body language will tell you of their displeasure.

The following information will help Western business professionals avoid the most serious problems that could jeopardise their ability to build relationships and trust with their Middle Eastern colleagues.

EVERYDAY TABOOS

Most everyday taboos stem from Islamic values, which we have previously described. This list should be considered a guideline for Westerners to avoid, at least in the company of religious Muslims. It is also important to keep in mind the legal status of many items on this list:

- No pork unless you are in a licensed restaurant and none of your dining companions is Muslim.
- No alcohol if you are with anyone who may take offence. In general, it's best to mirror the pattern of your host.

- Do not use the left hand for giving and taking 'clean' items, especially at meals, when handling business cards, or accepting tokens of hospitality.
- Do not show the soles of your feet to others, including crossing your legs.
- Do not wear shoes in houses.
- Do not bring pornography into the region.
- Be careful of importing other images that may be too risqué, especially in Saudi Arabia, including advertisements in otherwise benign publications.
- Never touch an Arab woman, especially in public.
- Never enquire after an Arab man's wife, daughters or any other female family member, especially Gulf Arabs and religious Muslims of any nationality.
- Do not publicly show physical affection between a man and a woman, even if you are married, although you may see other Western tourists doing so.
- Be aware of the risks involved surrounding any sexual behaviour between unmarried couples.
- Be aware of the risks involved surrounding any homosexual behaviour.
- Avoid talking about your pet dog; dogs are considered dirty.
- No gambling. Leave your lottery ticket at home.
- It would be very foolish to even contemplate illegal drug use anywhere in the region.
- Do not import over-the-counter drugs into countries where ingredients such as codeine are illegal.
- Avoid giving gifts that contain gold, silk or diamonds for men. Western men who wear a gold wedding ring or a silk necktie will not have a problem.
- Visiting most mosques; some mosques will operate tours for non-Muslims at specified times.

POLITICAL AND SOCIAL TABOOS

The art of small talk is a minefield throughout the world. Western business professionals should have a repertoire of topics when meeting people from the Middle East, especially at the beginning of business meetings.

Recommended topics of conversation

You will always be safe if you compliment your destination. Your hosts are very likely to ask you how you like Dubai or Bahrain; always answer in the affirmative, even if you are in the midst of a sandstorm.

Try to find common ground in sport. Many people in the Gulf follow football. Many people from cricket-playing countries are passionate about cricket. You may also have quite a lot in common with others if you play golf or have an interest in various water sports. From a traditional perspective, many Gulf Arabs are interested in falconry.

Showing interest in Islam and Islamic culture is a good idea, but be natural and sincere in your conversation.

Topics of conversation to avoid:

- Questioning Islam.
- Directly declaring your atheism or agnosticism.
- Making personal enquiries about local women.
- Criticising any of the ruling families in the Gulf, even whilst visiting a neighbouring country.
- All Israel/Palestine issues, although it is possible to show support for pro-Palestinian causes if you are well-informed from sources respected within the Middle East, i.e. beyond Western media.
- Showing support for Western involvement in the conflict in Iraq.
- Showing support for Western involvement in the conflict in Afghanistan.
- General references to the Middle East somehow being responsible for the world's problems with terrorism.

TABOOS FROM OTHER CULTURES

It is important for Western business professionals to remember that they are likely to be working with a number of people from other cultures, especially those from the Indian subcontinent in the Gulf.

Hindus

Hindus will not eat beef; many are also vegetarian. Although the religion does not forbid the consumption of alcohol, many Hindus are teetotal. Others are most certainly not.

It is important to keep these dietary practices in mind when working with Hindus from the Indian subcontinent – and beyond, as people of Indian origin who have migrated to the West will probably have retained at least some of their traditional religious practices. If you are hosting a business meal, it is best to avoid an establishment that specialises in beef, or that does not offer many vegetarian choices. If you are a guest, it is a good idea to learn a bit about Indian cuisine, as it varies tremendously from North to South. Be prepared to eat with your (right) hand instead of with cutlery in some traditional establishments found in the Gulf countries.

WESTERN CULTURAL BAGGAGE

Some Westerners also have their own cultural baggage that is not always appreciated in the Middle East. In general, some Westerners may have the attitude that, along with their business, they are importing a 'better' lifestyle into the Middle East, i.e. their own, as if somehow Western lifestyles are superior to others. Others may believe that most people living in the Middle East would migrate to the West if only they had the chance, when in reality, this attitude would be insulting.

Some Westerners may believe that they are 'helping' people to learn the ways of the modern business world, operating as if Western business practices are the only valid way of doing business. Even if the Westerners' intents are sincerely altruistic, in reality they will be seen as patronising. This is especially true if a Westerner tries to force task-orientated practices onto people who are relationship-orientated (*what* you know versus *who* you know), to criticise differing attitudes to time, or to ask a group of people to switch off their mobiles to avoid interruption to business when their value system is to do many things at a time.

It is also important to keep in mind that many people from the Middle East are quite familiar with the West, especially the USA and UK, as they may have gone to university or visited friends and family over extended periods of time, based in these countries.

Colonialist attitudes

It would be wise for Europeans to be aware of the legacy of colonisation, which includes the British, the French and in earlier times, the Portuguese. Turkish people also carry this historical baggage from the days of the Ottoman Empire. The British, in particular, would do well to avoid colonialist attitudes towards anyone living in the Middle East, including Arabs and other guest workers, especially those from other former British colonies.

Apartheid attitudes

The acceptance of post-apartheid South Africans into the global community has brought a large migration of skilled (mostly white) workers to the Middle East. Some of these people have exhibited behaviours and attitudes that can only be described as congruent with the values of the apartheid era. There is a fine line between acceptable, expected and abusive behaviour toward people employed in service occupations. Residual racism, even when considered within the context of hierarchical attitudes of the Middle East, should be avoided.

American patriotism

Given the recent political and military decisions made by the US government, especially during the administration of George W Bush, it is strongly advised that Americans travelling to the Middle East consider dampening their enthusiasm for their country, particularly if they are also prone to promoting their version of life as the best way, or only way, for others to live theirs as well. This behaviour, especially when coupled with a clear lack of history and understanding of the region is distinctly unwelcome.

However, it is also important to understand that the Arab and Muslim worlds do not hate all Americans. In fact, people from the Middle East in particular are very familiar with living in an environment where their personal opinions and attitudes can be at great odds with the official positions of their own government. Thus, those Americans who do not agree with their government's political and military policies affecting the region can expect their Middle Eastern counterparts to regard them by their own merits and not as an extension of their government.

Westerners' fear of the Middle East

There are many Westerners who react with fear when they learn they have been asked to do business in the Middle East. Americans in particular may have little or no exposure to the Middle East beyond the never-ending reports of the Israeli-Palestinian conflict broadcast on CNN, Fox News or the traditional national networks.

Unlike most other Westerners, who generally consider the Gulf countries the anchor of the Middle East, Americans are often referring to Israel or the Levant when they speak about the Middle East. Their geographical knowledge may not extend beyond this small part of the region. The author has witnessed several instances where Americans have needed clarification as to the location of Dubai, vaguely believing it is somewhere in Saudi Arabia. These same Americans then react with shock when they learn that several million Europeans routinely holiday in the Emirate each year.

Many Westerners who are fearful of the unfamiliar can convey their fear when doing business with the very people they may be uncomfortable around. Americans should be especially aware of their own demeanour if this applies to them, as their Middle Eastern colleagues are quite astute in picking up their feelings of apprehension, suspicion and fear. Try to relax and pick up on the courtesy and hospitality of your hosts; you will be welcomed much more quickly if you act in a trusting and accepting manner.

Proselytising

Some Western Christians appear to be keen to spread 'The Word' wherever they travel. Whether a conventional Anglican or the most fundamentalist of the American home-grown Christian sects, it is strongly advised that all attempts to proselytise the Christian faith are abandoned throughout the Middle East. This is for one's own safety in some of the most conservative parts of the region, including all of Saudi Arabia, as well as for practical reasons. An actively proselytising, Western Christian's chances of forging a good business relationship anywhere in the Middle East, even amongst local Christian communities approaches zero.

Popular Western body art trends

Although it is possible to see all sorts of personal expressions of individuality amongst Westerners who are working and living in the Middle East, not to mention tourists, there are some practices that should be given consideration if they apply to you.

In particular, tattoos are frowned-upon in Islamic culture in spite of some residual tattooing amongst some rural tribal people. If you have tattoos, you may want to consider concealing them, especially when in a business environment.

Body piercings can also cause confusion as well as offence. Whilst it is accepted for women to have pierced ears, other body piercings on a woman are not considered desirable. An exception is made for a nose piercing for women who originate from the Indian subcontinent. Nor are any piercings on a man desirable.

Finally, very long hair on men is considered feminine as well as undesirable unless it is for religious reasons, such as for Sikh men. However, as this is a less permanent expression of individuality, it is possible to see some Arab youths sporting long hair styles. Western businessmen are not expected to be enamoured of this desire, as the expectation is to be conventionally well groomed in the business environment. If you do have long hair for reasons that are not religious, it is a good idea to keep it tidy, and to tie it back if it is very long.

In the Arab world, long flowing, loose hair on women may be more associated with social functions as it comes very close to sexualising the woman, especially in some conservative environments. Keep in mind why many women wear the *shayla* from a religious point of view. Thus, Western women with long hair may want to consider tying it back in a business environment as well, as the long-haired author did whilst conducting business. This will give her a more business-like appearance and possibly assist her in being taken more seriously. It is also significantly more comfortable in the hottest months.

Disability

Much of the Middle East remains uncomfortable with or ashamed of disability. Often it is seen fatalistically, i.e. it was God's will, or that somehow the disability was brought on by a past negative event or behaviour. It is not unusual for families to 'hide away' a disabled member of their family, often for life, and often without ever specifically referring to that family member by name. Needless to say, disability legislation can be considered at best a future possibility, although some Middle Eastern countries are beginning to raise awareness of this issue.

For those Western business professionals who have a disability, they should be prepared for a range of reactions from their Middle Eastern counterparts, and indeed from other fatalistic cultures such as the Indian subcontinent. Western business professionals with a disabled friend or family member may wish to refer to the individual but not their disability, avoiding shame, embarrassment and possible discomfort for all parties.

12

Attitudes to Westerners

Many Western business professionals may be curious about attitudes that others living in the Middle East have about themselves. Are Westerners *really* welcomed? Are they simply tolerated, or are they looked upon favourably? Are Westerners losing their place in favour of the Far East and India? Certainly, especially with the advent of satellite television and other widely-accessible media throughout the region, it is important to keep in mind that most people in the Middle East will know a lot more about you than you know about them.

Of course, it is very difficult to generalise about such a large group of people who also have varying cultural values amongst themselves. However, some attitudes are prevalent in the Middle East. It should be noted that the following attitudes are mostly applicable to people from the EU, North America, Australia, New Zealand and South Africa.

THE GOOD

Westerners are usually seen as honest and trustworthy, at least compared to others. Westerners are generally seen to be fair. Westerners are regarded as relatively easy to understand, both in a motivational sense and linguistically.

Western technology, higher educational facilities and medical skills are unquestionably admired and desired. We also have the examples of engineering skills for the oil industry as well as military technology. It's not an accident that many of the Middle East's most highly regarded leaders have a background attending the likes of Sandhurst. Western IT companies have had a strong presence in the region since the mid 1990s. More and more outposts of Western universities are being established in the region. World-renowned medical partnerships are expanding.

Western consumerism continues to expand into the Middle East. It is nearly impossible to avoid British clothing retailers, American fast food outlets, French hypermarkets, Swiss luxury goods and German automobiles from the Gulf to Lebanon. The crowds, including in-country nationals, attest to their popularity.

Interestingly, Western popular culture remains very popular, although it is undoubtedly a topic that also generates much criticism. Excellent examples include fake/smuggled Coca Cola in Iran, baseball caps worn by some Saudi youth, localised versions of television shows as diverse as Pop Idol, MTV, Who Wants to Be a Millionaire (long before Slumdog Millionaire), and news formats both in Arabic and in English that will be familiar to viewers of the BBC or CNN.

THE NOT-SO-GOOD

Westerners are often seen as people who regard rules, plans, rigid time-keeping and procedural structure in general as higher priority than 'the important things', i.e. relationships, family obligations, religious holidays and even quality of life issues. Westerners are also seen to be in a hurry. Do not be surprised if your Middle Eastern partner misses a deadline and then advises you that it was because he ran into a friend – the relationship with the friend will always be more important than being 'on time' with you.

Most Westerners are seen as not being family orientated. It can genuinely shock some people in the Middle East if they learn you haven't seen an uncle, cousin or niece for months, or that your family only gets together for weddings and funerals. Closely related to this is a perception of selfishness in many Westerners. Of course, many Westerners operate in a much more individualistic manner than in Middle Eastern cultures. Whilst there is certainly no simple solution, it is a good idea for Westerners to emphasise their 'family values' and underplay their autonomy wherever possible.

There is an ongoing level of discomfort about many Westerners' social morals. Many Westerners' behaviour can be confusing to Muslims, who regard Islam as a way of life, including as a compass for their own social morals. When a Westerner doesn't have a strong religious compass, there is often a suspicion that the Westerner also has no social morals, regardless of the reality.

Many people in the Middle East also struggle with many Westerners' sexual behaviour. This can range from an expression of affection in public even between married couples, to the infamous case in Dubai in 2008 with the 'sex on the beach' British couple. Whilst many people in the Middle East are aware that many Westerners live together unmarried in long-term, stable relationships, the equivalent arrangement in their culture simply does not officially exist (and in fact, would be found only in the rarest of exceptions).

Homosexuality is another area that is difficult for most people in the Middle East to understand. It will undoubtedly take some time to gain acceptance of civil partnerships amongst most people in a region where homosexuality remains illegal and its very existence often officially denied.

Some Westerners' relationship with alcohol can be uncomfortable for many people in the Middle East. This is particularly true when Muslims – and indeed others – unavoidably encounter public drunkenness. It is also the reason why it is of paramount importance for Westerners who drink in the Middle East to make sure that, as well as choosing the correct company, that they also choose the appropriate venue that provides discretion and avoids offence, especially if you do become intoxicated. This can include restaurants, pubs, clubs and private homes. Special care should be given when departing these venues; you should take steps to minimise inflicting your drunkenness on to the public, however brief it may be.

Many Westerners are perceived as having manners that fall short of expectations. This is particularly true in Western cultures that value efficiency and the ability quickly to get down to business. People in the Middle East will not thank you for jumping into business straight away, no matter how important. There is no shortcut to courteous behaviour and hospitality, even when the Westerner is 'running out of time'.

ATTITUDES TO WESTERN WOMEN

One of the most common misconceptions about the Middle East, at least from Westerners, is the region's beliefs and attitudes towards women. Although we have been exploring many of these issues either directly or indirectly elsewhere in this book, it's worth taking a minute to explore our own beliefs and biases about Middle Easterners' attitudes towards women in general.

Many Westerners have expressed the following views about Middle Eastern women:

- women are oppressed
- women must walk three paces behind a man
- women cannot work
- women cannot drive
- women cannot own their own business
- women must wear the veil
- women are forced to marry someone they don't even know
- women have no say in marriage or family life
- women must accept additional wives
- women cannot divorce.

With the exception of some restrictions in Saudi Arabia, all of the above are false.

The preservation of honour is of paramount importance to most people in the Middle East. Although men are expected to behave honourably, it is women who are seen as the keepers of family honour. Thus, women's behaviour reflects not only on them, but also on their entire family. This reaches to the extended blood family as well as to the tribe. Honour is generally maintained through modesty as well as through actions.

Traditionally, men are considered to be the head of the family. Women are responsible for the wellbeing of their family and for the comforts of their family's home life, not unlike in much of the rest of the world. However, this remains a strong traditional role and is unlikely to be negotiable as it might be in some domestic family arrangements found in the West.

Men's and women's status within their family changes over their lifetime; it is particularly important for women. Additional status is gained once a man or woman has married, again when a married couple has a child, and again when they have a son.

Traditionally, many children are desired, although family planning is common amongst many women in the Middle East, particularly in parts of the Levant, in many educated families, and in many Christian families. However, most families will continue to have children until they have at least one son; it is not unusual throughout the region to see a large family of older daughters and one young son. Finally, a woman continues to gain status as she grows older.

How an individual woman's life is likely to play out depends to a great degree on her religious sect, piety, her nationality and above all, her education level. With the advent of the Gulf Countries' '–isation' programmes, many Gulf women are the first generation of their families who are in a position of paid employment. With their honour protected in the work environment, and with the encouragement of their ruling families, this trend is expected to continue. Women in Egypt and the Levant have had a longer tradition of employment, whether through personal choice or financial necessity.

GENERAL ATTITUDES TOWARDS WESTERN BUSINESSWOMEN

Historically, women have had a role in business since the beginning of Islam, as the Prophet Mohammed's wife Fatima was a businesswoman in her own right. Restrictions on women going out to work stem less from Islam and more from cultural practices, lack of suitable opportunity in poorer regions and a lack of education that has been a major obstacle for many women until recent times.

As a Western business professional, you are likely to encounter businesswomen from the Middle East. Who they are will depend on their nationality and personal background as well as the particular line of business in which your organisation is operating.

Educational opportunities have improved beyond all recognition for some women in the region. Most women in the Gulf Countries now have excellent opportunities to achieve higher education, including university degrees. In fact, most Gulf nationals are now more likely than Westerners to achieve a university level degree. Institutions range from gender-segregated, highly-respected local universities to branches of Western institutions. Other women travel abroad to complete their education, often to the US or the UK. Sheikha Mozah of Qatar has received global recognition for her work in improving the educational standards of women throughout the region. In Yemen, education remains a challenge for women as it does for many men.

Women in Saudi Arabia face challenges. Educational opportunities depend on the family's cultural values. Some families support girls' education; others do not. Some families support the education of their daughters, but do not support them working outside the home; others are happy for them to work, but only in a gender-segregated environment, which is possible in many professions throughout the Kingdom. Similar attitudes exist in Yemen, with the additional burden of financial hardship for many of Yemen's poor.

Many women in the Levant are well educated, with Lebanon leading the way. Elite families in Iran, Egypt, Jordan and Syria ensure their female members are included in all available educational opportunities. Queen Rania of Jordan is supporting work to improve the literacy rate of all women in Jordan, which has seen massive gains in less than a generation.

It is safe to conclude that businesswomen from the Middle East are from a relatively privileged background. Although they may come from a religiously observant family, they are unlikely to come from the most fundamentalist backgrounds. They will invariably have the support of their families in their roles as businesswomen.

Many people in the West may stereotype Middle Eastern businesswomen as being meek and mild. Whilst it is fair to say that most women will remain courteous at all times, the author is more than happy to dispel that misconception. In her experience, many of her most formidable business partners and competitors alike were businesswomen from Iran, Lebanon, Egypt and Palestine working throughout the region.

Finally, Middle Eastern businesswomen will expect you to respect them at all times, from both a professional and a personal perspective.

In a professional capacity

Western businesswomen are often placed in a position of privilege when working in the Middle East, especially when working in the Gulf Countries. This privilege is obtained partly through the woman's nationality. It is also obtained for the professional businesswoman by her job title.

In a business environment, the Western businesswoman's job title provides her with her status, which can be quite powerful, depending on her line of business, her local business partners and *wasta* within the region. Many Western businesswomen will find it no more difficult to do their job in the Middle East than they would in London, New York or Sydney.

However, stereotyping still exists, and it is almost a certainty that the Western businesswoman will encounter misconceptions about her professional role at some point in her travels. It is often enough for the woman to remind her counterpart gently of her job title, emphasising her authority, as more and more of the Middle East is becoming used to Western businesswomen working in all capacities.

However, some challenges for Western businesswomen remain, especially when working with very traditional or very religious colleagues. The most frequent situations that can be frustrating include speaking to the woman through a man who is also present, not looking directly at a woman when speaking to her, or assuming the woman must report to her male counterpart simply because of her gender. The woman should be reminded that these behaviours are rarely meant to be malicious, but are the traditionalist's belief in how to treat a woman 'properly'.

In these situations, the woman's status can be reinforced by reminding her counterpart that her organisation would never have sent her to the Middle East if they did not support her in her professional position. Any male counterparts who may be travelling with her should also be enlisted to confirm her status; this is especially important in a situation where a Western businessman is in a subordinate position to the Western businesswoman.

In public

Most Western businesswomen will quickly establish their status within the work environment. However, some of her 'privileges' may not follow her into the public environment. Although her gender does not always work in her favour, she will usually retain some of her status due to her nationality. Western women who hail from a non-Western background or ethnicity are, sadly, likely to suffer in public more frequently than their European counterparts, at least until their nationality is clearly established.

Common frustrations that Western businesswomen will almost certainly encounter throughout the region include various behaviours that can only be made sense of if one imagines that the woman has become invisible. Many women will find that men will ignore them in a queue, whether in a shop or at the airport. If a woman is in the company of a man, it is not unusual for a service person, such as a taxi driver or a waiter to enquire about the woman's needs through the man (even if it is the woman who knows the destination or is hosting the meal).

Social etiquette can also be a minefield. For example, lifts present an interesting social experiment. Does the woman get on first, sharpen her elbows so she has a chance to get on at all, wait for a man to invite her on, or wait for another lift that she does not have to share with a religious Arab man? In reality, all of these options are correct, depending on location and circumstances.

It is up to the woman to decide when to ignore behaviour that she may consider rude or offensive in public, as everyone has their own principles, frustrations and thresholds for tolerance. The author – not always known for her patience – recommends that Western businesswomen choose their battles.

WORKING IN SAUDI ARABIA AS A WESTERN BUSINESSWOMAN

In public

Western businesswomen who are contemplating working in Saudi Arabia have a host of additional challenges to consider. Western businesswomen can and do successfully work in a professional capacity in Saudi Arabia, but the realities are that it remains much more difficult than for her male counterpart.

Her first consideration is whether she will be able to obtain a business visa to get into the country at all. Factors that will enhance her chances of obtaining a business visa include, but are not restricted to:

- the importance of her company;
- how important she is (this is where a very prestigious job title can make the difference);
- how strongly her Saudi sponsors want her in the country;
- the amount of *wasta* her sponsors have within the Saudi government;
- when and how far in advance she applies for her visa;
- her nationality;
- her religion;
- her age.

Western businesswomen generally have a better chance of successfully obtaining a Saudi business visa if they come from the UK or US, especially in certain lines of business. They will also have a better chance if they are over 40 years old, although there are some exceptions made for women between the ages of 30 and 40. The author is not aware of any Western businesswomen successfully obtaining a business visa under the age of 30. However, this is not meant to be a discouragement to younger women to try. Women from a Christian, European background generally have a better chance than women from other religious and ethnic backgrounds. Jewish women should be theoretically treated the same as their Christian counterparts, but in reality may struggle, as will their male counterparts. They may wish to consider applying for their visa as a Christian if this is not an ethical issue for them.

For Western businesswomen who have been successful in obtaining a business visa, they must be aware of fundamental differences in how they must conduct themselves both professionally and personally whilst in the Kingdom.

Firstly, their sponsor must meet them at the airport (or at the land border in the middle of the King Fahd Causeway if travelling overland from Bahrain), as they are simply not allowed any further into the Kingdom without their sponsor, who will be acting as the woman's *mahram* (male guardian). Western businesswomen, just like all other women, must wear the *abaya* in public throughout the Kingdom unless visiting a Western compound. This includes throughout all public areas of her hotel. In Riyadh, she will also need to wear a *shayla* that covers all of her hair and her neck. Jeddah and the Eastern Province are less restrictive, although the *abaya* remains mandatory. Many Western businesswomen feel more comfortable continuing to wear a *shayla* in Jeddah or Damman as well, especially if travelling alone.

Women must travel with a *mahram* throughout their stay. This can be a driver supplied by their sponsor or organised through their hotel. If travelling with other business colleagues, officially she must not travel with an unrelated man in Riyadh, including other Western business colleagues, as there is a real possibility she could be challenged by the *mutawwa* and for the 'couple' to produce their marriage certificate. The best solution is to travel in a separate vehicle. Alternatively, some Western businesswomen may travel with a Western married couple, which is permitted as long as both husband and wife are present. However, this isn't usually practical in a business environment. Western businesswomen travelling in Jeddah or the Eastern Province are unlikely to run into difficulties travelling with an unrelated male if they keep a low profile, although it remains technically *haram*.

Women will struggle to function in many public environments, again especially in Riyadh. Women must continue to observe *hijab* in their hotel, except in their room. Women are not allowed to use many other hotel facilities, including the health club and the swimming pool.

Women must eat in the family section of all restaurants, which are generally either a separate room or is screened off from the main area of a restaurant, and where no single men are permitted to enter. This includes the restaurants in her hotel. Unfortunately, some businessmen are not keen on conducting business in an environment filled with families, especially when a lot of small children are present. More difficult is the fact that some restaurants do not have family sections at all; in this case, women are simply not allowed into the restaurant.

In Riyadh, the main public venues that a woman will be welcome in are in are in an upmarket hotel or a shopping mall. In Jeddah, she will have many more options, including the use of private facilities for water sports that are associated with the hotels. The author can attest to this personally, as she has managed to hire diving gear for a scuba excursion in Jeddah, where she set out in full veil from her hotel and ended up on the dive boat in a Western swimming costume and the diving gear, once the boat was a respectable distance from the shoreline.

Of course, women cannot drive, although this also means that women never need to worry about being arrested for driving offences ... or parking.

Interestingly, Western businesswomen are permitted to fly internally within Saudi Arabia without a *mahram*. Thus, a flight between Riyadh and Jeddah would be routine, although she still needs someone to meet her before she can leave the next airport. Women have access to business lounges and other airport facilities, although she must comply with any established family sections.

Occasionally, a Western businesswoman may find she is seated next to a very religious Muslim man on a flight, especially to a destination in Saudi Arabia. The man may be distinctly uncomfortable sitting next to her, sometimes to the point where he requests a change of seat. The author once found herself in this exact situation on a flight from Karachi to Jeddah where her neighbour asked the flight attendant to change the seating in the first class cabin. No other first class passengers were willing to change seats possibly as it was *Hajj* season. Fortunately, the gentleman accepted the opportunity to switch seats with an Irish passport holder originally seated in the business class cabin.

Happily, in the airport and indeed elsewhere in Saudi Arabia, Western businesswomen can generally expect to be pulled out of most queues, with their needs seen to separately and processed more quickly.

Women also have it slightly easier than their male counterparts during prayer times, when all business comes to an official halt throughout the Kingdom. Unlike men, who need to disappear from public view in many situations, women can simply sit quietly and respectfully in public until prayer time is over. The author found this time very useful for mastering a variety of games on her mobile phone once she ensured the sound was muted.

Finally, there are difficulties and annoyances that can be classified as nuisance level. Western businesswomen should keep in mind that even when wearing local dress, it is still obvious that you are an outsider by the way you walk, the accessories you carry and your general demeanour. Remarkably, many Western businesswomen may be the recipient of unwanted male attention, especially in their hotels. At the other end of the spectrum, some men will refuse to be anywhere near you in public, and may even suggest that you should not have come to Saudi Arabia. Invariably, these comments and behaviours will only happen when you are momentarily alone. Like almost anywhere else in the world, the best advice is to ignore the offending behaviour, as you are highly unlikely to be in any physical danger no matter how unpleasant it may be. In the unlikely event the offending behaviour becomes persistent, a quick comment about acting like a good Muslim should do the trick.

In a professional capacity

Although it might be overstatement to suggest that a Western businesswoman's situation is one of privilege when working in Saudi Arabia, her professional status does continue to have an impact on how she is treated. In short, once a Western businesswoman successfully obtains a business visa and travels to the Kingdom, she will be considered an 'honorary man' within the business environment.

A Western businesswoman will be able to go about her usual work at her sponsor's place of business, as this is her reason for being in the Kingdom in the first place. She will be invited to be present in traditionally male areas of business, such as offices, conference rooms and training environments, especially in a private setting. She will be invited to meetings, be able to lead a presentation or training course, negotiate a sale, or do whatever else is her normal remit as a part of her responsibilities. As long as the woman displays her competence and authority, her business decisions will be recognised and accepted.

A Western businesswoman has the additional ability of being able to interface directly with Saudi businesswomen without the restrictions imposed on her male counterparts. As the Kingdom is making tentative steps towards encouraging more women into the work force, this can be a distinct advantage for the Western businesswoman.

Meeting customers will be somewhat dependent on their general attitude towards working with women. Many Saudis will work with a woman in a normal business setting; some will even go out of their way to do so in their desire to be seen as modern and supportive. Others will insist on meeting in public, such as in the reception area of a hotel. A very few may prefer not to meet with a woman at all; again, this is most likely in Riyadh.

Western businesswomen should never try to shake hands in public anywhere in Saudi Arabia. However, if a man extends his hand in greeting (and it will happen), you should shake it briefly, with minimal eye contact. Make sure you keep a very respectful distance, almost to the point where you need to stretch your arm a bit to greet the man.

Western businesswomen should be aware that there are a few remaining difficulties within a business environment that will restrict her method of doing business. For example, it is nearly impossible for a woman to attend trade shows or other activities that introduce the potential for public displays of authority over a group of men, although the author predicts this may change in time.

Crucially, Western businesswomen will continue to have fewer occasions to socialise publicly with men in Saudi Arabia above and beyond restaurants. This will include *shisha* smoking, trips to the desert, and any public activity involving a group of men. Western businesswomen should consider whether they can send a male colleague who can take their place in these circumstances.

A final note regarding business opportunities with Saudis should be considered. Many Saudis are happy to escape the social restrictions of their homeland, and you may be the perfect excuse for them to leave the Kingdom, even if it is only for a short while. It is not uncommon for Western businesswomen to meet with Saudis in Bahrain or Dubai within the Gulf, and even further afield in Cairo or Beirut, especially in the summer months. Do not be surprised if these meetings are scheduled very near to the start of the weekend.

13

Communicating in the Middle East

English is the international language of business throughout most of the Middle East, including all of the GCC countries. English and French are both useful in parts of the Levant, especially Lebanon and to a lesser extent in Syria. Some Arabic may be necessary for those Western business professionals working in Yemen and Sudan. Many Iranians only speak Farsi unless they have spent time abroad.

ENGLISH LANGUAGE SKILLS WITHIN MIDDLE EASTERN POPULATIONS

Many people from the Middle East have been educated to a high standard, and speak, read and write English fluently. This is especially true amongst Arabs from the Gulf Countries as well as educated Arabs in the Levant, especially in the younger generation. Other Arabs may speak English reasonably well, but may not have the same level of written English language skills. The main exception is in Yemen, where English language skills remain poor, except amongst some of the elite.

American or British English?

English language usage varies tremendously throughout the region. In a professional business environment, it is important to establish whether English is used in a British or an American context. Broadly speaking, American English is more common in Saudi Arabia, Kuwait, Lebanon and, of course, Israel. British English is favoured in the UAE, Qatar, Bahrain and Oman. Syria, Jordan and Egypt will be influenced by both. Iranians who speak English will be influenced by friends and family abroad; thus, there is a higher chance an Iranian will speak American English.

Other English language usage

English dialects will also follow lines of business. Thus, most oil related businesses will use American English. Most businesses related to property development will use British English; so will most Western multinational organisations, including those with corporate headquarters in the US. Of course, there are other Western English language dialects throughout the region, including Australian, New Zealand, Irish and South African English.

Indian-owned businesses will almost certainly conduct their business in Indian English, as will most Indian professionals working throughout the region regardless of their clients. Educated Indians will invariably speak, read and write English fluently. However, there will be real differences in syntax, as well as different terminology, between Indian English and other dialects. Accents and cadence vary as well. Most Western business professionals will quickly become familiar with the most common expressions – don't be afraid to ask if you don't understand.

Throughout the Middle East, there is another important influence on the English language. Due to the sheer numbers of service people working in the region, other English language dialects are commonly heard. In particular, it will serve the Western business professional well to be able to understand some of the more common nuances of English spoken throughout the Indian subcontinent as well as Filipino English. Service people will generally have at least enough English to be able to perform their jobs; many others speak English fluently.

In general, it's a good idea to use Standard English throughout the Middle East, ideally British Received Pronunciation. Your colleagues are unlikely to be appreciative of your ability to use obscure Cockney rhyming slang, ghetto rap or incessant references to local culture or sport that do not travel.

All I want to know is yes or no!

Language is not simply a matter of dialect or accent. It is also contextual, i.e. it matters *how* words are spoken as much as *which* words are used.

One of the most common frustrations felt by nearly all Westerners working in the Middle East is the belief that they reached an agreement when, in fact, their business partner was really delivering an altogether different message. The Westerner may then conclude that their partner was not being honest. Communication has broken down.

Whilst there are no simple solutions to this problem, the Western business professional should realise a few fundamental differences in communication styles.

INTERPRETING INDIRECT LANGUAGE

Many Westerners, especially those from English-speaking Western countries or those from Northern European and Germanic countries, speak in a low context style, i.e. they tend to say what they mean and mean what they say. Subtleties, hints and innuendos are not generally relied upon to convey additional meaning; messages are delivered directly by an efficiency of clear words.

Whilst this may make it easy to understand the Westerner, it can also easily offend many other cultures as being too direct, especially when delivering bad news or being put into a position of needing to admit a problem. Indeed, this is one of the main areas where many Westerners can come across as rude in the Middle East, whereas they would be considered honest, genuine or easy to get on with at home.

Many people from other cultures, including Arab cultures of the Middle East, those from the Indian subcontinent and, indeed, most cultures throughout Asia, communicate in a high context manner. This means they choose their words very carefully, not only to represent their meaning but also to shape the impression, mood, and expectation of both the speaker and the listener. They may also speak to different people differently, depending on their relationship with the other person. This is especially true in an environment where the subordinate is expected to agree with the boss, regardless of their own knowledge, opinions or expertise.

For Western business professionals who are used to speaking directly, they may miss the real message of the conversation, which may be unspoken but delivered through tone, eye contact, body language, or other contextual cues. Whilst the Westerner may be somewhat used to the social 'white lie' (does my bum look big in this?), they are usually unused to applying the same communication principles in a work environment.

THE MULTIPLE MEANINGS OF 'YES'

Additional challenges may come into play when people translate words from another language into English. For example, in Arabic and in many Indian languages, there are several words for 'yes', depending on context. These subtleties are missing in English, where there is pretty much only one way to say 'yes'. Thus, it would be incorrect to assume your counterpart is intentionally misleading you; they may simply not have a word in English that captures the nuance of 'yes' from their own language.

Although this list is far from complete, it is a good start for the Western business professional to consider whenever they are entering into a conversation with their Middle Eastern counterparts, especially if they are Arab nationals, people from the Indian subcontinent, or people from farther east in Asia.

Yes:

- I am here
- I hear you
- I hear you but I don't understand you and won't admit it
- I acknowledge I have received your request
- I recognise your status

- I'm trying to please you
- I will pass your message to someone else who may or may not do something
- It is my intention
- I will do it if nothing else happens that's more important in the meantime
- I will deliver something on time, but it might be rubbish
- I will deliver the completed report by 16.00 GMT Monday.

If you think you are in danger of misinterpreting someone's 'yes', it is generally a good idea to ask them to repeat what they understand in a manner that forces them to describe the issue in their own words. If you simply ask them if they understood you, you will simply get another unhelpful 'yes' in reply.

Other nonverbal communication clues should be noted. Is the speaker unable to look at you directly? Are they addressing someone else in your group instead of the speaker? Is their body language in opposition to their words?

If you are speaking to someone from India (but not typically Pakistan or Bangladesh), you may notice that they often respond to a comment or request by performing what can be described as a 'head waggle'. It's not quite a nod, nor is it a side to side gesture. Instead, it's closer to a wobble, and can be very confusing to others, including people of Indian origin from elsewhere in the world. The head waggle can simply be interpreted similarly to the multiple meanings of 'yes' as described above; it is unlikely to be used when delivering bad news or disagreeing with the speaker.

AVOIDING SAYING 'NO'

As much as Westerners may become frustrated with the overuse of the word 'yes', they may be equally frustrated by the lack of use of the word 'no' throughout the Middle East. The motivation for avoiding the word 'no' also needs to be explored, as Westerners may also need to learn the multiple meanings of other words and phrases that are meant to convey 'no' by other cultures.

'No' is often considered too direct a response to delivering bad or disappointing news. In this instance, saying 'no' may also be considered rude. Within the cultural context of the Middle East, it is often more important to be polite and more 'correct' and to avoid saying 'no', even if it may introduce an element of confusion to those untutored in this etiquette. The motivation to be polite is stronger than the motivation to deliver a clear message that is certain to be understood by most Westerners.

In other circumstances, 'no' is avoided so that something can remain concealed, especially if it is also a source of shame or could cause someone to lose face. In a business environment, this may include not admitting a lack of knowledge, hiding a lack of authority, becoming embarrassed by not meeting an expectation, or not being able to confront an unpleasant or incorrect assumption. Sometimes, they may have simply not understood the speaker's English.

Of course, there are many contexts where the speaker is indeed conveying a negative message, which is not spoken directly and requires contextual interpretation. They said 'no' – did you hear it?

As with 'yes', here is a list of phrases that the Western business professional may wish to consider whenever they are entering into a conversation with their Middle Eastern counterparts, especially if they are Arab nationals, people from the Indian subcontinent, or people from farther east in Asia.

No:

- Let me see
- I'll look into it
- I will try
- It seems so
- It might be difficult
- It might be a problem
- I cannot accept.

It is generally best practice to deliver bad or difficult news face-to-face wherever possible. The next best choice is by telephone. Try to avoid delivering bad news by email, although email can be used to follow-up or notate bad news initially delivered verbally.

Use of analogies and metaphors

Once your Middle Eastern counterpart becomes comfortable with you, it is possible that their communication patterns will change when delivering bad news. However, this is only possible with certain people and only then once trust has been established. If you are fortunate enough to establish a relationship that permits your counterpart to speak more directly, you will observe that they will preface negative information with a variety of phrases, including:

- Permit me to say …
- I am ashamed to say …
- Frankly speaking …
- I am sorry to say …
- Forgive me for saying …
- With respect …

It is still of utmost importance that the Western business professional remains polite at all times, even when your Middle Eastern counterpart is 'frankly speaking'. It is strongly advised that you remain formal and respectful in reaction to receiving information delivered so directly, as the speaker has undoubtedly taken a psychological and social risk in speaking with you in this manner.

These principles should also be considered when the Western business professional is in a position where they must deliver bad news, negative news, or criticise a situation. In general, the negative message should be delivered gently, surrounded by praise both before and after the main message, as if the negative message is wrapped in cotton wool. Criticism in particular should not be delivered in public, especially if singling out an individual from a group.

UNDERSTANDING SILENCE

Most Westerners are uncomfortable with prolonged silence, particularly after asking a direct question. However, silence as a communication tool is quite common throughout the Middle East. Similar to the relationship with 'yes' and 'no', silence is a communication tool for the Arab world, the Indian subcontinent, and for most of the rest of Asia.

Silence, like other high context communication techniques, can be used in a number of scenarios, and may have many meanings depending on circumstance. Again, it is the challenge of the Western business professional to try to understand the various meanings of silence when confronted with it in a business or social situation.

Most often, silence is used:

- As a negotiating tool
- To gain additional time to gain consensus amongst colleagues
- To mask a lack of authority
- To mask a lack of knowledge, especially when it's assumed or expected
- To cover language or comprehension problems
- By people who do not have sufficient status, even if they are the most knowledgeable person in the room
- To avoid saying no
- To save face
- To avoid embarrassment or shame
- To conceal shock or disapproval
- To conceal anger or reacting offensively.

Many Westerners can compound difficulties when encountering silence by trying to fill it with conversation. It is best to try to resist this temptation, especially with negotiating, as many Westerners tend to fall into the trap of making additional concessions that they may not have otherwise made. In other scenarios, it is usually better to allow your Middle Eastern colleague to break the silence; they will usually do so by changing the topic, usually to the relief of all parties.

HUMOUR, SARCASM, IRONY AND SELF-DEPRECATION

The use of humour is tricky in the best of circumstances. Even when people speak the same language, humour does not necessarily translate across cultural boundaries. One of the most obvious examples is the British use of irony, which is very likely to be completely lost on an American audience.

Irony, sarcasm and self-deprecation are all styles of humour that can easily cause misunderstandings in the Middle East. It is not unusual for people who are communicating in a language that is not their native tongue to take words and their meanings literally, at least until they know the language – and you – very well. Of course, this can cause problems when presented with an ironic or sarcastic comment. Word play is also difficult to pick up, especially if the listener is trying to translate what has been said into their language.

Self-deprecation is a more complex minefield. Telling a joke at one's own expense can be confusing in cultures that are concerned about status and saving face. If you have just poked fun at or belittled yourself, it can be very confusing to someone who is motivated to preserve their reputation at almost any cost. For example, joking about how your company managed to meet their targets in spite of your feeble contributions (as the number one sales person) may be funny to you and your colleagues. However, this may cause your Middle Eastern partners to reconsider why they are working with someone who they may see as someone who cannot be relied upon.

This does not mean that the Arab world does not have a sense of humour – far from it. The best policy is to be very careful about cracking jokes or making sarcastic comments until you know your audience very well. This includes their comprehension of English and their cultural frame of reference.

Western business professionals would do well to steer clear of religious humour altogether, even if it's the one about the Pope, the Rabbi and the Dalai

Lama and doesn't touch upon Islam. Jokes that reference gender or sex are best avoided unless you are in an all male audience and you know your colleagues very well – sometimes, it will never be appropriate, especially with a religious or very traditional Arab.

It would be foolish to make any jokes about the ruling families or other government officials anywhere in the region. Not only would this horrify your Middle Eastern colleagues; it can also be dangerous in some countries. Thus, it is strongly advised even for Westerners to avoid making jokes along the lines of why Prince Charles really talks to plants. Your Middle Eastern counterpart simply cannot imagine making a similar comment about their ruling family. It is also considered highly disrespectful in a hierarchical context.

Finally, it is important to keep in mind that your Middle Eastern colleagues come from a variety of backgrounds. Thus, even if you find a level of comfort joking around with your Arab colleagues, the same humour does not necessarily translate with your Indian colleagues. Know your audience and err on the side of caution when in doubt.

Switching to Arabic

Although Western business professionals can expect business to be conducted in English, there are times when they find the conversation has switched to Arabic (or to another language if most others present speak, for example, Tamil or Urdu). If this happens, do not automatically take offence. Sometimes, it's simply easier for people to revert to another language to discuss a topic more clearly, especially if Arabic or other vocabulary is more suitable to the issue being discussed.

On the other hand, speaking Arabic at critical moments, such as when negotiating, can be used to conceal information, especially if the speakers presume the Westerner does not understand Arabic.

It is up to each Western business professional to determine their need, desire and ability to learn at least some basic Arabic. Many Westerners find it useful, at a minimum, to understand critical negotiating vocabulary, including numbers. Others never learn any Arabic beyond the basic courtesies, yet are just as successful working in the region.

ARABIC BASICS FOR THE WESTERN BUSINESS PROFESSIONAL

Do I need to understand any Arabic?

As previously established, English is the international language of business throughout most of the Middle East, including all of the GCC countries. Attitudes towards learning Arabic vary widely amongst Western business professionals. Many Westerners start Arabic language lessons once they discover they will be working in the Middle East; others never bother. There are Westerners who have been living in the Gulf for over 30 years who still do not speak Arabic.

Arabic dialects and accents

Arabic is a Semitic language. Perhaps not surprisingly, as it is spoken across such a wide geographical area, there are dozens of Arabic dialects. From a Westerner's point of view, the most distinct Arabic dialects are Gulf Arabic, Yemeni Arabic, Iraqi Arabic, Levantine or Mediterranean Arabic and Magrhebi Arabic. The Arabic of the *Qur'an* is Classical Arabic, which is written, but would not be used in spoken form.

Spoken Arabic also has many accents. Most native Arabic speakers can quickly place where another Arabic speaker is from, or at least where they learnt their spoken Arabic.

Western business professionals should be aware that there are many dialects of Arabic spoken throughout the Middle East, the *Maghreb* and throughout Islamic learning centres world-wide. Some of these dialects vary quite a lot from each other. For example, the author once worked with a colleague in a Gulf country whose mother tongue was Arabic. He was tasked to start up a business relationship with a prospective partner in Morocco. He quickly discovered that his Moroccan counterpart, although also a native Arabic speaker, spoke a dialect of Arabic so different from his own that they agreed to speak English in spite of Arabic being both of their mother tongues.

Modern Standard Arabic

Most language schools teach a form of Arabic called Modern Standard Arabic. Arabic speakers throughout the world will understand it, although it may sound a bit too formal when spoken in certain contexts. It is roughly analogous to Modern Received Pronunciation in British English.

Basic characteristics of Arabic

Many Western business professionals find learning Arabic to be very difficult. There are many fundamental differences between Arabic, English and most European languages with the exception of Maltese, which shares some characteristics with Arabic, although Maltese uses Latin characters.

Arabic Character	Character Name	English Equivalent	
ا	'Alif	A	(like in mall)
ب	Baa'	B	(as in bravo)
ت	Taa'	T	(as in tango)
ث	Thaa'	TH	('th' as in moth)
ج	Jiim	J	(as in Juliet)
ح	Haa'	H	(as in hotel aspirated)
خ	Xaa	KH	('ch' as in loch)
د	Daal	D	(as in delta)
ذ	Thaal	DH	('th' as in mother)
ر	Raa'	R	(rolled 'r' as *rioja*)
ز	Zaay	Z	(as in Zulu)
س	Siin	S	(as in sierra)
ش	Shiin	SH	(as in shadow)
ص	Saad	S	('s' with more air)
ض	Daad	D	(as in delta)
ط	Taa'	T	('t' with more air)
ظ	Thaa'	DH	('th' with more air)
ع	'Ayn		(expulsion of air)
غ	Ghayn	GH	('j' as in *junta*)
ف	Faa'	F	(as in foxtrot)
ق	Qaaf	Q	(as in Qatar)*
ك	Kaaf	K	(as in kilo)
ل	Laam	L	(as in lima)
م	Miim	M	(as in mike)
ن	Nuun	N	(as in November)
ه	Haa'	H	(as in hotel)
و	Waaw	W	(as in whiskey)
ى	Yaa'	Y	(as in Yankee)

* between a 'g' and 'k' sound

Arabic has its own alphabet, which is written from right to left. It contains some sounds that are not used in spoken English. This makes transliteration from Arabic to English or, indeed, any Western language, a challenge and an inexact practice, as translators may choose different ways to interpret Arabic in another written language.

The Arabic alphabet

There are further challenges for Westerners when attempting to learn Arabic. Arabic letters are written differently depending on their relative position within a word. Thus, an Arabic 'b' is written differently in each occurrence in the equivalent phrase 'baby lamb'.

English Character	Character Name	Final Position	Middle Position	Initial Position	Stand Alone
B	Baa'	ـب	ـبـ	بـ	ب

Furthermore, short vowel sounds are not written in everyday Arabic. Thus, in the English equivalent, it would be difficult to distinguish between the written words for batter, better, bitter and butter. Thus, Arabic words must also be taken in context within a sentence. Finally, Arabic is a gender-based language.

Arabic numbers

For purists, Arabic numbers are the digits we use in the West today. Arabic numbers as we know them in the modern world actually originated from India. There is only one symbol for each Arabic digit. Unlike Arabic text, Arabic numbers are written from left to right, just as they are in the West.

Arabic numerals

'Arabic' Digit	Character Name	'English' Digit
٠	sifr	0
١	waahid	1
٢	itneen	2
٣	talaata	3
٤	arba'a	4
٥	khamsa	5
٦	sitta	6
٧	saba'a	7
٨	tamsniya	8
٩	tis'a	9

Useful Arabic terms

It is beyond the scope of this book to provide Arabic language lessons. However, there are Arabic words and terms that the Western business professional may find useful when doing business in the region. This is not meant to be an exhaustive list, nor is this list professionally transliterated. It also assumes you are speaking to a man. However, it should help to get you started.

Courtesies

As salaam alaikum – Formal greeting, literally 'Peace be upon you'

Wa alaikum salaam – Formal response to above

Sabah khair – Good morning

Masa khair – Good afternoon

Tisbah khair – Good evening

Ahlan wa sahlan – Welcome

Ahlan bekum – Formal response to above

Marhaba – Hello

Ma'a salaama – Goodbye

Kayf halak – How are you?

Al hamdu lillah – Fine (thanks be to God)

Aywa/Naam – Yes

La – No

Mumkin – Maybe

Tayib – OK

Shokran – Thank you

Afwan – You're welcome

Min fadlak – Please

Assif – Sorry

Common expressions

Insh'allah – If God wills it

PBUH – Peace Be Upon Him

Y ani – Er, uh, I mean

Mabrouk – Congratulations

Mish mushkila – No problem

Ma'alesh – Never mind

Bit-tawfiq – Good luck

Hallas – Finished, done

Y'aleh – Let's go

Habibi – Friend, but women should sometimes be careful with this one

Daily living

Wasta – influence

Sharia law – civil and criminal laws as interpreted by Islam

Halal – permitted

Haram – forbidden

Nargileh – water pipe (for smoking)

Sheesha – water pipe (for smoking)

Diyya – fine paid to next of kin, aka blood money

14

Getting down to business

One of the biggest frustrations voiced by Western business professionals is the difference in attitudes to time. People from the Nordic and Germanic countries of Europe as well as English-speaking countries throughout the West are generally bothered more than people from Southern Europe.

There is a different rhythm to the working day in the Middle East, even in countries that have adopted the Western-style, straight (as opposed to split) day. This is reflected in punctuality, reprioritisation, multitasking and how to communicate when faced with unexpected problems, such as extraordinary traffic delays.

PUNCTUALITY

In the Middle East, punctuality is generally much less important than it is in most of the West. Indeed, throughout much of the Middle East, the attitude may be that if a person is always punctual, they may not be very important. This is also illustrated by the way you may request an appointment with your Middle Eastern colleague. Thus, it is not unusual to be told to 'call me when you get to Bahrain', 'come by in the morning' or 'I'll be in my office after *asr*'. It is also common to receive a call from your colleague advising you that 'I'm five minutes from your hotel'. All of these may seem vague to the Westerner, but are, in fact, appointments that you can be reasonably sure will happen. Such references should be considered as the speaker's intention to be broadly available during these ranges of time; the Westerner should not take most references to quantifiable time literally.

If you do have a fixed appointment it will be expected that you arrive on time. However, you may find that nobody is there if you arrive at the meeting venue 'on time', especially as the day goes on. Your colleague's previous meetings may have taken longer than anticipated (it is much better to allow a good meeting to run beyond its time and be late for the next meeting rather than to end the meeting in order to be 'on time' for the next meeting); they may have run into a friend, colleague or family member by chance (which requires the correct etiquette – and time); there may have been a nasty problem with traffic; they may not be clear as to your intentions and are dealing with more certain business first.

In general, you will be seen in time. However, it may be quite a bit later than you thought, or it may be with someone other than the person you thought you would be meeting – sometimes a subordinate, but sometimes a superior.

Patience is of paramount importance in these circumstances. It is also advised that, if you are the type of person who is uncomfortable 'doing nothing' that you find a way to feel productive during the time you are waiting. Blackberrys and other technology provide tools to solve many of these problems. You can also expect to drink a lot of tea or other beverage whilst waiting. Be careful never to refuse this gesture of hospitality no matter how impatient you feel.

REPRIORITISATION

As with many things in the Middle East, hierarchy and status is generally taken into account when your colleague is conducting business throughout the day. If you are not a high priority, it is possible to find that the appointment you thought was for 11.00 has slipped to sometime in the afternoon. Additionally, it's possible that your 11.00 appointment becomes a dinner meeting. In the latter instance, you have probably become a very high priority for your colleague, and should clear your diary to attend this meeting regardless of other plans you may have already made.

A good strategy for the Western business professional is to remain as flexible as possible. Try not to schedule too many fixed appointments in one business day, especially if they are physically far apart and introduce commuting challenges as well. Many plans result from a successful meeting; this strategy gives you time to accommodate these found opportunities into your working day. This can easily result in needing more time in the Middle East than you initially anticipated. Thus, it is strongly recommended that the Western business professional does not commit to an inflexible airline ticket where they have no ability to change their return flight out of the Middle East.

As reprioritisation is a normal occurrence, it is pointless to try to schedule precise, fixed appointments very far in advance. Of course, this can present problems for the Western business professional who is trying to plan their business, and especially so when trying to justify the expense of a business trip when their schedule appears to be so tentative. However, unless your Middle Eastern colleague is travelling away from the region, it is reasonably safe to assume that they will see you at some point during your visit, especially if they are considering doing business with you. You just may not know exactly when.

MULTITASKING

Once you meet your Middle Eastern colleague, do not be surprised by all sorts of other activity going on around you. In particular, your colleague is pretty much guaranteed to answer his or her mobile phone no matter who is calling. People may come and go in the office, or if you are meeting in public (Starbucks-type venues in shopping malls are popular), your colleague may well hold an extended conversation with someone walking by.

Some Westerners find this style rude or chaotic. It is almost a sure bet that your Middle Eastern counterpart feels their use of time is efficient and accomplished by so much activity. On the other hand, the common view of Westerners who give their full attention to one task at a time may seem to be a highly *inefficient* by their Middle Eastern counterparts. Is there one 'right' approach to time?

TIME EXPECTATIONS OF THE WESTERN BUSINESS PROFESSIONAL

Unfortunately for the Western business professional, time is pretty much a one way street in the Middle East. Even if your colleague is not punctual, you are expected to be. Even if you have other priorities, you are expected to be available when it becomes convenient for your colleague to see you, at least within reason.

It may not seem particularly fair, but it is generally a good idea to remain as cooperative as possible in these circumstances, especially when you are still building a business relationship and trying to establish trust. Sometimes, these techniques are actually being used as a test to determine your seriousness and commitment to the region or especially to their organisation.

If you find yourself in a situation where you are going to be late, make sure you ring your Middle Eastern counterpart and advise them of your delay. Make sure you have your contact's mobile phone as it is not safe to assume a message left at an office will reach your colleague. Apologise profusely. Make sure that if you are blaming a traffic problem, there really is one, as your colleague will almost certainly be aware of it (and may be stuck in it as well).

In addition, it is possible that your Middle Eastern colleagues will make assumptions about your general availability whilst visiting the region, i.e. your time is also our time. This is common with both Arab colleagues as well as with people you may be working with from the Indian subcontinent. Western organisations may also put a greater demand on your time than you might expect of them in the West, especially in the evening, when the Middle East really comes to life.

Don't be surprised if:

- your deadlines are regarded as flexible
- you are working all hours
- you are working hours convenient to your hosts
- you are working up to the last minute when your business does become your host's top priority
- you are asked to stay in the Middle East longer than you had planned.

IDENTIFYING AND INTERACTING WITH COLLEAGUES

There is little expectation of privacy in the Middle East from both a personal and professional point of view. Since a person is not regarded individually, but as a part of a group, the need to be alone is unlikely to be understood or even considered as a normal desire.

Once the Western business professional has been invited into their Middle Eastern colleague's office, they are often surprised by the number of people who are already in the room. These people will include your colleague's staff, who may have a variety of job roles. They will be present in greater numbers than at an equivalent meeting in most of the West.

There may also be others present who do not appear to be employees, but are clearly known to your host and have an interest in meeting you. They may be personal acquaintances of your host. There may be yet others present who remain silent throughout the meeting; it may not be obvious why these people are in attendance at all. These people could be anyone from young family members effectively apprenticing, to someone who has a specific working knowledge of a Western business trait and is present in an advisory capacity. On occasion, they may simply be there for their language skills. You may never be told the reason for their presence.

In addition, there may be people present who clearly have no direct interest in your meeting. As it is not unusual for many business people in the Middle East to multitask, these people may be there for a completely different meeting even though it is being conducted at the same time as yours! For the Western business professional, this will undoubtedly take some getting used to, especially if the intent is to discuss a sensitive or confidential matter.

Regardless of which scenario you find yourself in, you are expected to crack on with your business regardless. Do not expect any real opportunity to have a one-to-one conversation in the Middle East, as they generally simply do not happen. You may also need to learn the skills of noncommittal business small talk to protect confidentiality, at least until other people present at your meeting eventually leave.

If you are holding your meeting outside an office environment, do not be surprised if you are met by an entourage of people at the coffee shop or in the reception area of your hotel. The combination of people and their purpose will be similar to the office environment.

SEATING PLAN

There are some points that should be taken into consideration when attending a business meeting in the Middle East. Firstly, your host is very likely to invite you to sit in a specific seat in the office. Generally, the position of honour is the seat immediately to the right of your host. You should continue to follow your host's lead in greeting the other people present in the room; you will be introduced in the specific order that is appropriate by age, hierarchy and status. It is also possible that you may not be introduced at all to some people. Do not force an introduction if this happens.

Your seat position can indicate the pace of the next few minutes. If you are invited into a room full of other people and are immediately seated to your host's right, you can be reasonably confident that your presence has a high priority and that the other business matter will be concluded very shortly. If on the other hand you are led to a seat away from your host, you are likely to be in for a wait until the other business matter is concluded, even if it takes quite a bit of time. In either scenario, do not be surprised if other activity is taking place, especially on mobile phones.

On a related note, when walking into a room, give priority to the right.

THE DECISION MAKER

Although someone in a relatively senior role is very likely to conduct the meeting, they are not necessarily the most powerful person in the room. That person may be someone who appears to be in authority, yet remains mostly silent or asks a very few, pointed questions.

In other instances, the real decision maker is not even present at the meeting, but someone who will make a decision from input received from your meeting who has acted as their eyes and ears. Thus, it will take another meeting or other contact before the Western business professional can expect to learn about the outcome of their initial meeting. This can be frustrating when deadlines need to be met in the West, as there is no guarantee as to when the absent person intends to address your business or make a decision.

On occasion, someone will enter an office once a meeting is in progress. This is in addition to the usual latecomers. This person is usually an older man. He is rarely acknowledged directly, and the meeting continues as if he is not there. The Western business professional should follow the host's lead and continue their business as normal. Never proactively try to force an introduction or otherwise interrupt the flow of the meeting. However, you will probably detect a change in the atmosphere of the room, where those in attendance become more formal. This is because the elderly man is most likely the true decision maker; he may the senior member in a family-run business or a sponsor in the Gulf.

In general, access to the decision maker is limited, especially in large commercial organisations and in government and military institutions. In these circumstances, the challenge for the Western business professional is to find a way to make your business the top priority within your Middle Eastern counterpart's organisation. You may need to be persistent.

STATUS

It is important to keep in mind how status and influence come into play when conducting business in the Middle East. Status may come from *wasta* more than expertise, especially in senior positions.

Senior people will have complete control of a meeting. Their agenda will be the one that is followed; it does not necessarily resemble any written agenda if there is one. If there are any diversions, they will come from the person conducting the meeting. Westerners who initiate an agenda should be prepared to use it as a guideline only; chances are excellent that your meeting will not cover all items on an agenda or will go off topic.

For example, it is not unusual for someone in a meeting to remain silent if they are not in a position of influence, even if they have the knowledge or solution for a topic being discussed. In this scenario, their expertise is not as important as recognising and behaving according to status.

For the Western business professional who needs this information, the trick is working out a way to obtain the knowledge through another channel. This is where you may need to leverage your own staff, always keeping in mind that equals prefer to work with equals. Thus, you may need to find a way to obtain this information outside the main meeting, possibly through an informal conversation between subordinates.

Although people who come from a meritocracy may be uncomfortable with this, the best recommendation is to accept this is the way business is conducted throughout the Middle East. Learn how to develop and use your own *wasta*.

How can I really get their attention?

There is no one right or wrong formula for success in the Middle East. What works in one line of business may have no relevance in another line of business and may be a disaster for a third. However, there are some general guidelines that should be considered to assist the Western business professional.

Identifying the right people

Remember that in a typical Middle Eastern business environment, the boss leads and the subordinates follow. Some leaders like to manage tasks; others will delegate to their team, but undoubtedly retain their full authority. There will be strategists and those who implement in your meeting; their roles will be clear.

In some organisations, subordinates have permission to speak, although it is expected they will do so to reaffirm their leader's opinion. Other subordinates may be given permission to speak on their topic of expertise only. Still others may remain silent regardless of their level of expertise. In general, be prepared for your team to contribute on an equals-to-equals basis.

The most talkative person is not always the decision maker. There will be no debate or argument amongst individuals on a Middle Eastern team, especially with you present. Any further requirement needed to make a decision will almost certainly be obtained and made away from your meeting. You can expect to receive a decision in a subsequent meeting; the timing depends on the complexity of the decision, their priority of wanting to do business with you, and the availability of the person ultimately in authority.

PERSONAL DIGNITY

Never underestimate the importance of preserving the status and personal dignity of your Middle Eastern counterpart. The Western business professional should avoid causing any situation where either could be compromised. Remember that perception is reality in these circumstances.

Preserving personal dignity also applies to the Western business professional when speaking about themselves. In general, it is best to avoid discussing anything in your background or personal circumstances that could diminish your status in the eyes of your Middle Eastern colleague, even inadvertently. This can include describing your chronic health issues, relationship problems, being sacked from a previous job, or discomfort with anything 'too posh'. Try to refer to yourself in a positive but modest manner wherever possible.

Praise

The Western business professional will generally receive a positive response whenever they seek to praise. This can extend to even the smallest detail, and is used to great effect throughout the region. It goes a long way to explain why it is common to hear praise about Gulf rulers' most trivial comments or activities.

Blame

Another good technique that works well is to accept liability whenever appropriate. Appearing to accept the blame for not planning well, not fully understanding something, not explaining something clearly, or even resolving a disagreement will earn the Western business professional respect. The author found it effective to claim responsibility for being too early, implying the host could not possibly be ready for her visit, even though she arrived at the agreed time.

Face

Saving face is a strong motivation throughout the Middle East, as it is throughout Asia as a whole. It is strongly recommended that the Western business professional avoids putting their colleagues in a position where they feel they could lose face, even if it's inadvertent.

In the Middle East, it is possible to lose face by:

- not living up to expectations
- not keeping a promise
- being criticised in front of others
- requesting something inappropriate to one's status.

Giving face earns respect and loyalty. Courtesy and politeness will go a long way. Accepting blame can preserve face.

Face and Westerners

The Western business professional should also be conscious of the way they portray themselves; it is possible for them to lose face as well. The most common problems for most Westerners are displaying impatience and acting in a culturally insensitive or superior manner, especially if their behaviour also has colonialist overtones.

There is another consideration for Westerners that may not be as obvious. In many Western cultures, there is a pride in achievement, especially when it involves rising from a humble background or difficult personal circumstances such as raising a child with a disability. Many Westerners are proud of these achievements and are happy to describe how they have overcome these obstacles to reach the level of success they currently enjoy.

However, if these achievements are discussed in the Middle East, the reaction may be very different, as both Arab cultures and cultures from the Indian subcontinent are motivated to hide these characteristics, as they are factors that actually reduce one's status. Thus, it is strongly recommended that these details are not discussed, thus preserving your face.

COMMUNICATION

There are times where it may seem impossible to reach your Middle Eastern colleague. Even if you have checked holidays, time zones, and your sales manager's cousin's daughter's wedding date, there are circumstances where you still struggle to the point where is seems your communication has found its way into a black hole. Again, there are no simple answers, but there are proven techniques that should help Western business professionals minimise these frustrations.

Face-to-face

In general, the best way to communicate in the Middle East is face-to-face. This is where Western ex-pats, who are in the region full time, often have an advantage over business professionals who are coming and going from their home countries.

Throughout the Middle East, the traditional way to do business has been through a person's reputation, honour and word after building a good working relationship and trust. The ability to look your business partner in the eye and interpret all sorts of other non-verbal cues also play an important role in conducting business. Thus, this suggests you need to be physically present in the region.

The situation in the modern business world has not really changed very much. The pressure to open an office or to have employees based in the region (and preferably in country) remains strong. Although there are organisations which do manage to work successfully in the Middle East remotely, they are the exception. At a minimum, they will require a local partnership acting as an intermediary on your behalf, supplemented by very frequent travel from you into the region to provide face-to-face communication. 'You can't get anything done in the Middle East if you're not there' is an accurate mantra.

Your presence makes it possible to attend meetings that are invariably set up at the last minute (I'm five minutes from your hotel). You are able to respond to an urgent need, especially when your business has become your colleague's most important priority.

There is also a major advantage to having the authority to make decisions on the ground, as decision-making is expected to be quick once your Middle Eastern partner has made their own decision. If your Middle Eastern partner then has to find you, this seriously diminishes your chances of securing business more often than you may be aware.

The Western business professional should be prepared to make decisions on the ground without further consultation back to the home office. If this level of authority is not granted by the Westerner's organisation, their Middle Eastern counterpart may come to the conclusion that the Westerner does not have sufficient status for them to do business with. Be prepared.

However, it is not always realistic to be physically present in the region, especially in the early days when your organisation is establishing itself in a new market. In these circumstances, it's probably best to advise your Middle Eastern counterpart that it is the intention of your organisation to set up local presence at a future date, once you are able to justify your business model. You can remain vague as to how long this may take, at least for a while. In the meantime, you should give serious consideration to balancing the need to travel frequently into the region – often at short notice – with the need to remain flexible upon arrival. Travel logistics should be made accordingly.

Video conferencing

In many parts of the world, video conferencing is considered to be the next best thing to being there. However, video conferencing is generally less successful in much of the Middle East. The main exceptions may be Western, multinational organisations, especially those with an established, office-based staff. Even so, the chances of a successful video-conference would only be with other employees or between offices within the same organisation.

For more traditional organisations in the Middle East, especially with an Arab or Indian business subculture, there is simply too much physical movement outside of the office to make this option viable, especially amongst the very people who are in a position of authority.

There are a couple of circumstances where video conferencing may be effective. It may have some value as an exchange of information amongst subordinates or amongst people executing previously-made decisions, but it should never be considered an alternative to face-to-face meetings for the purpose of advancing business decisions.

Video conferencing may also be a useful tool if a Western businessman is working with female Saudi staff in a traditional Saudi business environment. Although the Western businessman may not be allowed to work in close contact with his female counterparts, video conferencing is generally an acceptable alternative where there is a genuine need to communicate.

The telephone

In general, the preferred method of doing business in the Middle East, for those who cannot be there, is by using the telephone. This is consistent with the traditional way of doing business through one's word.

Land lines

The use of land lines is diminishing fast and is thus becoming much less effective than even a few years ago. This is due to the popularity of both mobile phones and the internet, which are replacing the need to ring someone for many mundane tasks.

If you are working in a very traditional, office-bound line of work, you may still be ringing someone on their land line, but even so, it's a good idea to obtain your Middle Eastern colleague's mobile phone number as well. He or she is almost certain to give it to you.

Land lines do continue to serve the purpose of facilitating a conference call, as discussed above. However, if you are not using video conferencing, it is always a good idea to have a roll call or other formal introduction when conducting business by conference call. You may be surprised to find that you thought there are six attendees, where in fact there are twenty!

It is also important to establish a good working relationship with the office manager in all offices you are likely to be working with throughout the Middle East. This person used to have the coveted role of gatekeeper to the most important people in an organisation. Although this role may be somewhat diminished with the use of mobile phones, the office manager is still more likely than most to know the movements of their senior office personnel. They are also a good resource to help you understand everything from an organisation chart to the rhythm of how their organisation conducts business.

Mobile phones

As businesses continue to embrace the latest technology, there is no doubt about the popularity of mobile phones throughout the Middle East, where every business person seems to have the latest model. Then again, everyone from your driver to your colleague's eight-year-old daughter is likely to be carrying the trendiest model as well.

In today's business environment, it is strongly recommended that you obtain any prospective business partner's mobile telephone number, even if you have no other details about them except for their name and the company they work for. People throughout the Middle East are highly likely to answer their mobile no matter what else they are doing, with the possible exception of during prayer times. As much as this might be an irritant for those Western business professionals who do not like interruptions by people answering their mobiles whilst in the middle of doing something else, it is a distinct advantage when you are the person trying to contact someone.

Your mobile phone

There is no escaping the fact that mobile phones are also a status symbol and thus reflect on your status as well. Although there is no expectation for you to carry a jewel-encrusted version of Nokia's top-of-the-range model, you should be aware of the image your mobile portrays.

There is another concern that should be seriously considered by most Western business professionals, especially those who are working for organisations that have limited or no direct presence in the region. It is an excellent idea to obtain a SIM card that gives you a local mobile number in the country you are doing business in. This gives your prospective Middle Eastern business partners another indication that you are serious about establishing a long-term relationship with businesses in the region.

Obtaining a SIM card is now easy to do with most service providers based in the region, including the once-notoriously difficult Etisalat. If you are working in more than one Gulf country, it is usually sufficient – at least initially – to obtain one mobile number for the region; most people choose a UAE number unless their focus is one of the other GCC countries. If you are working throughout the region, you may wish to add at least one other Levantine or Egyptian number to your collection of SIM cards, as this will give an even better impression that your organisation is focused beyond the Gulf.

It's up to you as to whether you intend to carry several handsets or to swap SIMs in and out of your own handset. Don't forget to include your local mobile phone number on your business cards as soon as you have established it.

Email

Although emails are popular in business throughout the world, they are used very differently in different cultures, business environments and in different positions within an organisation.

In the Middle East, emails have their place, although they should not be regarded as very important compared to either face-to-face meetings or to the telephone, especially by decision makers. Written information generally is regarded in one of two ways by decision makers in the Middle East – as detailed information that is dealt with by subordinates and thus not requiring the specific attention of a senior person, or as documentation that acts as an insurance policy in case something goes wrong.

In addition, although many Arabs may have an excellent command of spoken English, they may have a lesser standard of written English, which they most certainly do not wish to reveal to you.

Thus, it is strongly recommended that the Western business professional does not automatically use email as their main tool for communication, no matter how convenient it may be for them, even when dealing with time zone, working week or other logistical challenges.

Emails are best used to summarise what has already been discussed and agreed to. They also have their place as a method to exchange a series of detailed information, such as between two engineers or legal secretaries. It is safe to assume that, when corresponding with a senior or influential person, an office manager or other administrative person will be reading and controlling the access of your email. This may even be true if you are aware that your Middle Eastern business colleague uses a Blackberry or other 3G device with access to email.

If you are in a position where an email is required, it is important to use the formalities as to style and content that you would use if meeting someone in person. Thus, you should open with a polite greeting, using titles as well as names; do so in transliterated Arabic if you can. The main body of your email should be short and to the point. Keep language simple, with one idea per paragraph. Using bullet points and other brief summaries generally works well. Nvr use txt spk and DO NOT SHOUT. If you are delivering bad news, make sure you have done so in person or on the telephone prior to summarising it in an email. Close respectfully. Where required, follow up in person or by telephone.

COMMITMENT

Another major frustration that is felt by many Western business professionals is disappointment when your Middle Eastern colleagues do not meet your expectations. This is another part of doing business where cultural values and attitudes should be taken into account.

Throughout the Middle East, in both Arab and Indian subcultures, the employee's motivation is to execute the instructions of their boss. However, this motivation can often compete with the motivation to treat guests well, and to try to please guests as any good host would do. We have now created an environment where mixed messages and misunderstandings can easily develop.

Although there is no one formula that can be used to untangle all of the difficulties a Western business professional is likely to encounter, there are some common behavioural characteristics they should be aware of that could lead to misunderstandings.

Saying one thing …

Initially, it is not uncommon for your Middle Eastern colleague to give you reassurances that something will be done or a decision will be made by a certain time. Your colleague is almost certainly trying to please you, and probably has a genuine belief that there is a good chance that your request will be met. His or her commitment often comes with the ubiquitous *insh'allah*. '*Insh'allah*' should not be interpreted as an 'insurance policy' against failure so much as an intent that the request is meant to be addressed. However, Middle Eastern intent and Western style commitment are not always the same thing.

Sometimes, a reassurance can be overly optimistic. For example, your colleague is hoping the boss will return from a trip in time or will consider your business to be a top priority – *insh'allah* it will happen. And in many instances, it does. However, when it doesn't, the Westerner shouldn't jump to the conclusion that their colleague was intentionally misleading them. Instead, they should try to read the signs that there may be a problem in meeting a commitment before it has serious consequences.

… and doing nothing

In spite of previous reassurances that may have been given, subordinates are waiting for direction from the top. Until they receive that direction, they will not take further action. This is true even if they have already promised to deliver something by a certain deadline. This is true even if they know exactly what needs to be done. This is also true even if they are simply waiting for a signature or other formality that they know is going to happen because it has always happened the same way for the last twenty years. At the end of the day, the boss has the power and the authority; it is their job to execute, regardless of reassurances, job title, or anything else.

Although it's not always possible to change the outcome, the Western business professional would be well-served by applying listening techniques to determine whether their colleague is saying 'no' indirectly.

As frustrating as this inaction can seem to the Western business professional, it is useful to try to understand it from your Middle Eastern colleague's point of view. In effect, the motivation is simply: 'If I don't do anything, then I haven't done anything wrong.'

It is nearly a sure bet that anyone who challenges their management's authority or takes initiative beyond what has specifically been delegated to them is seen as insubordinate behaviour. And unless this employee is a Gulf national, they are running the serious risk of losing their job and their right to live in the country. These are not risks very many people are willing to take, including Western expatriates.

FATALISM

Many Westerners find it difficult to operate in an environment that lends itself to so many disappointments. They may also observe that their Middle Eastern colleagues seem not to be bothered by missing a deadline or otherwise not delivering on a commitment.

It is a good idea for the Westerner to keep in mind that there are two belief systems in play for the majority of people doing business in the Middle East that can explain such a fatalistic attitude.

In Islam, the concept of *insh'allah* is a powerful tool. Most people will literally explain a disappointment as God's will, i.e. it wasn't meant to happen because *Allah* did not wish it to happen. There is nothing a human being can do about it, so there is no point in trying to change the outcome. Thus, your deadline was never meant to be met.

In Hinduism, *karma* serves a similar purpose. Whatever was meant to be was meant to be. It's very difficult to argue with a belief system that believes in pre-destiny. Your colleague intended to meet your deadline, but it was destiny that it was never meant to be met.

15
Business and socialising

GIFT GIVING

Gift giving is an important part of doing business in the Middle East. However, it is not always compatible with Western businesses' human resources policies, especially for those Western business professionals who work for American corporations or the American government. In addition, there are a number of cultural and religious considerations that must be taken into account.

When to expect gifts

Gift giving generally occurs when a major milestone has been achieved. Examples are if you have signed a contract with a new partner, you have achieved a major sales target because of your partner's contribution, or you have opened a new office. Gift giving is also expected when a very important person is visiting the region. In the case of the Western business professional, it is likely to happen if you are travelling with a very senior executive, especially if they are coming from your corporate headquarters.

Taboos

Never give a gift that contains a pork-related product. In general, never give a gift that includes alcohol, including liqueur-filled chocolates and perfumes. Wine or spirits should never be given to anyone in public in the Middle East, even if you are in a country that permits alcohol consumption.

However, it is possible to give a gift of very high quality alcohol in private, but only if you know someone very well and it does not jeopardise their reputation. Of course, this should be done with discretion and only in a country where it is possible to obtain alcohol legally. If in doubt, leave it out.

In general, Western ex-pats will appreciate a gift of alcohol, but again, only if given in private, as their reputation can also be damaged if alcohol is given in the presence of people who object to it, especially if they report to the person with the objection. This also holds true for other non-Muslims.

When giving a gift to a Muslim, images of immodestly-dressed people should be avoided. So should gifts clearly intended for a host's spouse, such as flowers, chocolates, or anything made of silk. If giving a gift to a very religious Muslim, images of any living being should be avoided, including depictions of animals.

Gift ideas

Gifts are given to the most important people within your Middle Eastern colleagues' organisation, even if your direct dealings with them are limited. Gifts are also given to senior management and to other people who are in key positions in your line of business. Junior team members, support staff and the like do not expect gifts; in fact, it would be awkward to include them.

It is nearly impossible for the Western business professional to 'out bling' their Middle Eastern colleagues, especially those from the GCC. There is simply no point in going down this path.

Instead, try to give a gift that is something thoughtful from your home country. Pottery, glassware and high-quality diaries that include national holidays are all good ideas. Find out if your colleagues support a football team in your home country – you'll be surprised how popular Manchester United memorabilia is in the region. So are cricket-related items for many colleagues, especially from the Indian subcontinent.

Gift ideas that have a direct business-related theme include pens, memory sticks, laptop bags and anything else that is practical and can be produced with your company logo. Take care to ensure that these items are produced with the highest appearance of quality in mind. For example, you can gold plate the memory stick (in this instance, the appearance of 'gold' is OK as a memory stick would not be worn by a man).

Etiquette

Never refuse a gift, no matter how inappropriate it may seem at the time. This would be a major insult and would probably cause irreparable harm to your business relationship. The exception to this rule is a gift of cash, which is not a gift at all, but a problem.

All gifts should be accepted graciously. Make sure you remember your manners and thank your host. Always accept a gift with the right hand or with both hands; this is another instance where the left hand is taboo. Gifts are opened in private throughout the Middle East.

Caution

If you think you are in violation of your company's policy, accept the gift and report it to your manager or HR as soon as possible.

BUSINESS DINNERS

Receiving an invitation

Business dinners are often elaborate affairs. If you have received an invitation from an Arab host, you are most likely to be invited to a Lebanese restaurant or to a restaurant in a prestigious hotel. The choice of restaurant will be one where the host is known to the proprietor, where excellent service can be relied upon.

Gulf Arabs will not invite their spouses to business dinners. You should not expect to receive an invitation for your partner in these circumstances, even if they are travelling with you.

However, Western businesswomen will receive an invitation to a business dinner – another instance of becoming an honorary man. There may be the need to dine in the family section of a Saudi restaurant, although the author has personally experienced a situation where her Saudi host used his *wasta* with the restaurateur to organise a table in the main restaurant where she joined the rest of the party in spite of her gender.

Levantine Arabs may or may not include their spouses; if this is the case, you will be made aware of this in advance. If you are travelling with your partner, they will receive an invitation to the business dinner as well. Your partner should accept the invitation regardless of any previous plans they may have made.

Be prepared for an all-evening affair, as business dinners will take several hours. Be prepared to eat late in the evening, especially in Egypt, where many restaurants do not even open until 23.00 or so.

Accepting an invitation

Try not to refuse invitations to business dinners, as they are great opportunities to establish a stronger relationship with your Middle Eastern colleagues and to build trust. This includes many of the usual challenges that the Western Road Warrior may routinely encounter on any business trip. Invalid excuses for refusing an invitation include:

- You have been out to dinner every evening since your arrival in the region
- You are on a diet
- You don't like Middle Eastern cuisine
- You need to catch up on emails, phone calls, etc.
- You need to prepare for tomorrow's meetings.

There are a very few circumstances where you may be excused from accepting an invitation to dinner. Valid excuses include:

- You must fly out of the Middle East or to another city that evening (and you do so) but be careful not to leave the impression that another customer or business partner is more important than the person who extended the dinner invitation
- You must be present on a long conference call as directed by someone of higher status than you.

It is strongly recommended that you use these excuses infrequently. If you do decide to use an excuse to avoid a business dinner, never get caught.

You should generally be able to plan your movements and advise your host in advance (or extend your stay as required). If you decide to use the conference call excuse, try not to use it often or you will compromise your authority. You should also be cognisant of time zones, etc. so your excuse is a plausible one.

If you accept an invitation to a business dinner, you must stay for the entire meal, as leaving early would be considered the height of rudeness.

Dining etiquette

When arriving at the restaurant, greet your host first, then everyone else present in order of hierarchy and age. Your host will undoubtedly have a seating arrangement in mind, with the guest of honour usually sitting to the host's right, as in the office environment. Follow your host's lead and wait to be seated.

Your meal will often be an extensive buffet. If not, your host will almost certainly order the meal for all of his or her guests. This will include a series of starters called *mezze*, which will be a combination of vegetarian and non-vegetarian dishes. They will be followed by several main courses, which will be a combination of lamb, chicken and, often, whole fish.

Never eat with your left hand, especially if you are eating something with your hand. Never pass any food with your left hand, including a bread basket or condiment. Although it is OK to use cutlery with your left hand, never serve yourself from a communal plate with your left hand. You should also refrain from using your left hand when drinking from a glass or cup. When using cutlery, 'continental manners' (using both the knife and the fork at all times) is the correct etiquette.

You will probably feel as though there is enough food at the table to feed a small army; this is a sign of a generous host and should never be criticised, even though it appears that a lot of food could be going to waste (it won't be).

Never refuse offerings of food and drink that have been specifically suggested by your host, as to do so would be considered an insult. You should always try something, no matter what your personal preferences are. In spite of rumours of food 'challenges' such as sheep eyeballs, the Western business professional can expect fewer unusual dishes than on many menus in France (or the variety of offal routinely found in the UK).

Be very careful about announcing Western-style food allergies, as somehow they don't seem to exist in the Middle East! If you do have a genuine food allergy, use your common sense. Try to eat the smallest amount possible if it is just a discomfort (the author cannot tolerate most dairy products, yet will take one bite of cheese-based products just to be polite). Of course, food allergies that could trigger an instant trip to the doctor are another matter altogether.

Vegetarians will be understood throughout most of the Middle East, even if vegetarianism is often considered to be an odd choice for a Westerner, as it is most often associated with Hinduism. Traditional Arab cuisine includes a lot of vegetarian options in *mezze*. Options are more limited in main courses, although those who eat fish will be catered for.

You will be expected to take second helpings of at least some of the main course – be prepared! Never leave a lot of food on your plate, as this is a signal that you did not like the food. Never leave a clean plate, as this is a signal that you are still hungry and that your host did not do a good job. Instead, when you are finished eating, you should simply leave 'one bite' on your plate.

Business dinners will be concluded with sweets and coffee. Once coffee is served, you should accept one cup and drink it. Do not ask for a refill. Once the guests have finished their coffee, the meal is over. People will leave very quickly at this point, as it is not customary to stay back for any further small talk.

Taboos

Do not expect to be offered pork when dining with Arab colleagues in the Middle East. There will be no pork on the menu at Lebanese restaurants or any other traditional Middle Eastern restaurants. Nor will there be pork on the menu in any Indian restaurants even if they serve other meat.

If you are invited to a restaurant where pork products are on offer, such as in a restaurant in a hotel, do not order them unless you are only dining with other Westerners.

Alcohol is a much trickier matter, especially if you are the guest of an Arab national in a hotel that serves alcohol. The best advice is twofold; when in doubt, leave it out; however, if your host accepts an alcoholic beverage, follow their lead.

In reality, you are most likely to be dining with a large group of colleagues from a number of cultural and religious backgrounds. In this case, it is most important not to offend your host, but you should also take your fellow diners into account.

If your host does not approve of alcohol, your business dinner will be completely alcohol free.

Other hosts may not drink alcohol themselves, but do not mind if others do. In this instance, follow your host's subordinates' lead. If they drink, then you could order a pre-dinner drink. Wine may be served with the meal; if so, it's OK to have one or two glasses. But keep the quantity very modest.

If your host chooses to drink alcohol, then it is strongly advised that you do so as well, even if you don't particularly wish to. In these circumstances, it is strongly advised that you do not exceed the quantity of alcohol consumed by your host. Keep in mind that there will probably be a mix of drinkers and non-drinkers in this scenario. However, as a Westerner, it will be assumed that you will join in with the host.

Do not be surprised if some of the host's subordinates drink alcohol at times when the host is not present. Others may choose not to drink in a public setting, such as a hotel lobby, but may do so in a private function room of a restaurant or at someone's home.

One final word of caution. Throughout the Gulf countries, it is technically illegal for Muslims to consume alcohol anywhere, including in licensed restaurants and other licensed venues. However, these restrictions have been typically ignored in recent years. Whilst the author has no reason to believe this will change in the near future, these decisions are ultimately made unilaterally by the powers that be in each country.

Paying the bill

Don't ever offer to pay the bill as a guest, as this would be considered a direct insult to your Arab host. This also applies to hosts from the Indian subcontinent. Western ex-pats will practise this convention as well. In short, as a guest, do not expect – or even pretend to try – to pay the bill for a business dinner anywhere in the Middle East.

Hosting a dinner

Western business professionals who are not resident in the Middle East will invariably be considered guests. This severely limits their opportunity to host a business dinner. In general, it is better to leave this to your Middle Eastern colleagues. You should instead reciprocate with an elaborate dinner when your colleagues visit you in your home country.

Business dinners with Indian colleagues in the Middle East

Much of the same etiquette applies with both Arab hosts and hosts from the Indian subcontinent. The main differences are that you may be dining with an Indian host's extended family, especially in a family-run business. In some circumstances, this could include granny, the baby and your host's 15-year-old, bored nephew.

Taboos are dependent on your host's religion. Hindus don't eat beef and are often vegetarian. Pork remains unacceptable for most Indians in the Middle East for practical as well as possible religious reasons. On the other hand, they may drink alcohol, at least once the female members of the family and children depart the scene.

You can expect a selection of freshly-squeezed juices prior to the start of your meal. Indian meals generally do not include beverages during the meal; water is usually served once the food is finished. You may need to ask for water if you don't think you can manage to get through the meal without it.

You may be expected to eat with your hand, especially in very traditional restaurants. You will undoubtedly be eating a specific regional Indian cuisine that reflects your host's preference, usually their region of origin in India or Pakistan. Unless you have spent time working in India or Pakistan, this cuisine may be completely unfamiliar to the Western business professional, even to those who think they are well acquainted with curry.

OTHER ENTERTAINMENT

Although you will most often be invited to a business dinner, you may also receive an invitation for other functions.

Traditional entertainment

Western business professionals may be invited to join their Arab colleagues on a trip to the desert, especially in Saudi Arabia. Whilst there are tourist-style desert adventures available in Dubai and some other Gulf countries, invitations to the most authentic desert trips will be extended by Saudis. They will invariably be a male-only event.

Although not a common practice, it is possible you may be invited to a horse or camel race. Additional consideration should be given to camel racing, in particular, where there is ongoing controversy as to the suitability of the camel jockeys, who are often very small boys from the Indian subcontinent. Many of these boys may not be in the country of their own free will and may have little to no say in their role in this sport.

Western business professionals who express an interest in falconry may be rewarded with an invitation to this activity once you get to know your Arab colleague very well.

Western influenced entertainment

European-style fine arts are another option in the Levant, with concerts and festivals on the agenda, especially in Lebanon. Jordan and Egypt have an increasing range of events throughout the year. Syria is taking tentative steps in this direction as well. These events are currently in short supply in the GCC, although there will be a growing range of cultural events as various countries continue to expand their fine arts portfolio.

Live concerts by Western musicians remain relatively rare, although they occasionally find their way to Dubai or Abu Dhabi. These shows are invariably popular with the Western ex-pat communities throughout the Gulf.

Of course, if you are working with a number of Western ex-pats, you can expect to receive invitations to Western-orientated events, similar to those you would receive back home. This can include bars and nightclubs, golf and other sport. If you go to a bar or nightclub that advertises live music, chances are very high that the entertainment will be provided by a Filipino band singing cover versions of familiar Western pop songs.

Do not be surprised if you are working with a subset of Arab colleagues who are also interested in going out to bars and nightclubs – you may be exactly the excuse they need, although more and more Gulf nationals, in particular, are entering licensed establishments of their own accord, often in full national dress. This is usually suggested after a business dinner has finished. In general, the same rules apply about accepting these invitations, regardless of your own desire to attend. If your party includes people from Iran, Kuwait or Saudi Arabia in particular, you may be in for a long night.

Arabs from the Levant have much more access to bars and nightclubs in their home countries; as a result, their attitude to them is not unlike that of Westerners.

Other ethnic entertainment

For those Western business professionals who work with people from the Indian subcontinent, there may be opportunities to experience live Indian music, especially in Dubai and Oman. Do not be surprised if you are accompanied by your colleagues' families in certain circumstances.

AN INVITATION TO SOMEONE'S HOME IN THE MIDDLE EAST

In general, invitations to an Arab's home are earned. They will typically be extended only after a good relationship and trust has been established. They should be considered an honour by the Western business professional and should always be accepted.

Even so, it is quite rare to receive an invitation to an Arab national's home in parts of the Gulf, especially in the UAE and Qatar. It is slightly more likely in Bahrain, Kuwait and Oman. Women are almost never invited to a Saudi's home in most normal business circumstances. Invitations to an Arab's home in the Levant are more common, and are somewhat dependent on the background and religion of the family. Levantine Christians often extend invitations to their homes, for example.

It is unlikely that you will receive an invitation to an Indian colleague's home. Invitations to a Western ex-pat's home are quite common.

Inside a traditional Middle Eastern home

You will be invited into a room that is used to receive male guests. Western businesswomen are likely to be invited into this room too, again in her role as an honorary male. Do not expect to be invited to other areas of a Gulf Arab's home, especially further to the centre of the property, as this is the part of the home where women and girls will be located, although Western businesswomen may be at an advantage in this situation. You are much more likely to meet the entire family in a Levantine home, including female members of the family and children, who are invariably on their best behaviour.

Etiquette

Never bring a gift to an Arab's home that could even remotely appear to be for a woman only.

The safest gift to bring when accepting an invitation to an Arab's home is Lebanese sweets. Ask colleagues or your hotel concierge where to find a high quality Lebanese sweet shop near to your hotel or near your guest's home if you are arriving in your own transport and it's very hot outside. Lebanese sweet shops can be found everywhere throughout the Middle East.

Make sure you bring more than enough sweets for everyone to enjoy; they are ordered by the kilogram! If you are unsure of what items to include, ask someone working in the shop as they will certainly help you. It's also a great chance for you to sample some yourself, as most shops will be very accommodating. You should make sure the sweets are packed in a gift box, which will also be provided by the shop.

Present your gift as soon as you arrive. They may be served later in the evening.

As in a restaurant, greet your host first, followed by others present in order of hierarchy. If you don't know everyone present, then err on the side of caution by greeting elders before younger people.

It will be expected that you remove your shoes when entering traditional Arab homes, although this may not be necessary in some homes in the Levant. Be careful not to show the soles of your feet, even if it is difficult if sitting on a low cushion or sofa.

Always accept a drink, dates, sweets and other courtesies prior to the main meal. Expect the meal to be served after a period of small talk. The meal may be served by staff, or it may be buffet-style. Your host will ensure that you receive the best morsels of the meal. Always accept this courtesy with graciousness. Expect to eat at least one refill of the main course – it's always best to pace yourself so you do not become full too quickly. As in a restaurant, it is polite to leave one bite to signal that you are finished.

Finally, do not admire anything in the house too enthusiastically, as your host may feel an obligation to offer it to you!

HOSTING ARABS IN THE WEST

At some point, most Western business professionals can expect to host their

Middle Eastern colleagues in their offices in the West. This is generally a good sign, as the business relationship is getting serious. However, visits can be a very dangerous time if the Westerner's office and colleagues are not prepared to recognise some potentially very different expectations. Without preparation, cultural misunderstandings could seriously damage your Middle Eastern partner's trust in doing business with your organisation.

The 'minder'

Ideally, Western organisations should consider assigning an employee to look after the Middle Eastern guest's needs. This person should be the one the guest can turn to for assistance and advice throughout their visit.

The 'minder' would most often be a junior member of staff who is perceived to be up and coming within the organisation – they may eventually work in the Middle East themselves. Of course, the minder should have some working knowledge of the Middle East and should be comfortable in the company of their guests. Employees from an administrative or human resources position are usually not a good fit, as they will most often be seen by the guest as of insufficient status or are an unlikely person with whom to build an ongoing business relationship.

The minder should be prepared to deal with the guest's travel-related needs, acting as a link with drivers, hotel staff and the airlines if the guest needs logistical assistance. The minder is also responsible for ensuring the guest gets from the hotel to the office or other meeting venue. The minder should also be in a position to assist with local knowledge, advising on shopping and other leisure activities.

Upon arrival

Business trips to the West may be of any duration. However, in many lines of business, it is most likely that your Middle Eastern guest will visit for approximately one business week. They may or may not spend all of this time with you as they may have other business or other interests in your country as well.

Many guests from the Middle East will arrive in the West on a Sunday, as it is likely to be their first working day of their week. They are most likely to depart on a Friday, although many may leave on Thursday as well if they wish to be home for their weekend.

Most Middle Eastern colleagues will appreciate and, in fact, expect a 'meet and greet' service upon arrival at the airport, as this is the norm for visitors of any significant status throughout the Middle East. The minder should ensure their personal presence at the arrivals hall of the airport to facilitate the guest's visit from this point forward. In fact, many people from the Middle East may consider it an insult if they are not personally met at the airport, especially if visiting your organisation is the main purpose of their visit.

Ground transport should be organised by the Western organisation by providing a high-status car and well-dressed driver; taxis are not usually seen as of sufficient status. In general, the minder should not personally drive the guest from the airport as this would be regarded as a diminishment of their status. However, in some provincial cities in the US, Canada, Australia and New Zealand, they may have little choice but to provide this service as well.

Hotels and other accommodation

Hotel status is important in the Middle East; it is considered equally important for your Middle Eastern colleague when staying in the West as well. In general, most Middle Eastern guests are likely to favour five star standard, internationally-recognised brand name hotels from the West or in some instances the prestigious properties of the Far East or the Indian subcontinent. As more Western hotels have an affiliation with elite Middle Eastern brands (such as the Jumeirah Group), these options may be viable as well.

Less popular are boutique hotels or properties that advertise their historical or themed appeal unless they are of a five star standard. Even so, the Middle Eastern guest should be made aware of the precise nature of the property prior to booking, as some quirks may not appeal. Hotels that advertise their self-catering facilities or other long-stay advantages are generally unsuitable, even if they are popular with Western business professionals.

Hotels should be suitably staffed to provide a full suite of services expected of a five star property. Ideally, this should include European-style concierge services as opposed to the North American-style 'concierge floors'.

Although the practice is much less prevalent than as recently as ten years ago, there may be an expectation from your Middle Eastern guest that your organisation will pay their hotel bill. If this is the case and your organisation agrees to this arrangement, it is important to define exactly which services will be covered. Usually, organisations will fund business-standard room costs, taxes, meals and reasonable room service charges. An understanding should be reached well in advance if the guest expects an elaborate suite or similar accommodation, or if they are travelling with a family entourage and thus require several rooms.

Sensitive issues should also be dealt with prior to the guest's arrival. Beverage charges should also be negotiated if your organisation's hospitality does not extend potentially to Dom Pérignon or a wine selection from the hotel's exclusive cellar. Care should also be given as to whether an organisation also wishes to fund the possibility of an extravaganza of adult movies, consumption of the entire contents of the mini bar, the possibility of the acquisition of outside entertainment services, or any other surprises. For other guests, it is prudent to have the alcoholic contents of the mini bar removed from the guest's room.

In the office

A few considerations should be given to the Western offices prior to the arrival or your Middle Eastern guest. An official greeting in your office reception area will often be appreciated if the nature of your business is not security-related. However, it is imperative that you get the hierarchy correct as well as the spelling of the names of all guests. Make sure all employees who are likely to come into contact with your guest know how to pronounce their names.

The minder or other intermediary should check prayer requirements well in advance of the visit. If observant Muslims are visiting, check the prayer times for your city and provide this information to your guests. Schedule meetings accordingly. If your office does not already have a prayer room, provide a clean, private, quiet place where your guest can retreat to pray.

Always keep in mind that pork products should never be offered to your Middle Eastern colleague, including during tea breaks. If lunch is being catered, ensure that there are no pork-based ingredients used in food preparation or alcohol used in cooking.

Dealing with the pub

If your office typically patronises your local pub at lunch or after work, care must be taken as to whether this venue is appropriate for your Middle Eastern guest. As is ever the case surrounding the presence of alcohol, some guests would be offended, others will remain teetotal but will not be bothered in the presence of alcohol, and others will enthusiastically join in. This is another job for the minder if you do not already know your guest's disposition.

In the evening

Although business dinners can be an excellent way to host your Middle Eastern guest, they are not always welcome. It is generally a good idea to approach your guest by asking if they already have plans for the evening or, indeed, for the week prior to making any plans with your organisation.

Many people from the Middle East prefer to leverage their considerable connections in the West whilst travelling on business. This may include visiting friends and relatives living in your country. They may have attended school or university in the West and wish to catch up with classmates and other connections established from this time in their lives. They may wish to have some private time to go shopping or to visit the tourist attractions of your city, although in this instance, the minder should provide assistance where required. Finally, they may wish to pursue outside activities that may not be acceptable back home and wish for total privacy in order to preserve their reputation.

PERSONAL RELATIONSHIPS IN THE MIDDLE EAST

Although the main intent of this book is to cover business related matters, there is a chance that some Western business professionals may be considering the possibility of entering into a personal relationship with a Middle Eastern national.

Whilst it is not the intention of the author to judge the motivation of anyone who may explore these options, the Western business professional should consider the following realities before taking the plunge.

Western women and Middle Eastern men

Whilst it may be tempting for some women to establish a personal, social relationship with a Middle Eastern national, she should make her decision only after careful consideration. Risks include:

- loss of respect and honour by Middle Eastern colleagues if the relationship is discovered
- loss of status as an honorary man in a business environment
- fuelling the stereotype of Western women's loose morals
- falling foul of local laws regarding unmarried sexual relations with a man.

Having considered the above points, many Western women can and do enjoy a personal relationship with an Arab man, including platonic as well as discrete, intimate arrangements. However, she should also keep in mind that the Gulf, in particular, operates like a small village; it is nearly guaranteed that her discrete relationship is not as much of a secret as she may think.

Should a Western woman's personal relationship progress to a more committed status, it is strongly suggested that she fully researches her legal position before marrying an Arab national, especially as regards her personal rights and those of any future children. For example, although a Muslim man can legally marry a Christian or Jewish woman whether or not she converts to Islam, their children will be regarded as Muslim. She may need the permission of her husband to travel freely outside of her adopted country, even if she is married to an Arab Christian. If the marriage breaks down, it is highly likely that the man will have full, unilateral custody of their children.

Several other social restrictions apply to everyday life. The Western woman should ensure that she is fully informed before making a final commitment. Her original nationality will not protect her after marriage, in most circumstances, if resident in the Middle East as a married woamn.

Western men and Middle Eastern women

Western men have vastly greater challenges and run much greater risks as regards establishing a personal relationship with an Arab national woman.

Firstly, his chance of meeting and spending time alone with a Gulf national woman is remote at best and nearly impossible in Saudi Arabia. He may have a better opportunity to get to know a Levantine woman, especially if she is an ex-pat herself. Similar opportunities exist to meet an Iranian woman.

Although Middle Eastern men will generally recognise and possibly bond with a Western man's general interest in sexual relations with women, they will most certainly *not* appreciate your interest in a Middle Eastern woman. Thus, the Western man's risks are actually greater than those of Western women, including:

- losing the respect of your Middle Eastern business colleagues
- falling foul of local laws regarding unmarried sexual relations with a woman
- deportation if discovered by the authorities
- being banned from re-entering the Middle Eastern country where the relationship took place if the relationship was with a host national woman
- bringing dishonour to the woman's entire family
- potentially putting the woman's life in danger if her family believes in revenge for honour.

For those few Western men who manage to establish a personal relationship with an Arab woman, they should also keep in mind that the relationship may be more of an open secret than desired.

Should a Western man's personal relationship progress to a more committed status, it is also strongly suggested that he fully researches his legal position before marrying an Arab or Iranian national. If the woman is Muslim, he will be expected to convert to Islam before marriage. Although he may be welcomed into the woman's family, he will always be regarded as an outsider, and may not enjoy the same relative status as the other men in the family.

Homosexual relationships

Although Western men may have the opportunity to establish a homosexual relationship with an unmarried Middle Eastern man, it should be remembered that there will almost certainly be pressure on the man from his family to marry and live an outwardly heterosexual lifestyle. It would not be unusual for the man's family to deny that he is gay or in some instances to even acknowledge that gay men exist in the Middle East.

Married men in the Middle East may also seek a homosexual relationship outside marriage; it would be unwise for the Western male partner to think there is any realistic chance of divorce in this situation.

Due to the illegality of homosexual activity throughout the Middle East as well as strong social taboos, Western business professionals should do their utmost to keep any relationship under the radar, especially if it involves an Arab national.

Western women will find the opportunity to establish a lesbian relationship with a Middle Eastern national to be more difficult as her chances of meeting a willing woman will be much less than for a gay male relationship. However, if she does establish a lesbian relationship with an Arab woman, it is much more likely that it is assumed to be a close, platonic friendship and thus 'safe'.

16

Getting results

There is no one formula for success in the Middle East. Different lines of business may be looking for different criteria to fulfil their goals and objectives for anything from choosing a strategic partner to setting profitability targets.

However, there are recognised practices that the Western business professional may wish to keep in mind, that often make the difference between a successful outcome and frustration.

PRESENTATIONS

Whilst it is unlikely that the Western business professional will be able to avoid giving presentations whilst working in the Middle East, they should not be the main technique relied upon to advance business in the region. In general, presentations should only be given once a relationship is on the way to being established between your organisation and your prospective business partner.

Planning

When planning a presentation, remember that you are unlikely to start at the time you requested. People may try to arrive at the venue at the time published, but they will invariably socialise for a period of time before expecting to get down to business. Other invitees simply won't plan to attend, but may be reluctant to tell you so. It's generally a good idea to ring around just before the event to remind – and sometimes reprioritise – your audience. Try to schedule presentations well away from prayer times. In general, expect to start your presentation up to 30 minutes after the officially scheduled time, or once everyone has greeted their colleagues and has had a cup of coffee or tea. Make sure you provide elaborate snacks or a buffet with soft drinks, depending on the time of day.

Don't be surprised if people continue to arrive and leave in the midst of your presentation. It's simply best to continue without acknowledgement. This may include the most important person attending your presentation. Other activities that you can expect during your presentation are mobile phones ringing, people conducting an entire conversation on their mobile without leaving their chair, and people chatting about totally unrelated matters, especially those sitting further away from the presenter, and the occasional attendee who finds your presentation the perfect time to catch up on their sleep.

Style

Your presentation style should be carefully considered, especially if you are conducting business with a mostly Arab audience. For example, they are much less interested in your organisation's humble origins, the history of its founder, presence elsewhere in the world, forecasts, future promises or market share. They most certainly do not care how much your shareholders earned on last year's profits. Emphasising your organisation's pedigree, stability and family values instead is a better idea.

In general, most Arabs will respond best to a presentation that highlights the strengths and advantages of your product or service – to them. However, avoid directly telling them what they want or why they want it from you. Products and services that represent high quality, value and status will generally get attention.

During your presentation, the speaker should be well groomed, have an air of authority, and ideally be a charismatic speaker who appears comfortable with their audience. The speaker should also have an excellent command of the English language with an easy-to-understand accent regardless of their country or region of origin. Always thank the audience for their attendance when opening your presentation; it is also a good idea to compliment the Middle Eastern organisation's hospitality or something about the host country in general. Speakers should strive for as much eye contact with key members of their audience wherever possible.

There will be an expectation that the presenter is an expert in his or her topic of conversation; make sure the speaker is well prepared in this regard. Do not rely on speaker's notes or other tools that may be perceived as 'crutches' to your audience. In a region that relies on both oral tradition and rote memorisation throughout their formal education, the Western business professional should also be seen as capable of telling their 'story' through the force of their personality as well. However, vast technical detail can be given by an expert or provided elsewhere, especially when addressing a group of relatively senior people, who will undoubtedly delegate this task to more junior staff.

If you are presenting to an audience that comprises predominately executives from the Indian subcontinent, many of the same tips will apply. However, the Western business professional may also encounter some differences in these environments. In the main, they may be called upon to provide much more detail about their product or service than with an Arab audience. The presenter must be prepared to provide this information, generally within the context of the presentation. Be prepared. Secondly, this audience is likely to be much more price-sensitive than their Arab counterparts. Thus, it is usually important to emphasise value for money as well as the quality of your product or service.

Western business professionals who are working with large multinationals with a large number of Western expatriate employees can expect to deliver a presentation in a more Western style. However, it is still important to keep in mind that these multinationals are also working in an Arab environment. Thus, they may still be sensitive to many of the factors discussed above. Know your audience as quickly as you can to determine the correct presentation style for these Western organisations.

After the presentation

Don't be surprised if you don't get immediate feedback once you have finished your presentation. The audience will invariably need to discuss what they have heard before coming to any conclusion. They may also need to inform senior management in their organisation about the presentation if they were not in attendance and await instruction from the decision maker before progressing further.

Never push for a reaction at this time. It is also strongly advised that the Western business professional does not set any specific time constraints for a reply, even if they are facing internal deadlines such as end of quarter or a planned visit to the region from a corporate VIP. Nor is your imminent departure from the region at the end of your business trip a motivator, as your Middle Eastern colleague will expect you to return frequently if you are serious about establishing business in the region.

TRAINING

Planning

Planning a formal training session is similar to planning a presentation, especially as regards time. However, as some training sessions last longer than a typical presentation, additional considerations should be made. A prayer room should be provided. Try to schedule the training so a break is made during this time. If training will continue through lunch, it is imperative that the meal is catered so that all religions can find something suitable to eat. Buffets tend to work well; all food should be identified as to its ingredients.

Style

A similar style works with training as it does with presentations. However, the trainer should keep in mind that both Arab audiences and audiences from the Indian subcontinent are highly reluctant to be singled out in a large, public group. Thus, the trainer would do well to avoid calling on the audience to answer a question as an attempt to engage the audience. This will avoid the possibility of losing face, boasting or other individualistic behaviours that can make both groups uncomfortable in an open forum. Role play and similar techniques do not usually go down well as they can compromise the status and personal dignity of the attendees, although some group activities are possible. In short, do not design your training session to be interactive.

If it is at all practical, it is a good idea to have samples at the training session so the audience can touch and feel your product. However, if you do so, make sure it is either a working product or it is clearly labelled as a non-working sample that has the same quality, look and feel as the finished product. Prototypes do not generally go down well. Other tokens and handouts are also a good idea, including good quality brochures, key rings and the like.

After the session is over

Although it would be unusual for a member of the audience to ask a question of the trainer in an open forum, that doesn't mean the audience has no questions. In fact, they may have quite a few.

It is an excellent idea for the trainer to linger long after the training session is over. This will allow members of the audience time to organise their thoughts and work out how to approach the trainer once the official session has ended. It would not be unusual for a group of attendees to gather together and casually nominate someone to approach the trainer to ask all of the group's questions. If this is the case, usually the group leader will approach the trainer, followed at a distance by the others, who will invariably come closer to listen once the conversation has started.

One way to make it easier for the audience to approach you is to invite them to come and take your business card for their collection. Make sure you offer your business cards on a stand or other holder that gives your audience the excuse to approach you. Sweets can serve the same purpose of enticing the audience to your podium, panel or desk.

NEGOTIATION

By the time Middle Eastern businessmen (and women) had established the frankincense and incense routes of the Third Century BC, they already had 3000 years of negotiating experience. It is safe to assume that on average, your Middle Eastern counterpart will consider complex negotiations as part of the natural rhythm of doing business. As a Western business professional, you may not have the same level of comfort, especially if you hail from Northern or Western Europe or North America.

In general, expect negotiations to be a main part of the process of any significant business practice. Even many very trivial transactions are not considered a good deal unless negotiated, such as a request for 'an extra sweet for my son' in a shop or *souq*.

Bargaining

There will be an expectation that an initial business proposal or offer will be drawn up with significant room for bargaining, both for price and for more favourable terms and conditions. Western business people who are used to supplying pricing and/or terms and conditions that are nearly at their bottom line will need to rethink their entire strategy. Failure to leave room for bargaining will either leave the impression that they are too inflexible, are not showing enough recognition of the business relationship, are not serious about doing any business at all with their Middle Eastern colleague, or are exhibiting an appalling lack of knowledge about how business is conducted in the region.

During the negotiation process, it is important to keep a sense of control, honour and integrity. Your Middle Eastern partner is quite likely to use emotion when bargaining, focusing much more on the business relationship than simply on price, although price should never be considered unimportant.

It would not be unusual for your Middle Eastern partner to express his or her desire to 'touch and smell' the proposal on offer, as they may be relying heavily on their intuition to reach a decision more than on the facts alone.

As a Westerner, you should always strive to show patience, courtesy, and deference to authority, even if your counterpart does not always follow these practices.

Negotiations can be drawn out and time consuming, especially if someone in the chain of command is not available or has other priorities. The Westerner's need to close a deal in time to receive revenue recognition at the end of the financial quarter will generally be of little or no consequence for your Middle Eastern counterpart.

During the negotiation process, never forget what has been said in the lead-up to presenting your proposal, as your word is often more important than what is simply written in the document. A stray comment or casual promise, even one that was made months ago or only in passing will almost certainly be remembered and reintroduced during the negotiations.

In general, your Middle Eastern counterparts are in a more favourable position to draw on their usually excellent memories, which have been developed through the traditions of story telling as a way of recounting history as well as through memorisation of the entire *Qur'an*. Again, most traditional teaching methods throughout the Middle East and the Indian subcontinent reward rote memorisation of a vast amount of information. This is where the Westerner's memory is unlikely to be in the same league unless they were diligent in taking notes along the way (which is actually frowned upon, as it can look like compensation for a poor memory). Of course, during negotiations, your Middle Eastern counterpart may also be very good at recalling their memory selectively.

In the Middle East, it is not unusual to go through a series of negotiations at many levels within their organisational hierarchy. Thus, each level of management can be seen to have negotiated a good deal within their level of authority. This can present quite a challenge for the Westerner, who will be expected to concede something in the deal during each of these steps. Again, it is important to consider terms and conditions at least as much as price. The quality, status and prestige of the Westerner's goods or services should also be emphasised; ideally, a selection of quality levels should be offered in any major deal.

Make sure you know who the real decision maker is, as you will want to make sure you have held something back for them as well. The real decision maker may only reveal themselves at the end of the negotiation.

Women and negotiation

Women will be in a position to negotiate commensurate with their job title; their gender is generally not an issue with their Middle Eastern counterparts by this stage in their professional relationship. Again, to avoid any doubt, Western women should make it clear from the onset of negotiations that they are in a position of authority to execute any agreement reached on behalf of their organisation. Receiving the backing of their Western colleagues should dispel any residual concerns.

MARKETING CAMPAIGNS

Marketing campaigns, including advertising, are utilised throughout the Middle East. It is not unusual for the Western organisation to sponsor targeted marketing events to promote a new product or indeed, to shift a product that is reaching its end of life or that never realised its projected sales potential. Providing samples and other giveaways are another technique that generally works well throughout the region.

Do not be surprised if your business partners push heavily for an allocation of marketing funds from your organisation, especially in manufacturing and distribution channels. When considering any marketing campaign, it would also be wise to establish a procedure of checks and balances to ensure that any negotiated marketing funds will be used in the manner in which they are agreed, along with specific timelines as to when the campaign starts and finishes.

Western business professionals should be conscious of marketing campaigns that could offend their Middle Eastern audiences. They should be especially sensitive to activities that could be seen as against Islam. This includes gambling and other games of chance. Venues should be chosen carefully; bars and nightclubs should be avoided unless the targeted market is exclusively Western. The rhythm of the business year should also be considered; *Ramadan* is generally inappropriate, although *Eid* promotions can work in certain lines of business. Keep the weather in mind as well – for example, has your potential market left the region during the height of summer?

It is also a good idea to consider the reach of your Middle Eastern partner's market impact and expertise. Some organisations are truly effective throughout the Middle East. Others may have strengths in one region and little or no presence elsewhere. This is particularly common between the Gulf and the Levant. Some organisations may specialise in a small area, for example Jeddah in Saudi Arabia or Abu Dhabi in the Emirates. Considering a multiple market approach may make sense for the Western business professional in these circumstances.

ADVERTISING

Advertising campaigns are also popular throughout the Middle East, including print and broadcast media. Utilisation of the internet continues to grow in effectiveness, with B2B and B2C e-shots and other common practices.

Although there are good local advertisers in each country in the Middle East, the Western business professional should be aware that many advertising organisations and business publications are run out of Dubai. Most of these organisations have a regional reach, and often publish in both English and Arabic.

Advertising should also be culturally sensitive to the region. Keep in mind that images of immodesty that may be ignored in Dubai may be banned in Riyadh. Advertising appeal can be very different in each country; what may appeal in Beirut may be shunned in Egypt. This is where local knowledge can make the difference between a successful advertising campaign and a waste of money and resources.

Some Western business professionals may be required to follow internal guidelines established by their own corporation when advertising and promoting their brand. However, consideration should be given as to how your corporate image translates culturally as well as linguistically throughout the region. Examples of difficult logos and other images the author has encountered in her consultancy role include risqué cartoon characters, devils, naked women, crosses, alcohol consumption and pigs.

It is important to trust any translation services that you may employ for both words and context. Initials and acronyms can be troublesome as well, as FCUK has no doubt considered. Remember that Arabic is read from right to left. This is particularly important to remember in any advertising or schematic that illustrates a flow chart or any other story board. For example, showing a pile of dirty laundry in frame 1, your company's washing powder in frame 2, and a neatly folded stack of clean clothes in frame 3 may work fine in English but will take on an entirely different meaning when translated into Arabic if the frames are not reversed!

PUBLIC RELATIONS

Many Western organisations also consider the use of public relations resources when establishing a presence in the Middle East as well as at other critical moments in their business cycle. PR firms can be particularly useful in brokering relationships with local and regional media, including introducing you to the correct journalists for your line of business. They can also provide you with up-to-the-minute information on the trends and difficulties on the ground that are of interest to your organisation. They are also often a source of competitive information, whether deliberate or unintentional.

Perhaps unsurprisingly, PR firms are concentrated in Dubai, ranging from globally-known organisations to niche players. Be careful in your selection, as it may be a better choice to work with a small, but well positioned organisation that has exactly the right connections you need to raise the profile of your business in the right circles. It is also important to consider their effectiveness throughout the Middle East if you intend to work throughout the region. A strong PR firm in Qatar may have little or no impact in Lebanon and may have no contacts at all in Jordan.

CONTRACTS AND OTHER LEGAL DOCUMENTS

As business progresses between the Western business professional and their Middle Eastern partners, there will eventually come a time to commit to a legal document. This may be a sponsor or partnership agreement, a joint venture, preparations to open an office in a free trade zone, or formally agreeing to the terms and conditions of a negotiated proposal.

Which law?

Different countries in the Middle East follow different legal practices. In general, most countries now have a combination of the laws of their previous coloniser (if applicable) along with Islamic law for family matters. For example, Lebanon, Syria and Egypt's legal systems draw heavily from Napoleonic law inherited from the French. Jordan retains some Ottoman legal practices. Most of the Gulf countries practice a combination of English Common Law and *Shari'a* law.

It is important for Western business professionals to understand the ramifications of the local laws that apply in the country in which they are negotiating agreements and signing contracts. Although it is beyond the scope of this book to offer legal advice, the following points should be considered whenever entering into a legal agreement in the Middle East.

Exclusivity

Historically, many businesses based in the Middle East used to ask for exclusivity in their contracts, obliging the Western organisation to provide their goods or services solely through their organisation. Of course, this was very risky for the Western organisation, not least because it would make them vulnerable if their local partner became a non-performer. The days of exclusivity are now in the past, although newcomers to the region may be tested by their prospective partners. Beware.

Partners and sponsors

Any organisation which is establishing a formal relationship with a partner or sponsor will need to ensure they are working with an organisation that is well established in their region as well as in their line of business. For example, establishing an agreement with a Riyadh-based organisation may be good for business in Riyadh and possibly even in the Eastern Province, but is not necessarily the correct choice to do business with in Jeddah. Make sure these details are clarified in your agreements.

Written versus oral agreements

The days of doing business solely on the strength of one's word are over in the Middle East, similar to the nostalgia of the gentleman's agreement in the UK. Your Middle Eastern partner will expect Western-style contracts. They will also expect you to meet their oral as well as written agreements. This should be considered when drawing up formal documents.

However, in a region with a long and rich oral tradition, lengthy US-style contracts are generally to be avoided, as they often carry a tone of mistrust. A straightforward, clear document that fits within the local law of the land is generally a better option. Try to keep the wording simple, amiable and to the point.

Language

It is imperative that all parties understand the legality of official contracts and other formal documents. In some countries, English (or French) language contracts are valid. In other countries, where contracts are written in both Arabic and another language, it is almost certain that the Arabic language version will be considered the official version of the contract in the event of any dispute.

Thus, the Western business professional must ensure that they have engaged a trustworthy interpreter and translator for all Arabic language requirements. This resource should never be taken on recommendation from your prospective partner, but instead should be sourced from an independent third party, or from your home country's support services in the region, such as the British Council.

Which calendar?

Similarly, it is important to define which calendar is being referred to in a legal document, especially as a *Hijra* year is ten to 11 days shorter than a Western year. This is certainly significant when drawing up a lease, for example.

Final agreement?

In much of the West, a signed contract assumes that the terms and conditions negotiated remain in force until the expiry/renewal date of the contract or if a specific clause is violated. This is not necessarily the same attitude that your Middle Eastern colleague may hold. It is not unusual for your partner to attempt to reopen negotiations if a condition has changed, especially if it is to their disadvantage. This can include anything from an unfavourable currency fluctuation to a unilateral change in local law imposed by a ruling family to a religious objection after the fact. In this regard, the contract can be considered more like a Western-style Letter of Intent. This may cause significant discomfort to some Western organisations.

Try to make sure you have a firm and final agreement at the time you are prepared to sign the formal document. Imposing fixed validity dates often helps. Try to anticipate events that won't affect a contract and which ones will, closing these loopholes wherever possible.

Trusting your local partner

Although Western style contracts have become the norm in doing business throughout the Middle East, do not lose perspective. Your relationship with your local partner will still be the best guarantee of a long and prosperous business partnership. In the words one of the author's Gulf partners, 'I'll sign your contract now because I like you and trust you, and it will help you back at your headquarters. I will also put it in my desk drawer and forget about it, because if I ever have to open the drawer, we don't have any more business together anyway'. This business partnership remained one of the author's most successful for years.

MANAGING EXPECTATIONS BACK HOME

Timelines

Western business professionals who have started to master their business environment in the Middle East will often complain that they are under pressure to meet unachievable targets, goals and other quantifiable expectations from their Western, corporate offices. These expectations are usually regarded as unrealistic due to the application of timelines that may work in the West, but are certainly a recipe for failure in the Middle East, especially in the initial stages of a partnership.

Sometimes, the hardest challenge for the Western business professional who is making steady inroads into Middle Eastern business culture is setting realistic expectations back home, especially as regards timelines. Many organisations fail at a point where they think they should be seeing substantial financial returns, when in fact relationship building and testing the waters are still in progress.

The author often uses the following graph that is a simple illustration of this classic clash of expectations:

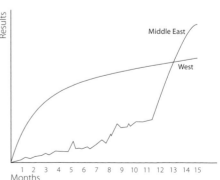

In much of the West, including most of Western Europe as well as English speaking countries, organisations like to see a quick return on their efforts. This is illustrated in the rising curve.

In countries where relationships are important, including the Middle East, organisations will spend a lot of time establishing relationships and building trust before very much measurable business gets done – this is the jagged line found in the diagram. The ups and downs in this illustration can be explained by anything from a religious holiday to a gap in the Westerner's visit to the region, or a miscommunication that takes time to resolve.

Simply put, has your organisation given you enough time to achieve your long-term goal of establishing a solid business model that gives you a true chance of success in the Middle East? Organisations who are focused predominately on short-term results may consider their efforts in the Middle East as a failure, especially if measured on a quarterly basis.

In the illustration above, most Western companies would probably accept the three month situation, but could start getting nervous after six months and positively upset after twelve months. They could even abandon the market at this point in time if they are a very impatient organisation or one that cannot adjust their short sales cycle mentality. However, if they had a bit more patience, results are starting to improve after thirteen months, illustrating the Middle East's belief in the Westerner. And as is often the case in the Middle East, once a solid and trusting relationship has been established, it is often the Middle East demanding a quicker response from the Westerner, as can be seen in this example after fourteen months.

Friday

It is astonishing how often Western organisations seem to forget that Friday is the weekend, is the Muslim holy day, and is the one day that people do not work in the Middle East (except in Lebanon). As a business professional to the region, you may need to remind your colleagues of this fact firmly and often. Do not expect a warm reception if you try to conduct business with your Middle Eastern colleagues on this day, even though they might not express their displeasure overtly, and even if you must do so under the duress of management instructions.

Sunday

Many Western business professionals with responsibilities in the Middle East may prefer to shift their own working week to mirror that of their region, i.e. also work a Sunday to Thursday work week, even if they remain based in their home country in the West. With the growing acceptance of working from home, access to corporate VPNs and the reliability of other technology, there is no practical reason for employees in most professions to travel to their corporate office.

Your Middle Eastern colleagues will recognise this gesture as a solid sign of your commitment to the region, especially if you work for an organisation that has yet to establish a physical office locally. Working on Sunday is also often an excellent strategy to keep ahead of any competition also based in the West who wait for Monday to start their work in the region.

Dealing with corporate 'bean counters'

Western organisations often expect detailed cost justifications for travelling to any business territory. This is especially true in times of economic difficulty, where corporate travel budgets are often scrutinised more closely. However, there are realities on the ground that should be taken into account when travelling to the Middle East that Western financial staff may not be aware of.

Unfortunately, it often falls on the shoulders of the Western business professional to educate their own accounting or travel department when planning their business trips to the Middle East. The following points highlight the business areas that may cause the most concern between the Western business professional and their colleagues who hold the power of getting their trip authorised or their expense report paid.

Demanding a detailed agenda before authorising travel

As we have explored, it is nearly impossible to publish a firm, detailed agenda that would accurately reflect the Western business professional's whereabouts once they arrive in the Middle East. The author recommends that the traveller who is faced with this requirement draws up an agenda that reflects their best attempt at accuracy, with the condition that it is probable that the agenda will be altered once in the region.

Inflexible travel plans, especially airline tickets

Many corporations strive to purchase the least expensive airline tickets that get their employee to their destination safely. This often involves highly restrictive or even non-refundable air fares.

This decision is particularly dangerous for travellers to the Middle East, who must often adjust their itineraries, especially at the last minute when business may be progressing to a positive conclusion at the end of their stay. Their Middle Eastern counterpart would surely expect them to postpone their return home so they can conclude their business. In this instance, a non-refundable airline ticket would be a false economy – this scenario happens more often than most people who set corporate travel policies would like to accept.

The stigma of flying economy
Long haul into the region

Until the advent of mainstream tourism in the Gulf in the early 2000s, it would diminish a Western business professional's status to do business in the Middle East in most lines of business if their Middle Eastern counterpart learnt they travelled to the region in economy class. Traditionally, that is the class of service flown by service staff and guest labourers. In the Middle Easterner's eyes, Westerners who flew economy were either showing their ignorance of the region or were causing their Middle Eastern counterpart to wonder if their organisation had the financial means and commitment to do business in the region.

Times have softened this perception somewhat, mostly to the detriment of more junior staff of some Western organisations. Senior executives, including new business development managers who are opening the Middle East for their organisation, should seriously consider flying in business class at a minimum (first class is no longer expected for all but very senior VIPs). This is commensurate with their assumed status, the importance of which should not be underestimated, especially during the early days of a business relationship.

Internally within the region

With the advent of regionally-based, low-cost carriers, it is now possible to fly on all-economy class airlines. This may be acceptable when the Westerner is travelling alone or with other Westerners, especially if you justify the choice of airline by saying it has a more convenient scheduled departure time.

However, extreme care should be taken if the Western business professional is travelling with a Middle Eastern national. The latter may insist on flying with a full service, scheduled airline, most often in business or first class. In this instance, the Western business professional should travel in the same class of service as their Middle Eastern colleague.

The stigma of staying in a budget hotel

Although the stigma of flying economy is loosening somewhat, your choice of hotel remains an important symbol of your status and of your organisation's seriousness in its capacity to doing business in the region. Western business professionals should stay in internationally-recognised four or five star hotels that have a business as opposed to a holiday reputation. These hotels can be owned by Western, Asian or Middle Eastern chains, and must be seen to have sufficient status in the country where you are travelling. Acceptable prestigious boutique hotels are arriving in the region as well.

The location of these hotels should also be taken into consideration due to considerable traffic challenges. It would not be unusual for your Middle Eastern colleague to have an agreement with a particular hotel that offers a discount to their business partners. It is often a good idea to enquire as to whether they have a preference of hotel for you to stay in, especially in the early days of doing business in the region.

It is also important to remember that your behaviour in the hotel will not go unnoticed by hotel staff, who may be subsequently asked to describe their impression of you as a guest to your Middle Eastern colleague.

No receipts

Although receipts are routinely available from hotels, upmarket restaurants and shopping malls, they are not always available from taxi drivers (especially in the Levant and Egypt), local eateries such as *shwarma* stands, and *souqs*. In some instances, the services provider may not be able to write in English (or in any other language, for that matter). It is strongly recommended that the Western business professional logs these undocumented, yet legitimate, business expenses in a journal, recording dates, time and place the expense occurred in accordance with the accountancy laws of their country of residence.

Conducting business outside the office

It is improbable that, as a guest in the Middle East, you will incur costs for activities conducted outside the office with your local colleague, such as trips to the desert, water sports, golf, nightclubs and live entertainment. However, it can sometimes be perceived by Western colleagues who are unfamiliar with business practices in the Middle East that you are staying in the region longer than necessary on a jolly.

As we have explored elsewhere in this book, these activities are legitimate business practices as much as giving a PowerPoint presentation in an office would be. It is a sometimes frustrating, but necessary task for the Western business professional to convince their management that their participation in outside activities should be considered to be another legitimate business activity that might involve additional expense.

BUSINESS ETHICS AND VALUES

At some point during their engagement with the Middle East, most Western business professionals will give thought to their personal business ethics and values and how they may be at odds to those they may be working with in the region. Amongst the most common issues that are raised by Westerners are the following:

Big picture issues
- Disagreement with local politics
- General discomfort with religious issues
- Inability of non-Muslims to practise their religion in Saudi Arabia

■ Human rights issues

■ Environmental/green issues

■ Freedom of speech and press issues.

Business practicalities on the ground

■ Dealing with colleagues who have obtained their position due to their *wasta* and not on their own merits, particularly if they appear to be incompetent in their job

■ Working in an environment where it is perfectly legal for your Middle Eastern counterparts to be working on different pay scales simply due to their nationality, especially in the Gulf

■ Working in an environment where local laws can be applied so that the Westerner has little practical recourse in the event of a business dispute

■ Being asked to reciprocate for favours that may be uncomfortable or considered to be an imposition

■ Working in certain environments without regards to Western style health and safety standards

■ Working in certain environments where there are few smoking restrictions.

Incongruities with Western HR policies

In addition, there are many practicalities that must be taken into account when considering the choice of individual employees about to work in the region. Some of the most common concerns are:

■ Requesting a Jewish employee to travel to an Arab country where his or her religion is requested on a visa application form (for most Westerners, this applies to Saudi Arabia)

■ Selecting an employee to travel to the region who has personal or family ties to Israel

■ Requesting a gay employee to travel to the region as it would generally be expected that he or she would not reveal their sexual orientation for their own effectiveness and, sometimes, safety

■ Asking women to accept social restrictions if working in Saudi Arabia

- Asking women to accept the need to wear an *abaya* and *shayla* in Saudi Arabia
- Asking women to accept the need to wear a *manteau* and headscarf in Iran
- Making a decision about whether to send an employee into the region due to their gender, age, marital status, nationality or ethnicity
- Considering the physical and acceptance-level challenges of sending a physically disabled employee into the region.

It is beyond the scope of this book to provide specific advice for employees and their organisations when facing these ethical and value issues. Some people will make decisions as to whether they are suited to working in the region on principle; others will take a more pragmatic view. However, organisations should have a policy in place where employees can raise issues that could potentially cause difficulty prior to their first assignment that involves travel into the region.

CLOSING THE SALE

As always, the particulars of successfully winning a deal depends on your line of business, the sales cycle, expectations of partners and customers, and any number of additional factors. The following information is intended to be a general guide for Western organisations in the commercial or private sectors doing business with Middle Eastern nationals or other expatriates located in the Gulf countries. Many of these pointers will apply to organisations doing business with local governments as well.

Timescales

Sales cycles will generally take longer than in the West, especially in the early days of establishing a relationship and building trust with your Middle Eastern partner. As we have previously explored, the Western business professional must determine whether they have a capacity to invest in the time needed to nurture a business relationship with their Middle Eastern counterparts on both a corporate and a personal level.

Priorities

Be aware of when your business is a priority for your Middle Eastern partner and when it is not. Keep in mind likely obstacles such as religious holidays or other times when business is less likely to be conducted, such as in the summer for many countries in the Gulf.

Try to find a way to make your opportunity the top priority with your host, who is very likely to be asking 'What's in it for me?' Try to steer your business proposal so that it is perceived to be the solution to your host's problem, an enhancement to their status or is the most prestigious (and ideally first) product to arrive in the region.

Professionalism

Always submit well put-together, professional proposals and bids. Make sure you are professionally put-together as well; pay attention to dress and personal grooming. Again, it's not about the money as much as it is about the prestige, status and quality of your deal. Don't be surprised if you are repeating yourself, especially if you are asked the same questions over and over – it might be a test of your loyalty and trustworthiness.

Keep in mind the power of the written word in the Middle East before committing anything to paper, email or a text message: 'If it is written down, it must be so.'

Focus

When pitching your product of service, many of these techniques work well in the Middle East.

Focus on:

- Strength of the relationship
- Personal synergies more than simply on the facts
- The advantages gained by your partner in doing business with you
- Anything unique, prestigious, or that will enhance your host's status
- The quality of your entire team.

Avoid

Try to avoid the 'cheapest price' trap. Know your arguments for quality. Try to sell to the strengths of whatever feature or service you can offer that will make your Middle Eastern counterpart's job easier and make them look good, both within their organisation as well as in your market in general.

Try to avoid the 'quickest delivery' trap. Once your Middle Eastern counterpart has indicated that they are ready to do business with you, this will already be expected!

Use subordinates effectively

Subordinates can test the waters without their activities being 'registered' higher up the chain of command. They can deliver a message that cannot be seen to be coming from someone in a higher position of authority. Subordinates can help save face in an awkward situation (and shoulder the blame if it doesn't work out).

Sponsor

Wherever possible, and whenever the budget permits, the Western business professional should consider sponsoring events where appropriate to build relationships with their Middle Eastern business associates. Ideas that generally work well include sponsoring *iftars* during *Ramadan*, visits to the Westerner's home country, conducting prestigious seminars or technical exchanges in the region, or hosting an event that recognises a professional qualification or high status as a prerequisite for attending. In the last example, follow up by providing certificates of completion to further enhance the attendee's status.

Deadlines

Try to set realistic deadlines with your Middle Eastern counterpart. With a belief in *insh'allah*, this will not be easy, but it is still worth a try. It is generally best to negotiate a date together with your business partner, as their reputation will be tied into delivering on their promise.

Try to ensure the date isn't too soon, as it may be unrealistic for your partner to meet. It is equally important to ensure the date isn't too far into the future, even if it does sound realistic – your counterpart will have too many opportunities to reprioritise your business in this instance.

Controversially, some Western business professionals have developed the skill to apply the strategic use of double agendas. This can be effective in the instance where the Westerner cannot be seen to have internal dates and forecasts slip within their own organisation, yet must project detailed timescales to their management. Of course, this requires an excellent memory and will often test the Westerner's organisation skills to the limit. It also provides a cushion for the all-too-frequent occurrence of missed deadlines within the region.

Persistence

In some Western cultures, it is normal to try to accelerate the sales process by applying the hard sell. In other Western cultures, there is a tendency to 'wait and see' once the official sales pitches are over and the time to make a decision draws near. Neither technique is likely to work in the Middle East. Instead, don't push, but be persistent … and patient.

GETTING PAID

During the sales cycle, the Western business professional should have made payment terms and conditions very clear, with specific dates and figures referenced. Internationally-recognised financial instruments such as letters of credit through a reputable bank should be utilised. The Middle Eastern organisation should have been financially vetted as to its financial stability (and credit worthiness if applicable). Meeting all obligations, both contractual and verbal will be expected from both the Western business professional and their Middle Eastern counterpart, although slight discrepancies may be overlooked amongst those with an otherwise excellent working relationship, if mutually agreed.

Western organisations which have established a solid business relationship can generally expect that their Middle Eastern counterpart will honour their payment agreement. However, as with so many other activities discussed throughout this book, paying the Western organisation may not always be at the top of your Middle Eastern counterpart's priorities. The key to getting paid on time and in full depends very much on the strength of your business relationship. If it is good, usually a quiet word will do the trick if the payment date has passed.

If the Westerner's organisation is having difficulty receiving payment, the softly, softly approach is initially the best one to take. In the case of a missed or partial payment, the Western business professional should approach their trusted Middle Eastern counterpart and have a private word about the problem. Leveraging this relationship should always be undertaken first. For example, it would be a big mistake for a Western organisation's accounts payable team, who have probably never met anyone in the Middle Eastern organisation to make their first contact with your partner a demand for payment.

If this technique does not work, then a good strategy is to ask what else the Westerner must action or provide in order to complete the payment. This is better than directly confronting your partner; always avoid negatives, such as 'Why aren't you paying me on time' or 'what's wrong?' Once the problem has been identified and rectified, then ask permission for your accounts payable team to contact the appropriate counterpart within the Middle Eastern partner's organisation.

CONTINUING THE RELATIONSHIP

Unless your organisation intends to withdraw from the Middle East once you have made your initial sale, it is imperative that the Western business professional continues to nurture their business relationship with their Middle Eastern partner. This includes during periods of inactivity in the region – all it takes is a simple telephone call to say hello and to remind your partner that you value their business and their relationship. This will pay off when you are ready to introduce your next product or service into the region.

OPENING AN OFFICE IN THE REGION

Once your organisation has won business in the Middle East, pressure will increase for you to open an office in the region. The Western business professional should give serious consideration as to the best strategy for them, as it may no longer be realistic to do long-term business in the region without a local presence. Many companies start by opening an office under their own name in a free trade zone, usually in Dubai; others establish a relationship with a local partner.

Whichever choices your organisation considers, the most important strategy is to show ongoing commitment to the Middle East.

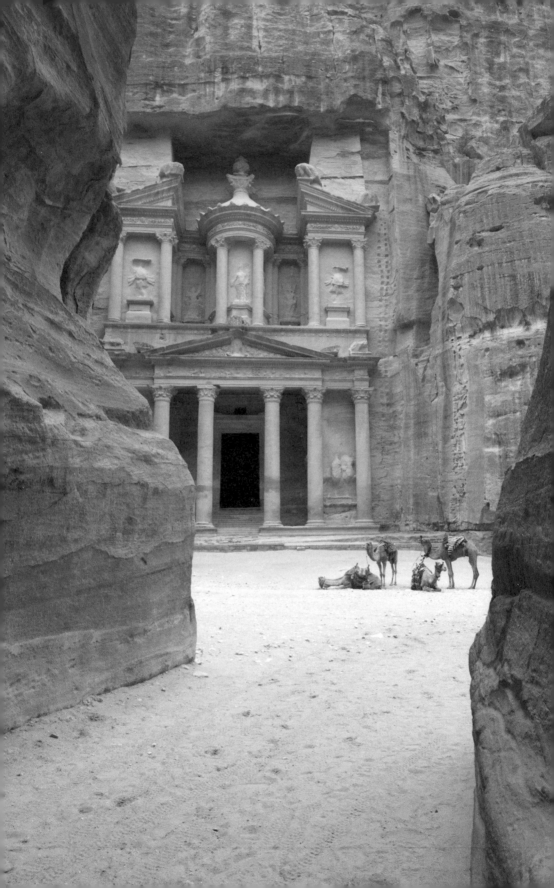

17
Free time

There are many books, websites and other resources that can provide reliable tourist information for every destination in the Middle East. For example, Lonely Planet or Rough Guides are typically recommended for destinations in the Levant. The author is a big fan of the Explorer Series of Complete Residents' Guides for the Gulf Countries, as these books are aimed at Western expatriate audiences and are more comprehensive as well as orientated to Westerners, both expatriate and frequent business visitors. It is not the intention of this book to replicate these sources.

Most Western business professionals to the Middle East are in the region for business, often with no spare time for any activity other than business. Occasionally, however, they might find they have a spare day or possibly a free weekend where they may be able to explore their destination. Thus, the following information concentrates on the most popular activities or local points of interest that are most likely to appeal to the Western business professional who has very limited time.

BAHRAIN

Base: Manama
One day

- Have tea at the restaurant in the centre of the King Fahd Causeway
- Check out the Bahrain National Museum
- Walk around the old *souq* of Manama
- Visit the Bahrain Fort
- Wander around Muharraq admiring the traditional architecture
- Don't bother with the Tree of Life

Weekend
- Take a weekend resort break on the Hawar Islands

EGYPT

Base: Cairo
One day
- See the pyramids and the sphinx in Giza just after sunrise
- Shop in the Khan al Khalili bazaar
- Go to the Egyptian museum
- Explore the City of the Dead
- Check out the Coptic museum and hanging church
- Take a *felucca* ride on the Nile

Weekend
- Fly to Sharm el Sheik to enjoy the Sinai Peninsula and water sports in the Red Sea. Choose Sharm over Dahab or Taba on the peninsula or Hurghada on the Red Sea coast
- Visit St Catherine's monastery at Mount Sinai at sunrise
- Fly or take a train to Luxor to see the Valley of the Kings and the Tomb of King Tut
- Fly to Aswan to enjoy a relaxing weekend in Nubian Egypt. Leave Abu Simbal to when you have more time

IRAN

Base: Tehran
One day
- Visit the National Museum and the Glass and Ceramics Museum
- Visit the Golestan Palace
- Visit the Niavaran and Saheb Qaranieh Palaces of the last Shah
- Visit the public parks of North Tehran
- Snow ski in Dizin or Shemshak – this is also a good weekend getaway

Weekend
- Make a trip to Esfahan your top priority. The city's Imam Square is jaw-droppingly beautiful. Explore the mosques, *souq* and polo palace, all surrounding the square
- Fly to Shiraz, where gardens and poetry live in harmony
- Visit the World Heritage Site of Persepolis
- Fly to Yazd to explore Zoroastrian culture

JERUSALEM

One day
- Explore the Old City's four quarters
- Go in the morning to visit the Temple Mount and Al Aqsa mosque
- Visit the Church of the Holy Sepulchre
- Have a meal at the King David hotel in West Jerusalem
- Visit the Mount of Olives
- Have lunch in the courtyard of the American Colony Hotel in Arab East Jerusalem
- Travel to Bethlehem to see the Church of the Nativity and to experience crossing through the controversial 'security fence' aka the 'apartheid wall'

JORDAN

Base: Amman
One day
- Tour the Roman ruins of Jerash
- Relax at a resort on the Dead Sea. Choose the Marriott or the Movenpick

Weekend
- Try to spend two entire days exploring Petra
- Drive down the King's highway. Stay in the Taybet Zaman Hotel
- Skip Aqaba – there are better Red Sea resorts in Egypt
- Save Wadi Rum for when you have a bit more time

KUWAIT

Base: Kuwait City

One day

- Walk around the Kuwait Towers
- Walk along the Corniche if the weather is favourable
- Visit the Al Qurain Martyrs Museum
- Visit the Grand Mosque

Weekend

- Check out the Friday Market
- Find a relaxing, clean beach resort for a detox weekend
- Don't go off road without reliable local knowledge due to land mines
- Don't try to approach the Iraqi border

LEBANON

Base: Beirut

One day

- Walk along the Corniche
- Explore Hamra and area around the American University of Beirut
- Check out Martyr Square, including the photos taken during the civil war
- Check out the nightclubs in Jounieh
- Experience the Jeita grotto

Weekend

- Tour the Roman ruins of Baalbek in the Bekaa Valley
- Tour the Roman ruins of Byblos
- Visit a Lebanese vineyard; Chateau Ksara run tours
- In the winter, snow ski at the Cedars or Mzaar ski resorts

OMAN

Base: Muscat
One day
- Check out the Mutrah *souq*
- Wander from fort to fort around Muscat's walled city
- Tour the Sultan Qaboos Grand Mosque
- Visit the Oman Dive Centre in Bandar Jissah for a full variety of water sports

Weekend
- Visit Ras al Jinz during turtle-egg laying season
- Weekend in the oasis town of Nizwa and the Fort
- Tour the mountain sights around Jebel Shams
- Camp in Wahiba Sands to for an authentic experience of the sand dunes
- Fly to Salalah to see frankincense in its natural environment
- Save the Musandam Peninsula until you need an escape from Dubai

THE PALESTINIAN TERRITORIES

Base: Ramallah
One day
- Visit Jericho
- Visit Nablus
- Visit Bethlehem

Weekend
- Make your own pilgrimage to Christian sites in the Holy Land
- Touring Hebron is not recommended for the casual tourist, but is of interest
- Touring Gaza remains off limits at the time of publication

QATAR

Base: Doha
One day
- Walk along the Corniche
- Explore the *souqs*
- Visit the excellent Museum of Islamic Art

Weekend
- Do a 4x4 camping weekend to Khor al Adaid, the inland sea near the Saudi border
- Hire a car and explore Qatar independently

SAUDI ARABIA

Base: Riyadh
One day
- Visit Diriyah, the ancestral village of the Saudi ruling family
- Visit the National Museum
- Check out the Kingdom Tower
- Check out the shopping malls, Riyadh's only real form of 'public entertainment'

Weekend
- Contact your embassy to gain access to other social opportunities
- Fly in to visit Madain Saleh, Petra's twin city in the Northwest of the Kingdom. Make sure you organise travel permits in advance of visiting this World Heritage Site

Base: Jeddah
One day
- Explore the old city on foot
- Walk along the Corniche
- Check out a private beach resort through your hotel

Weekend

- Dive the Red Sea
- Travel overland to Taif
- Visit the Asir mountains and national park
- Never attempt to visit Mecca if you are not Muslim

Base: Eastern Province

One day

- Walk along Khobar's Corniche
- Make friends with an ex-pat who will invite you into the ex-pat social scene

Weekend

- Check out Tarut island
- Visit Al Hasa Oasis of Al Hofuf
- Pop over the causeway to Bahrain if you have a multiple entry visa to KSA

SUDAN

Base: Khartoum

One day

- Check out the *souq*
- Visit the camel market
- Tour the national museum

Weekend

- Always check out the political climate before travelling outside of Khartoum
- Organise a weekend away in Nubian northern Sudan
- Scuba divers should consider a 'liveaboard' boat to explore the Red Sea's best dive sites

SYRIA

Base: Damascus
One day
- Visit the Omayyad Mosque
- Visit the old city in Damascus
- Shop in the Damascus' al Hamidiyya *souq*

Weekend
- Visit the wooden water wheels in Hama
- Visit the castle at Krak des Chevaliers
- Visit the dead cities on the road from Hama to Aleppo
- Spend a weekend exploring the old *souq* in Aleppo
- Visit the ruins of Palmyra

UAE

Base: Abu Dhabi
One day
- Tour the Sheikh Zayed Mosque
- Have a meal and a look around the Emirates Palace Hotel
- Watch for the opening of the Guggenheim museum and other cultural developments

Weekend
- Weekend break in Al Ain
- Check out the resort built on the Royal Nature Reserve of His Highness Sheikh Zayed Bin Sultan Al Nahyan at Sir Bani Yas island

Base: Dubai
One day
- Visit the Deira gold *souq* in the evening – the bling will amaze
- Join a desert safari in the late afternoon. Try to avoid the summer months
- Check out a shopping mall (the Mall of the Emirates has the ski slope)

- Check out Meena bazaar for a taste of shopping Indian style
- Get your hotel 'bling' fix at the Burj al Arab. You need to book in a restaurant to gain admission. Skip the Atlantis
- Cross the creek on a traditional *dhow*
- Take time to visit the Dubai museum in Bur Dubai

Weekend

- Check out the latest nightlife around Dubai Marina or wherever the trendiest hotspot of the moment is
- Retreat to Hatta for a spa weekend
- Travel to Fujairah for a weekend of water sports
- Better yet, include Dibba and points north on the Omani side of the Musandam peninsula
- Explore the northern Emirates by car along the west coast, arriving in Ras al Khaimah at your leisure

YEMEN

Base: Sana'a
One day

- Always obtain local knowledge to determine personal safety before travelling anywhere in Yemen
- Explore the *Souq* al Milh of Old Sana'a
- Climb to the top of a traditional Yemen skyscraper
- Check out the National Museum and art galleries featuring Yemeni artists
- People watch, especially in the afternoon when *qat* chewing is in full swing

Weekend

- Fly to Aden to relax on the beach or to see a bit of the old British Empire
- Fly to Socotra island to enjoy this culturally distinct outpost
- Visit Wadi Hadramut if it is safe – the situation constantly changes
- Never travel anywhere in Yemen without the correct government permit

A FEW HOURS' BREAK

Here are a few ideas if your time is even more limited.

- Wander in the old *souqs* of any city
- Buy fresh spices, carpets, brassware, frankincense, *oud, nargila*
- Check out Indian bazaars found in most Gulf cities, especially for fabrics
- People watch in any shopping mall
- Go to a beach club
- Many health clubs will organise a day pass
- Get a massage
- Wander around older neighbourhoods to see traditional architecture
- Check out a traditional coffee house, but be aware most are for men only
- Smoke a *shisha*
- Check out a neighbourhood restaurant that doesn't cater for tourists
- Organise a round of golf
- Go to a horse race or camel race, but be careful of child jockeys
- Try Ski Dubai
- Go to Wild Wadi water park
- Find out which clubs and pubs are favoured on certain nights by ex-pats
- Hook up with a team for a pub quiz
- Buy excellent Lebanese or Jordanian wine if you can manage the 100ml rule
- Eat on a Nile riverboat restaurant
- Find a venue playing live Arabic music
- Find a venue showcasing authentic Indian music or dance
- Get a good recommendation from a local to see authentic belly dancing
- Go to an *iftar* during *Ramadan*
- Join in holiday celebrations from *Eid* to *Diwali*
- Check out an event at your country's embassy

ACTIVITIES TO AVOID

Although there are some variations by country, it is strongly recommended that the Western business professional generally avoids the following activities:

- Card games
- Gambling
- Public drunkenness
- Consuming illegal drugs
- Attending loud parties with live music during *Ramadan*
- Chatting up local women
- Wearing fancy dress that offends the local population, including national dress for men
- Wearing an inappropriate swimming costume on a public beach
- Sex on the beach

18

Is working in the Middle East for me?

In attempting to unveil the Middle East to the Western business professional, we have explored a multitude of information: geopolitical facts and figures, the impact of religion, business practices, cultural norms, traditions and preferences, and curiosities that are simply part of life's rich pattern.

It is up to each individual to determine whether working in the Middle East is compatible with their personality, style of doing business, tolerance for what will inevitably be very different to 'back home' and comfort level in adapting to values and behaviours that may sometimes directly challenge one's individual beliefs and principles.

Whilst this book cannot make this decision for you, there are a number of questions you may wish to consider before committing to your organisation, family and friends. Here are a few to get you started:

YOUR PERSONAL CHECK LIST

- ☐ Can I adapt to working in an environment where my principles may be challenged or I may have to accept some very fundamental practices I don't agree with?
- ☐ Am I OK working in a country where the political and legal systems may not offer me the same protection that I am used to back home?
- ☐ Do I mind wearing certain clothes or wearing *hijab* when forced to by law?
- ☐ Can I manage to cope with very hot and humid weather?

- [ ] Can I officially manage to do without alcohol or pork in certain environments?
- [ ] Do I have any personal issues that worry me? Am I female, gay, left handed, an ethnic minority from my home country, atheistic or agnostic, very young, unmarried, a single parent, cohabiting, disabled, etc.?
- [ ] Can I tolerate people asking me a lot of personal questions?
- [ ] Am I able to adapt to working in unfamiliar or unpredictable situations?
- [ ] Can I empathise with others?
- [ ] Am I comfortable socialising with a wide range of people who I can eventually learn to rely upon in a business and social environment?
- [ ] Do I have the ability to see an opinion or point of view from someone else's perspective?
- [ ] Do I know when to express my opinion and when to stay silent?
- [ ] Can I manage the expectations of my colleagues in the Middle East at the same time as those within my organisation?
- [ ] Can I remain calm and courteous when faced with a perceived injustice?
- [ ] Am I patient?
- [ ] Can I learn to be patient?
- [ ] Am I really up to the challenge of learning what I need to know to be a success in my job in the Middle East?

FINDING COMMON GROUND

Within any culture, people are people. Regardless of culture, people's beliefs, characteristics and behaviour will fall into a Bell Curve distribution. Within any two cultures, there will always be an overlap between these two curves, as is illustrated in the diagram. The variable is the degree to which they overlap.

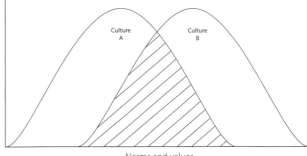

Norms and values

As we can see, it would be highly unlikely that, as an individual, you would fall within a distribution where you have nothing in common with an entire culture; if you do, then maybe an assignment working in that other culture is not for you.

A good coping mechanism is to find out what your Middle Eastern colleagues already have in common with you. By doing so, whether it's scuba diving, fondness for the latest technology, the desert, or poetry, you are beginning your journey towards building a relationship.

QUESTIONS TO ASK YOURSELF

- What do we already have in common?
- What's different, interesting and something I like?
- What's just different?
- What's different and may be more difficult for me?
- What's immediately important to get right, and what can I learn along the way?
- What are my strengths for working with the Middle East in general and Arabs/host country nationals in particular?
- How do I plan to manage my concerns?

Patience, patience, patience!

19

Finally …

With the impact of globalisation, the Middle East will continue to experience rapid change. As people from the West and elsewhere gain confidence and expand their business into the region, the Middle East will also become familiar to more and more people. The impact of satellite television, the internet, mobile phones and the ease of travel all provide opportunities to understand each other better than ever before.

Who knows what further changes will come to the region in the next 20 years? However, it is undeniable that cultural intelligence will continue to be of utmost importance.

It is the author's hope that reading *The Middle East Unveiled* proves to be useful to Western business professionals from a broad range of organisations. Watch out for the big issues – the smaller issues can be managed over time. Mind your manners – if in doubt, behave in a way that would make your grandmother proud!

REMEMBER …

- It takes a lifetime to unveil the Middle East.
- Focus on common values and interests rather than differences.
- Plan for the long haul.
- Enjoy your opportunity!

Recommended reading

It would be impossible to recommend a complete reading list covering all aspects of doing business in the Middle East. However, the author has found the following books to be useful when consulting with a number of corporations and other commercially orientated organisations setting out to do business in the region:

Recommended for expatriates and very frequent Western travellers to the Gulf Countries. These guides are regularly updated, so check for the latest edition before purchasing:

The Complete Residents' Guide Abu Dhabi (Explorer Publishing 2009)
The Complete Residents' Guide Bahrain (Explorer Publishing 2006)
The Complete Residents' Guide Dubai (Explorer Publishing 2009)
The Complete Residents' Guide Kuwait (Explorer Publishing 2006)
The Complete Residents' Guide Oman (Explorer Publishing 2009)
The Complete Residents' Guide Qatar (Explorer Publishing 2008)
The Complete Residents' Guide Saudi Arabia* (Explorer Publishing ,
    *projected publication date December 2010)
Saudi Arabia, The Business Traveller's Handbook, Andrew Mead (Gorilla
    Guides 2007)

Recommended for organisations about to set up business in Dubai:

Dubai Red Tape (Explorer Publishing 2009)
UAE Free Zone Investment Guide, (Excelencia FZ LLC Publishing 2005)
Dubai & Co., Aamir A Rehman (McGraw Hill 2008)
Setting Up in Dubai, Essam Al Tamimi (Excelencia FZ LLC Publishing
    2006)

Recommended for organisations about to set up business in the GCC:

The New Gulf: How Modern Arabia is Changing the World for Good,
    Edmund O'Sullivan (Motivate Publishing 2008)
Inside the Kingdom, Robert Lacey (Hutchinson 2009)
Middle East and North Africa Media Guide, Edited by Ben Smalley
    (Mediasource 2008)

General etiquette pocket-style guides:

Culture Smart! Egypt, Jailan Zayan (Kuperard 2006)
Culture Smart! Iran, Stuart Williams (Kuperard 2008)
Culture Smart! Oman, Simone Nowell (Kuperard 2009)
Culture Smart! Saudi Arabia, Nicholas Buchele (Kuperard 2008)
Culture Smart! UAE, John Walsh (Kuperard 2008)

Learn more about Islam:

The Holy Qur'an
Teach Yourself: Islam, Ruqaiyyah Waris Maqsood (Teach Yourself
Publishing 2006)

Learn Arabic:

Teach Yourself: Arabic, Jack Smart and Frances Altorfer (Teach Yourself
Publishing 2003)

Customised Language Courses in your home country:

Readers who are interested in learning more about the Arabic language
should determine the Arabic dialect correct for their needs. Many
Westerners learn Modern Standard Arabic, which suits the Arab speaking
world, but it not an exact match for everyday conversations. The reader may
also wish to consider learning Gulf, Levantine, Egyptian, or Maghrebi
dialects if they wish to focus on a particular region of the Middle East.

Useful websites

GENERAL WEBSITES

www.islamicfinder.org   useful everyday Islamic information

www.oanda.com   currency conversion

GOVERNMENT WEBSITES

These provide information on countries of the Middle East, including travel advice.

www.smarttraveller.gov.au   Australian Government Department of Foreign Affairs and Trade

www.voyage.gc.ca   Foreign Affairs and International Trade Canada

www.safetravel.govt.nz   New Zealand Ministry of Foreign Affairs and Trade

www.dfa.gov.za   South Africa Department International Relations and Cooperation

www.fco.gov.uk   UK Foreign and Commonwealth Office

www.travel.state.gov   US State Department

Glossary

abaya   a long black robe that covers a woman's body from the shoulders to the ground, or at least to the feet, as worn in the Gulf Countries and by law in Saudi Arabia

abu   father of

agal   the double strand of heavy corded fabric that secures the man's headscarf in place

Ashura   a religious holiday for *Shi'a* Muslims. It is the day of martyrdom of Ali, the grandson of the Prophet Mohammed (pbuh) and an important *Shi'a* figure

asr   the third prayer of the day, held in the late afternoon

ayatollah   a *Shi'a* religious scholar, recognised by the community, who interprets Islamic law

azan   the call to prayer that emanates from the minaret of a mosque

balto   a long black robe that covers a woman's body from the shoulders to the ground, or at least to the feet, as worn in Yemen

bidoon   'without' in Arabic. Refers to stateless people living in Kuwait, sometimes for generations

bin   son of

bint   daughter of

bisht   an outer robe, worn over the *thobe* either for special occasions or by men with very high status *caliph*   a successor to the Prophet who is a qualified and recognised head of a Muslim religious community

chador   a simple semi-circle of fabric worn over a woman's head and body without fasteners. It is typically worn by devout *Shi'a* women

dhuhr   the second prayer of the day, held just after the midday sun

dishdash   a long robe, usually white but sometimes of another pastel colour, that covers a man's body from the shoulders to the ground, or at least to the feet, as worn in the Gulf Countries. Used most often in Oman, Qatar and the UAE. Similar to *kandura* or *thobe*

diwaniyya

a special public room in a home that is used to receive guests

diyya   blood money paid as compensation to a person or their family by the guilty party

Eid al Adha

a religious holiday that starts immediately after the *Hajj* is complete, known as the Festival of the Sacrifice

Eid al Fitr

a religious holiday that starts immediately after *Ramadan* has ended, known as a time of feasting and celebration

fajr   the first prayer of the day, occurs at the first sign of changing light at the end of night

fatwa   a religious opinion that is meant to guide Muslims in achieving a moral way of life. It is not a death sentence *per se*, as is often believed in the West, although an opinion could include death

galabaya   a long robe, usually of a dark, solid colour most commonly worn in rural or traditional areas of Egypt and Sudan

ghutra   a male headscarf, usually white in colour that is worn in the Gulf countries

hajj   the fifth pillar of Islam; the pilgrimage to Mecca required of every able-bodied Muslim who is also financially able to fulfil this obligation once in their lifetime

halal permitted. In general, a practice that is allowed in Islam. In the West, most often associated with the ritual preparation of meat for human consumption

hadith the oral traditions regarding the words and deeds of the Prophet

haram forbidden. In general, a practice that is not permitted in Islam. In the West, 'harem', which is derived from the same root word, is most often associated with women's quarters in a house, which would be off limits to men

hijab modest dress. In the West, often misinterpreted to mean a woman's headscarf, although a headscarf may be a component of modest dress

hijra the Islamic calendar, consisting of twelve lunar months, for a total of approximately 354 days per Islamic year

hookah water pipe (for smoking)

Ibadi the majority Muslim sect found in Oman, neither *Sunni* nor *Shi'a*

iftar the meal eaten to break the day's fast at sunset on each day during *Ramadan*

ihram the formal intention to perform *Hajj*. Often associated with clothing worn during the pilgrimage to Mecca, usually two pieces of simple white cloth or a simple robe

imam respected community member who leads prayers

infidel a person who does not believe in religion, or believes in a polytheistic religion, depending on usage

insh'allah literally, 'if God wills it'. Often used to describe an event that is in God's hands

isha the fifth prayer of the day, held at the end of twilight

Islam   submission to *Allah* (God). A person who believes in Islam

ism   personal name, first name, *never* referred to as Christian name

jambiya   curved daggers often worn by Yemeni men

jihad   a struggle or ongoing attempt to live one's life in compliance with how *Allah* would wish both morally and ethically. It does not mean a Holy War as is often believed in the West

Jumu'ah   Friday midday prayers, the most important prayers of the week

Ka'aba   the holiest site in Islam. It is believed to have been first built-upon by Abraham, and was the site of prayer for the Prophet Mohammed. Muslims pray in the direction of the Ka'aba

kandura   a long robe, usually white, but sometimes of another pastel colour, that covers a man's body from the shoulders to the ground, or at least to the feet, as worn in the UAE. Similar to *dishdash* or *thobe*

keffiyeh   a black check male headscarf, usually worn by men of Palestinian origin who have performed the *Hajj*

khanjar   curved daggers often worn by Omani men

khatib   someone who leads the sermon during Friday prayers (*Jumu'ah*)

kummah   embroidered male Islamic skullcap, most often worn by men from Oman

kunya   a name used by a parent in recognition of a child, most often a first born son. Translated most often as father of or mother of the child's given name

Levant   Middle Eastern countries that border or nearly border the Mediterranean Sea, probably derived from the French '*soleil levant*' or rising sun

madrassa   is a place of learning, i.e. a school. The quality and range of subjects taught varies from world standard to sole rote memorisation of the *Qur'an*

Maghreb Arab countries of North Africa that border the Mediterranean Sea, probably derived from the Arabic meaning west

mahram a woman's male guardian required whilst in public in much of Saudi Arabia

manteau an over garment worn by less religious women in Iran that is worn similar to an overcoat in the West. It is borrowed from the French word for coat

Mashreq Middle Eastern countries that border or nearly border the Mediterranean Sea, probably derived from the Arabic meaning the land east of Egypt

masjid a place of worship for Muslims. It is the Arabic word for mosque

Mawlid the Prophet's Birthday. A public holiday in some, but not all, Middle Eastern countries

Mecca the holiest city in Islam, located in the West of Saudi Arabia near Jeddah, and the main *Hajj* destination

Medina the second holiest city in Islam, where the Prophet's tomb is located, and a *Hajj* destination

misbaha prayer beads

muezzin man selected to perform the call to prayer

mufti a *Sunni* religious scholar, recognised by the community, who interprets Islamic law

Muslim person who adheres to the Islamic faith

muttawa/mutawween
  Saudi religious police

nargila water pipe (for smoking)

niqab a face veil that covers all or part of a woman's face

nisba surname, last name, or family name

oud   a stringed musical instrument. *Oud* is also fragrance derived from agar wood and often used in Middle Eastern perfumes

pbuh   in English, Peace Be Upon Him. Used when referring to the Prophet Mohammed

qat   a bush grown in Yemen whose leaves provide a mild narcotic effect when chewed

qibla   an indicator that designates the direction of the Ka'aba in Mecca

Qur'an   Islam's holy book. Muslims believe that the *Qur'an* is a correction and completion of Jewish and Christian teachings

Ramadan/Ramzan
           the ninth month of the Islamic calendar. A time of piety, fasting, sacrifice, and good deeds

salaam   peace

salat   the second pillar of Islam. It is the call to prayer, and is performed five times per day by religious Muslims

Sahel   the Arabic word for the African continent located below the Sahara desert

sajada   prayer rug

Salafi   a group of ultra-conservative Islamic sects who believe they practise the purest form of Islam

sawm   the fourth pillar of Islam, it means fasting and is adhered to during *Ramadan*

shahada the first pillar of Islam, the profession of the faith that there is only one God and that Mohammed is his prophet

shamagh a red, check, male headscarf, usually worn by men who have performed the *Hajj* and are either of Jordanian origin or come from a country with a royal family

Shari'a law
comprehensive Islamic law covering criminal and civil matters

shayla a woman's rectangular headscarf, usually associated with the *abaya* and worn throughout the Gulf countries. It may be plain black or embroidered with an increasing number of designs and styles

Shi'a one of the two main branches of Islam, which believes religious power is transferred through the lineage of Ali, the Prophet Mohammed's son in law, whose wife Fatimah was a daughter of the Prophet

shisha water pipe (for smoking)

shurooq sunrise

souq/souk market

suhoor pre-dawn meal eaten during *Ramadan*

sunnah the traditions and practices of the Prophet. It can also be described as a way of life

Sunni one of the two main branches of Islam, which believes religious power is transferred through *caliphs* chosen from the Muslim community, subject to a number of qualifications

taqiyah a white, knitted skull cap most often worn by Gulf national men

talib a student. The Taliban were originally a group of students

tasbih prayer beads

thobe/thawb
a long robe, usually white, but sometimes of another pastel colour, that covers a man's body from the shoulders to the ground, or at least to the feet, as worn in the Gulf Countries. Used more often in Bahrain, Kuwait and Saudi Arabia. Similar to *dishdash* or *kandura*.

ulema religious scholars

ummah the world's Muslim population

umrah   pilgrimage to Mecca that takes place at any time of the year other than *Hajj*

Wahhab   *Sunni* Muslims who believe in following the teachings of the *Qur'an* and the *hadith*, emulating the way of life found during the first years of Islam during the time of the Prophet Mohammed

wajib   mandatory practices, such as adherence to the five pillars of Islam

wasta   influence, contacts, connections

wudu   a proscribed set of ablutions that must be performed prior to entering a mosque and prior to prayer

zakat   the third pillar of Islam. It is the giving of alms, which are calculated by using a formula applied to a person's wealth based on their savings and assets

Index

About the author

Donna Marsh first travelled to the Middle East in 1978. She has worked as a businesswoman in her own right for much of her 30-year career in corporate sales, marketing and new business development roles in the fields of banking and information technology, travelling throughout the Levant, Egypt and the Gulf Countries, including Saudi Arabia. She has managed a variety of business partnerships that included Indian and Western multinationals, Gulf and Levantine family businesses, and conglomerates from the Far East. She also has extensive experience working throughout the Indian subcontinent.

As founder of Culture Unveiled, Ms Marsh provides a wide range of cross-cultural business consultancy services, focusing on best practices for businesses and their employees expanding into new territories throughout the Middle East and Indian subcontinent. She has worked with a variety of FTSE 100 organisations and other multinationals from diverse professions, including finance, insurance, legal, oil and gas, pharmaceutical, healthcare, FMCG, technology, manufacturing, aviation, defence and for the British Government. Learn more at www.cultureunveiled.com

A British/American dual national, Ms Marsh lives near London.